Tangent: SUPERMAN'S REIGN

Volume Two
DISCARD

History Lesson

Ron Marz
Writer

Andie Tong
Penciller

Mark McKenna
Inker

Travis Lanham
Steve Wands
Letterers

Dom Regan
Colorist

Tangent: Superman's Reign

Dan Jurgens
Writer

Wes Craig (Chapters 7 & 8)
Carlos Magno (Chapters 9-12)
Pencillers

Dan Davis (Chapters 7 & 8)
Julio Ferreira (Chapters 9-12)
Inkers

Travis Lanham
Steve Wands
Sal Cipriano
Letters

Kanila Tripp
Colors

Tangent: Superman's Reign
Volume Two

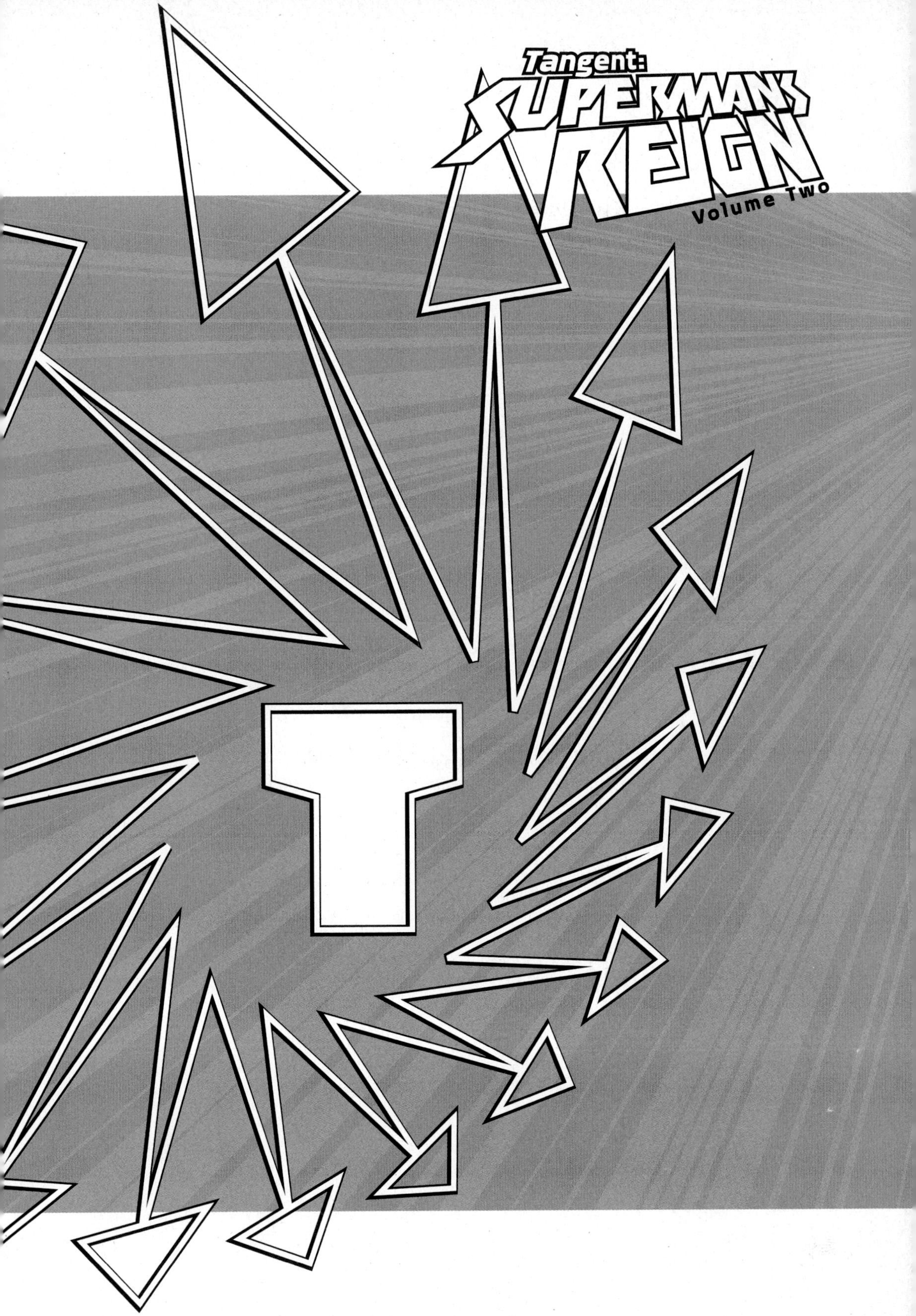

Superman created by Jerry Siegel & Joe Shuster

Dan DiDio
SVP-Executive Editor

Nachie Castro
Adam Schlagman
Editors-original series

Bob Harras
Group Editor–collected editions

Sean Mackiewicz
Editor

Robbin Brosterman
Design Director-Books

DC COMICS
Paul Levitz
President & Publisher

Richard Bruning
SVP-Creative Director

Georg Brewer
VP-Design & DC Direct Creative

Patrick Caldon
EVP-Finance & Operations

Amy Genkins
SVP-Business & Legal Affairs

Jim Lee
Editorial Director-WildStorm

Gregory Noveck
SVP-Creative Affairs

Sue Pohja
VP-Book Trade Sales

Steve Rotterdam
SVP-Sales & Marketing

Cheryl Rubin
SVP-Brand Management

Cover by Ivan Reis and Joe Prado
TANGENT: SUPERMAN'S REIGN VOLUME 2

Published by DC Comics. Cover, text
and compilation Copyright © 2009
DC Comics. All Rights Reserved.

Originally published in single maga-
zine form in TANGENT: SUPERMAN'S
REIGN 7-12. Copyright © 2008, 2009
DC Comics. All Rights Reserved.
All characters, their distinctive
likenesses and related elements
featured in this publication are
trademarks of DC Comics. The stories,
characters and incidents featured in
this publication are entirely fictional.
DC Comics does not read or accept
unsolicited submissions of ideas, stories
or artwork.

DC Comics, 1700 Broadway, New York,
NY 10019

A Warner Bros. Entertainment
Company
Printed in Canada. First Printing.

ISBN 978-1-4012-2474-5

 Fiber used in this product line meets the
sourcing requirements of the SFI program.
www.sfiprogram.org
CERTIFIED PWC-SFICOC-260
SOURCING

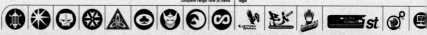

HISTORY LESSON:
CHAPTER SEVEN

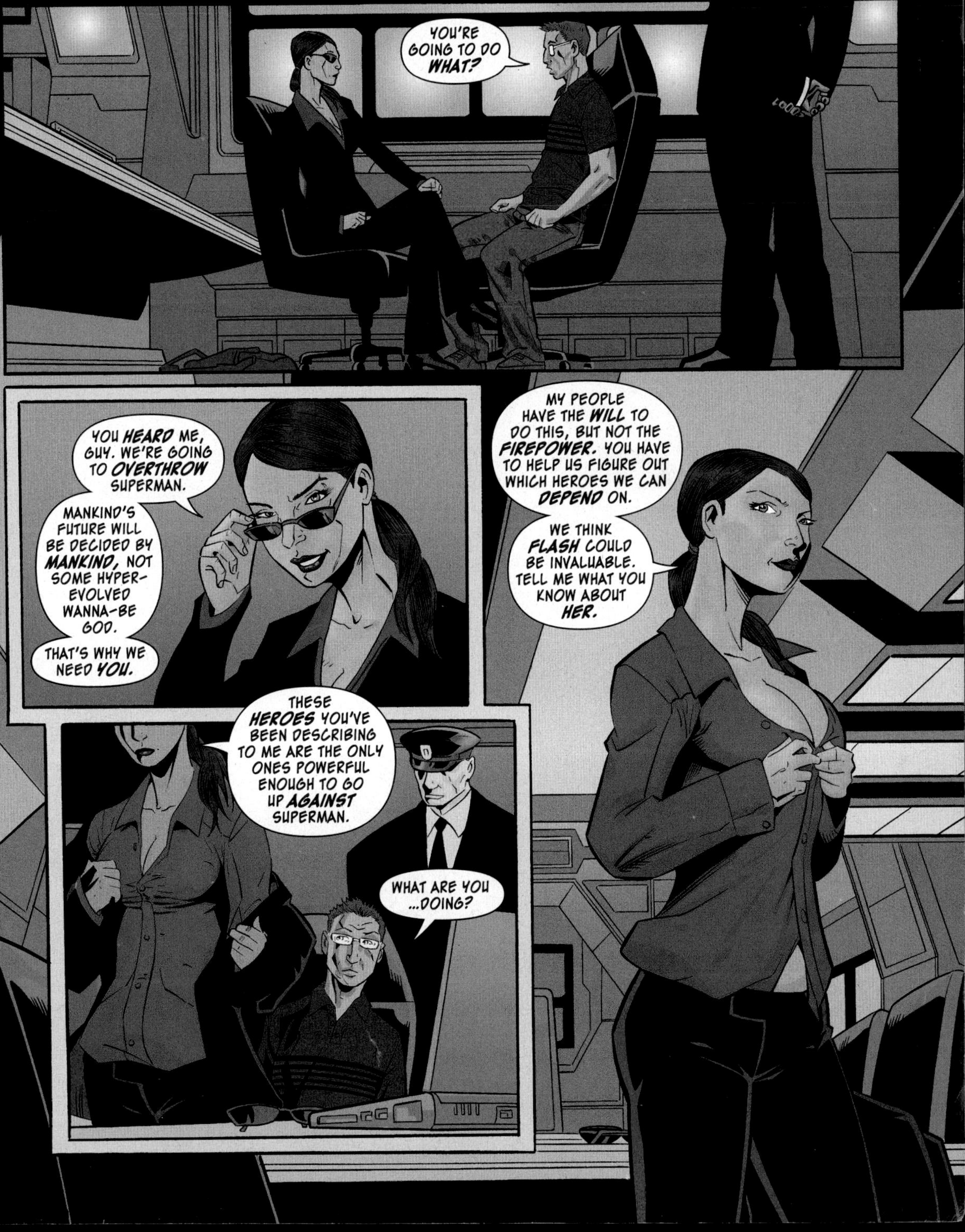

YOU'RE GOING TO DO WHAT?
YOU HEARD ME, GUY. WE'RE GOING TO OVERTHROW SUPERMAN.
MANKIND'S FUTURE WILL BE DECIDED BY MANKIND, NOT SOME HYPER-EVOLVED WANNA-BE GOD.
THAT'S WHY WE NEED YOU.
MY PEOPLE HAVE THE WILL TO DO THIS, BUT NOT THE FIREPOWER. YOU HAVE TO HELP US FIGURE OUT WHICH HEROES WE CAN DEPEND ON.
WE THINK FLASH COULD BE INVALUABLE. TELL ME WHAT YOU KNOW ABOUT HER.
THESE HEROES YOU'VE BEEN DESCRIBING TO ME ARE THE ONLY ONES POWERFUL ENOUGH TO GO UP AGAINST SUPERMAN.
WHAT ARE YOU ...DOING?

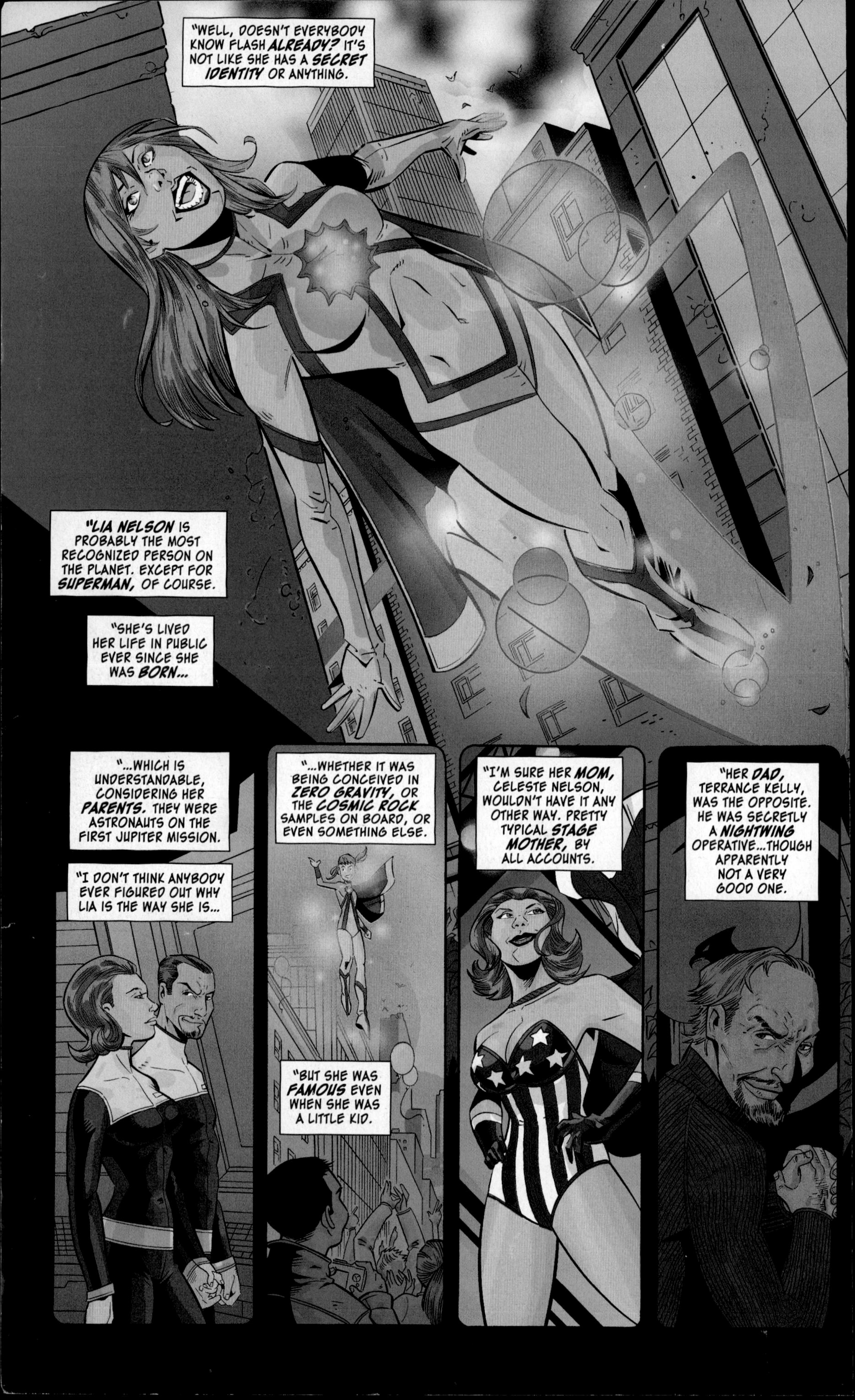
"WELL, DOESN'T EVERYBODY KNOW FLASH ALREADY? IT'S NOT LIKE SHE HAS A SECRET IDENTITY OR ANYTHING.
"LIA NELSON IS PROBABLY THE MOST RECOGNIZED PERSON ON THE PLANET. EXCEPT FOR SUPERMAN, OF COURSE.
"SHE'S LIVED HER LIFE IN PUBLIC EVER SINCE SHE WAS BORN...
"...WHICH IS UNDERSTANDABLE, CONSIDERING HER PARENTS. THEY WERE ASTRONAUTS ON THE FIRST JUPITER MISSION.
"I DON'T THINK ANYBODY EVER FIGURED OUT WHY LIA IS THE WAY SHE IS...
"...WHETHER IT WAS BEING CONCEIVED IN ZERO GRAVITY, OR THE COSMIC ROCK SAMPLES ON BOARD, OR EVEN SOMETHING ELSE.
"BUT SHE WAS FAMOUS EVEN WHEN SHE WAS A LITTLE KID.
"I'M SURE HER MOM, CELESTE NELSON, WOULDN'T HAVE IT ANY OTHER WAY. PRETTY TYPICAL STAGE MOTHER, BY ALL ACCOUNTS.
"HER DAD, TERRANCE KELLY, WAS THE OPPOSITE. HE WAS SECRETLY A NIGHTWING OPERATIVE...THOUGH APPARENTLY NOT A VERY GOOD ONE.

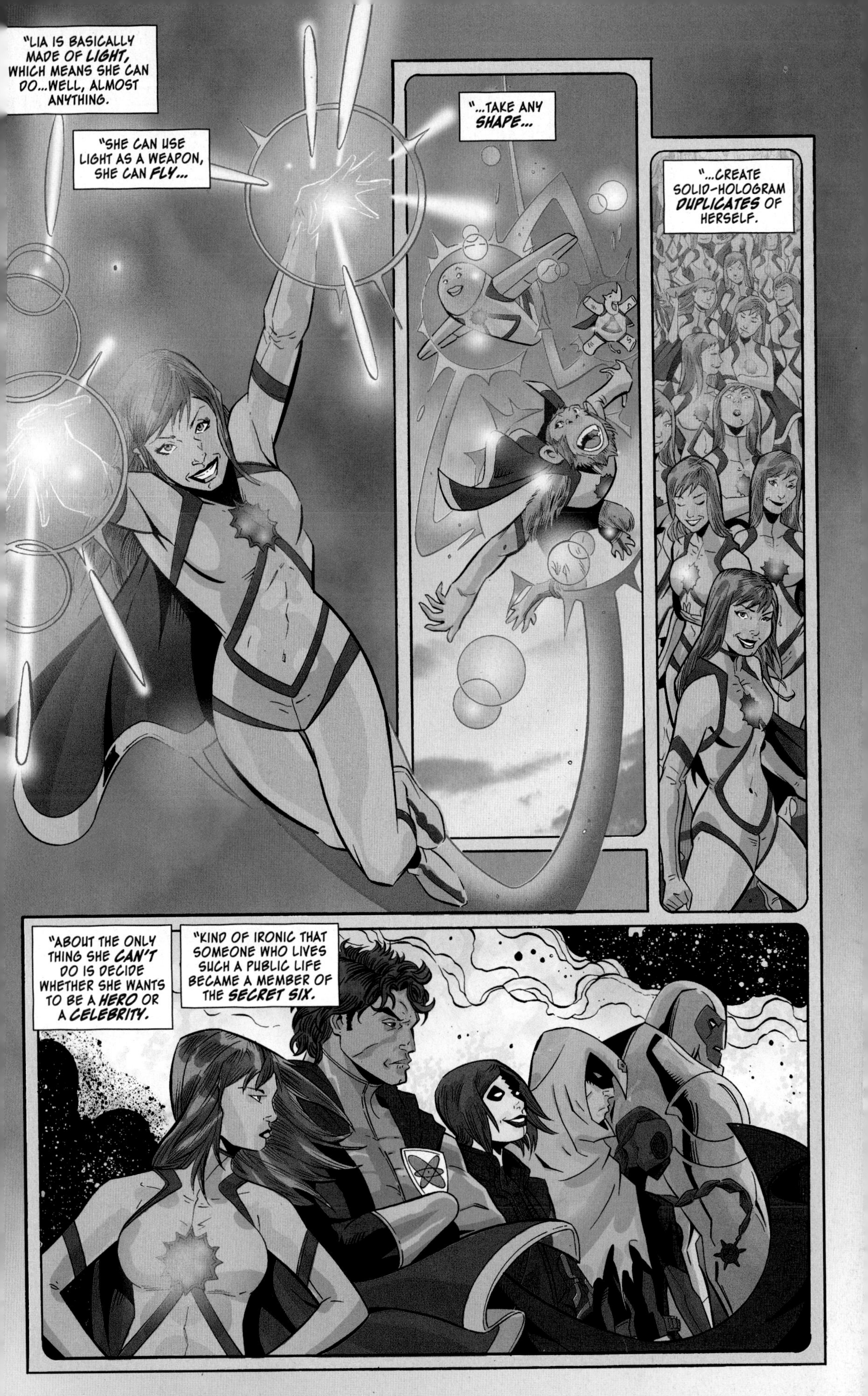
"LIA IS BASICALLY MADE OF LIGHT, WHICH MEANS SHE CAN DO...WELL, ALMOST ANYTHING.
"SHE CAN USE LIGHT AS A WEAPON, SHE CAN FLY...
"...TAKE ANY SHAPE...
"...CREATE SOLID-HOLOGRAM DUPLICATES OF HERSELF.
"ABOUT THE ONLY THING SHE CAN'T DO IS DECIDE WHETHER SHE WANTS TO BE A HERO OR A CELEBRITY.
"KIND OF IRONIC THAT SOMEONE WHO LIVES SUCH A PUBLIC LIFE BECAME A MEMBER OF THE SECRET SIX.

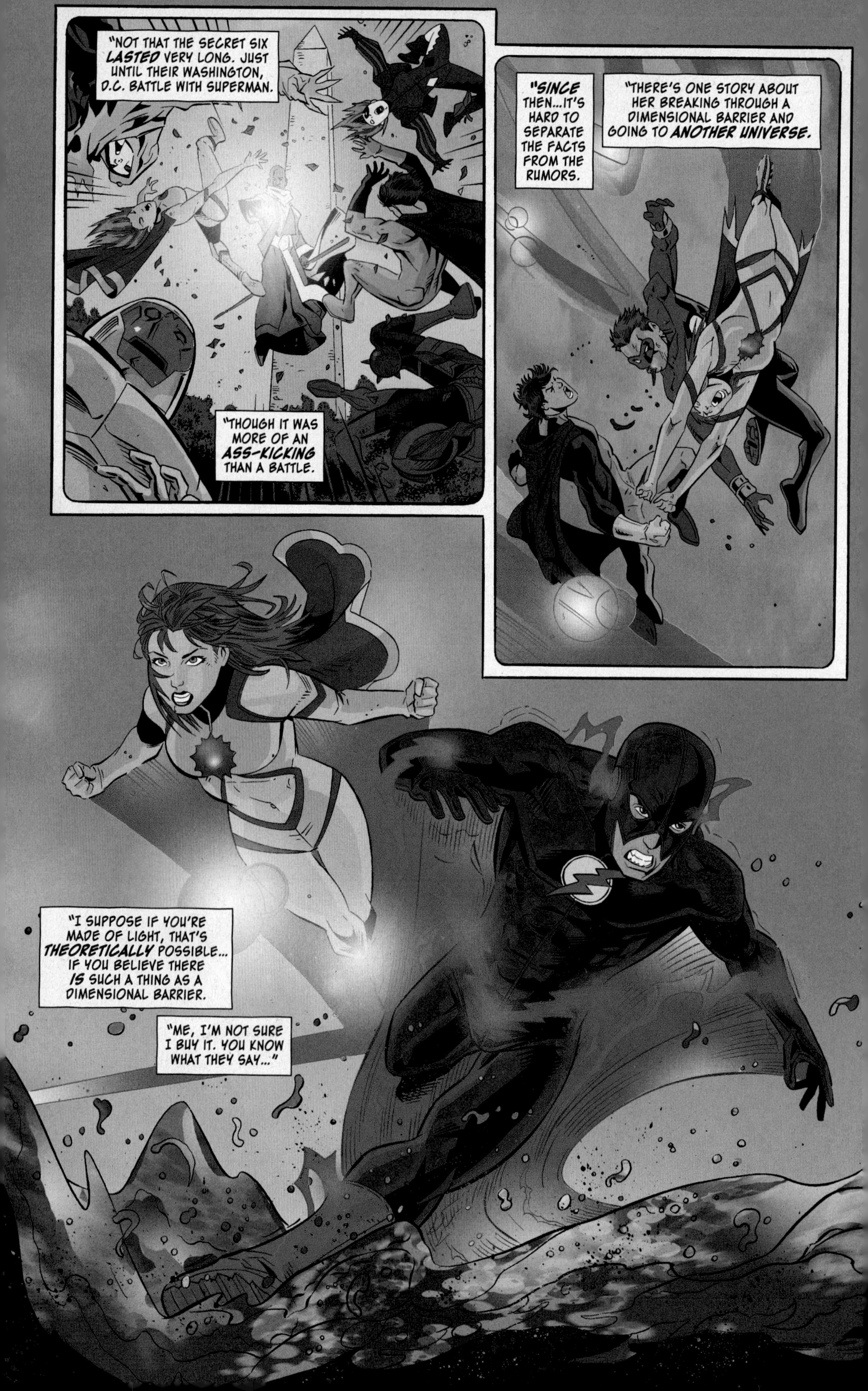
"NOT THAT THE SECRET SIX LASTED VERY LONG. JUST UNTIL THEIR WASHINGTON, D.C. BATTLE WITH SUPERMAN.
"THOUGH IT WAS MORE OF AN ASS-KICKING THAN A BATTLE.
"SINCE THEN...IT'S HARD TO SEPARATE THE FACTS FROM THE RUMORS.
"THERE'S ONE STORY ABOUT HER BREAKING THROUGH A DIMENSIONAL BARRIER AND GOING TO ANOTHER UNIVERSE.
"I SUPPOSE IF YOU'RE MADE OF LIGHT, THAT'S THEORETICALLY POSSIBLE... IF YOU BELIEVE THERE IS SUCH A THING AS A DIMENSIONAL BARRIER.
"ME, I'M NOT SURE I BUY IT. YOU KNOW WHAT THEY SAY..."

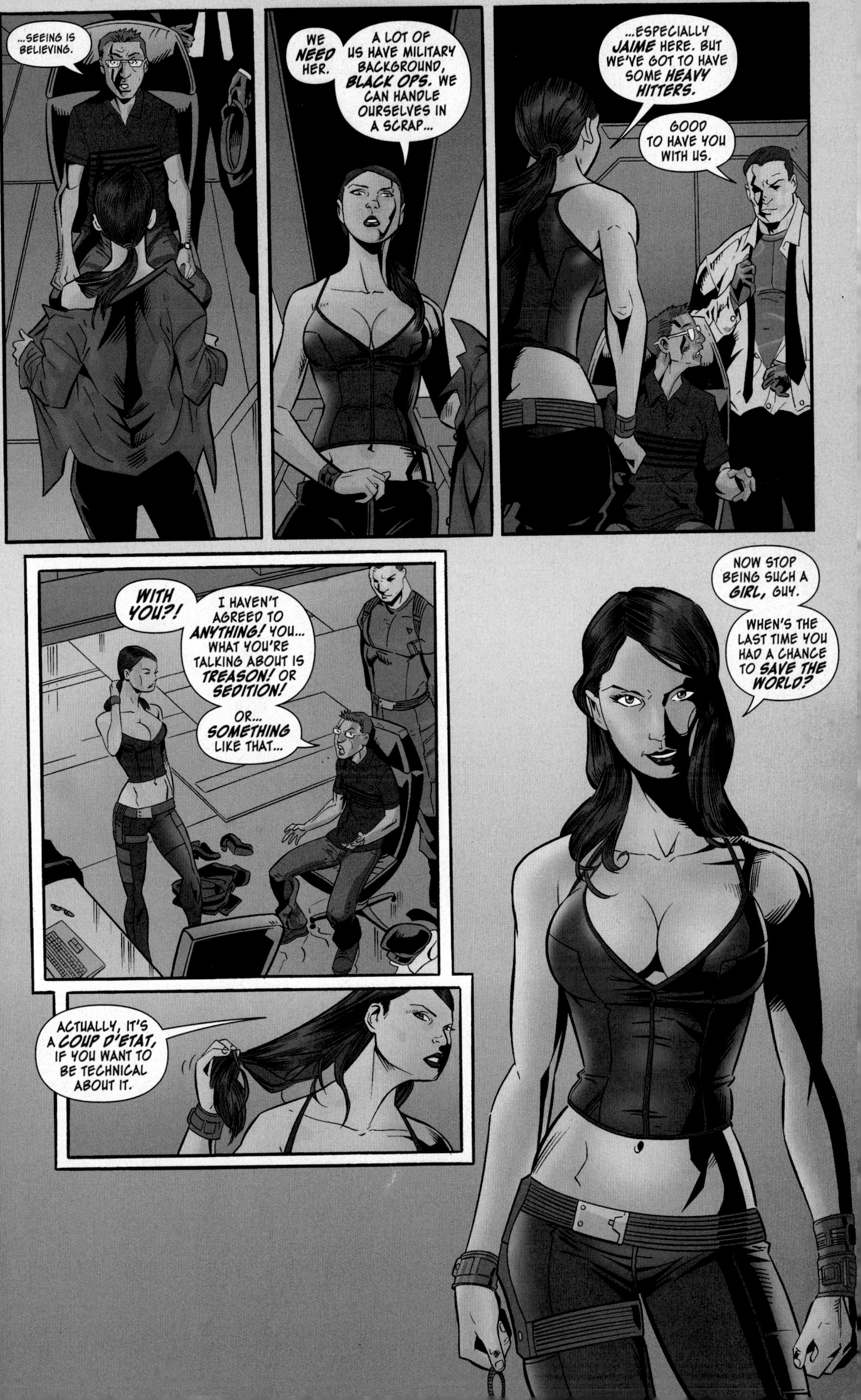
...SEEING IS BELIEVING.
WE NEED HER.
A LOT OF US HAVE MILITARY BACKGROUND, BLACK OPS. WE CAN HANDLE OURSELVES IN A SCRAP...
...ESPECIALLY JAIME HERE. BUT WE'VE GOT TO HAVE SOME HEAVY HITTERS.
GOOD TO HAVE YOU WITH US.
WITH YOU?!
I HAVEN'T AGREED TO ANYTHING! YOU... WHAT YOU'RE TALKING ABOUT IS TREASON! OR SEDITION!
OR... SOMETHING LIKE THAT...
ACTUALLY, IT'S A COUP D'ETAT, IF YOU WANT TO BE TECHNICAL ABOUT IT.
NOW STOP BEING SUCH A GIRL, GUY.
WHEN'S THE LAST TIME YOU HAD A CHANCE TO SAVE THE WORLD?

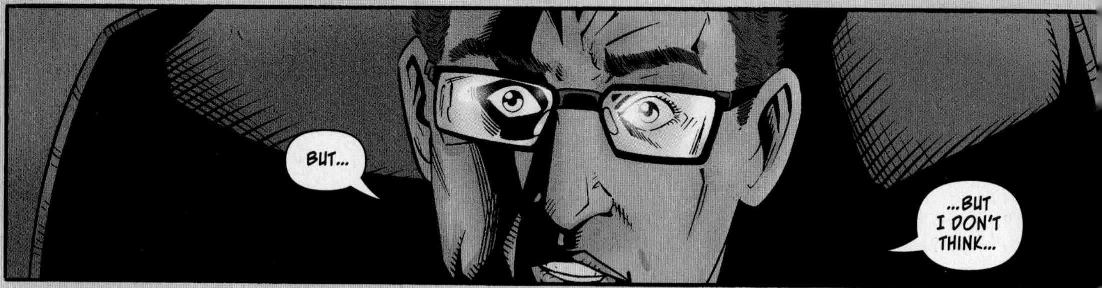
BUT...
...BUT I DON'T THINK...

HISTORY LESSON:
CHAPTER EIGHT

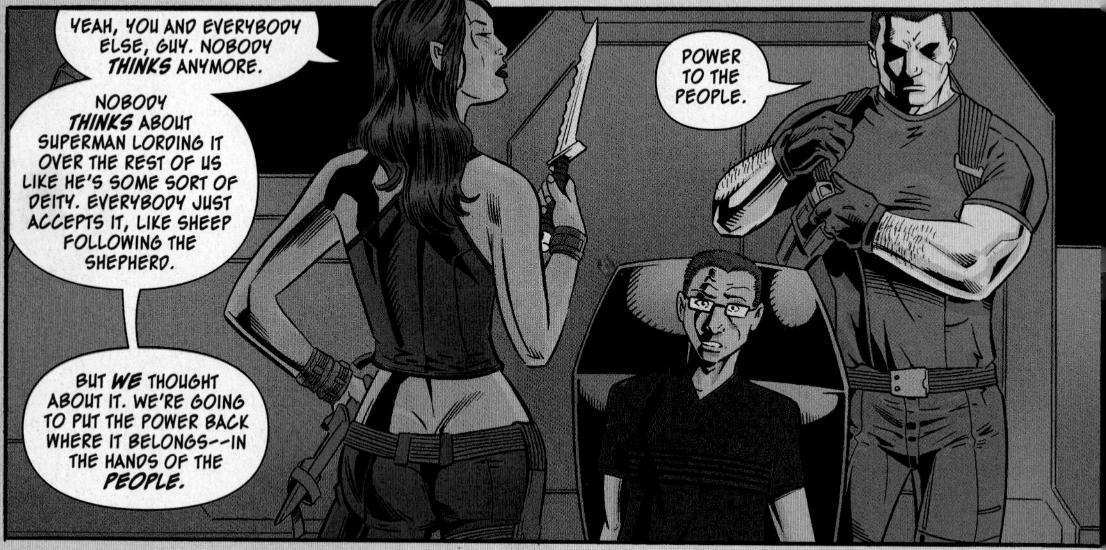
YEAH, YOU AND EVERYBODY ELSE, GUY. NOBODY THINKS ANYMORE.
NOBODY THINKS ABOUT SUPERMAN LORDING IT OVER THE REST OF US LIKE HE'S SOME SORT OF DEITY. EVERYBODY JUST ACCEPTS IT, LIKE SHEEP FOLLOWING THE SHEPHERD.
POWER TO THE PEOPLE.
BUT WE THOUGHT ABOUT IT. WE'RE GOING TO PUT THE POWER BACK WHERE IT BELONGS--IN THE HANDS OF THE PEOPLE.

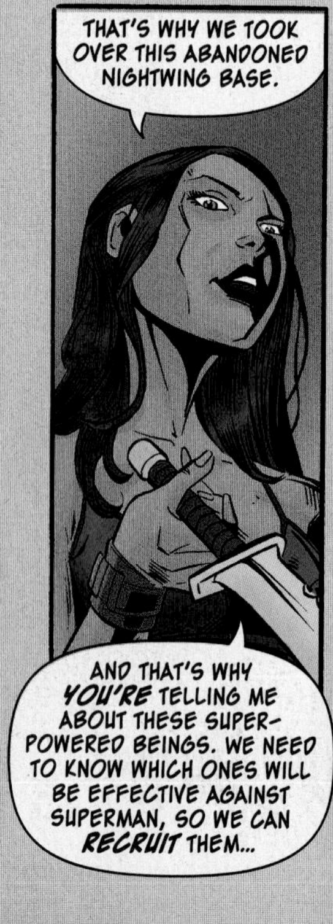
THAT'S WHY WE TOOK OVER THIS ABANDONED NIGHTWING BASE.
AND THAT'S WHY YOU'RE TELLING ME ABOUT THESE SUPER-POWERED BEINGS. WE NEED TO KNOW WHICH ONES WILL BE EFFECTIVE AGAINST SUPERMAN, SO WE CAN RECRUIT THEM...

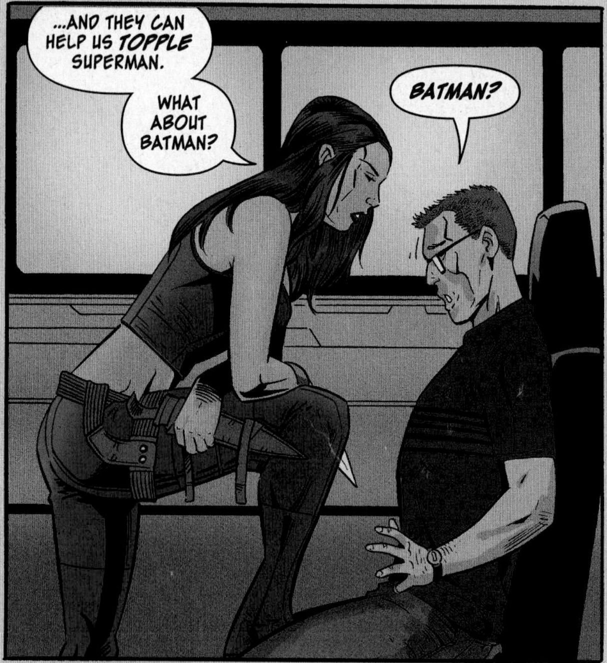
...AND THEY CAN HELP US TOPPLE SUPERMAN.
WHAT ABOUT BATMAN?
BATMAN?

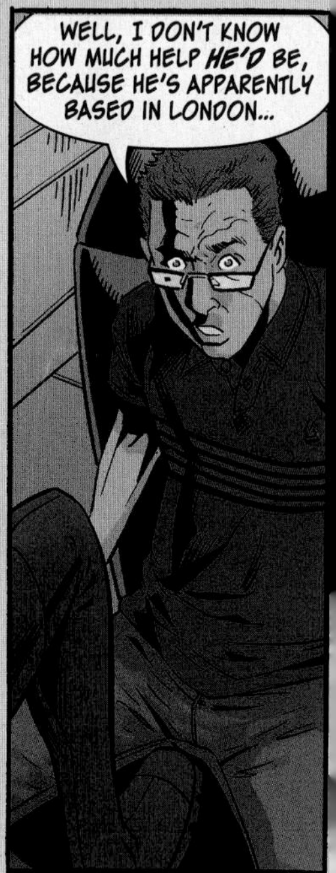
WELL, I DON'T KNOW HOW MUCH HELP HE'D BE, BECAUSE HE'S APPARENTLY BASED IN LONDON...

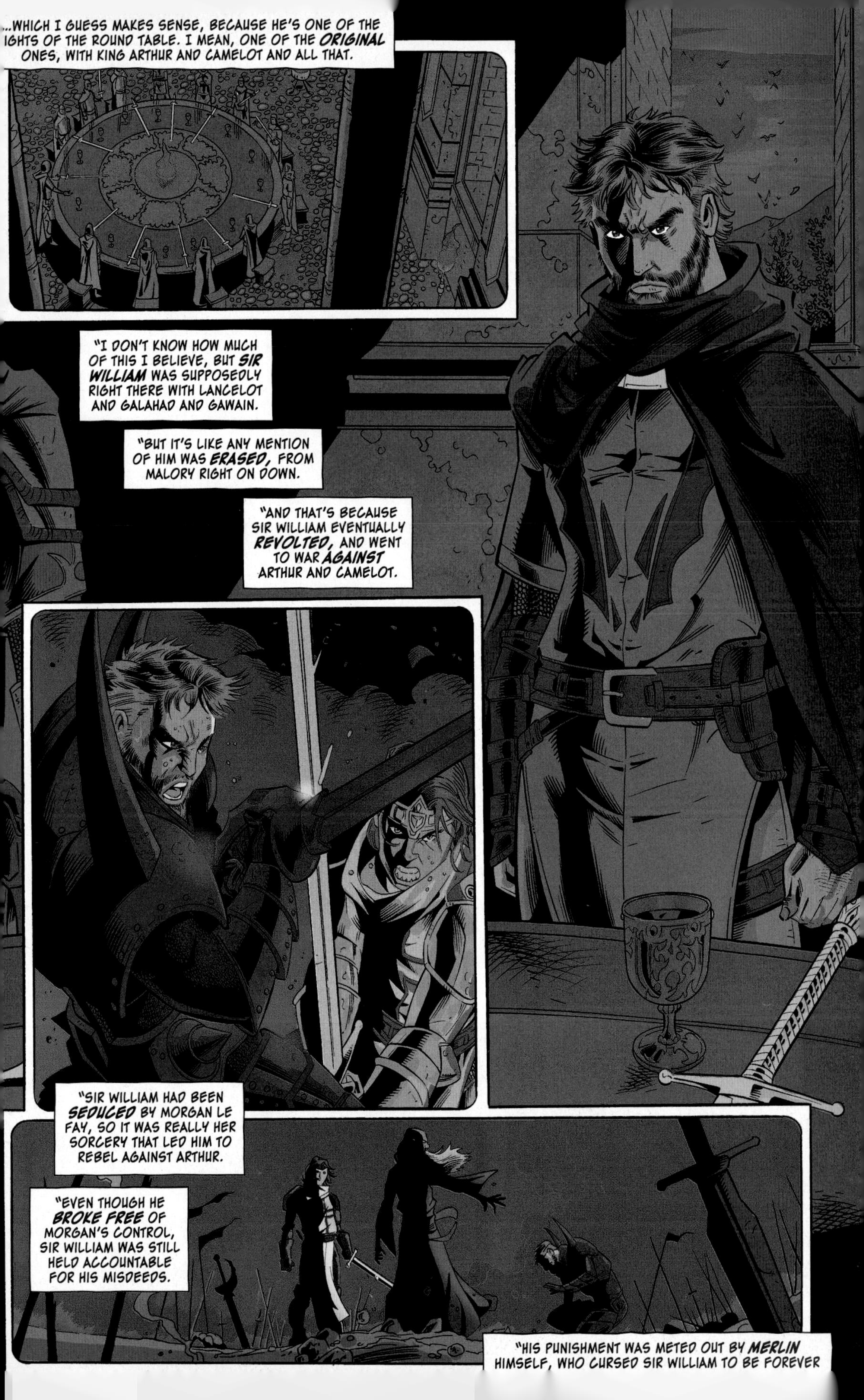
...WHICH I GUESS MAKES SENSE, BECAUSE HE'S ONE OF THE IGHTS OF THE ROUND TABLE. I MEAN, ONE OF THE ORIGINAL ONES, WITH KING ARTHUR AND CAMELOT AND ALL THAT.
"I DON'T KNOW HOW MUCH OF THIS I BELIEVE, BUT SIR WILLIAM WAS SUPPOSEDLY RIGHT THERE WITH LANCELOT AND GALAHAD AND GAWAIN.
"BUT IT'S LIKE ANY MENTION OF HIM WAS ERASED, FROM MALORY RIGHT ON DOWN.
"AND THAT'S BECAUSE SIR WILLIAM EVENTUALLY REVOLTED, AND WENT TO WAR AGAINST ARTHUR AND CAMELOT.
"SIR WILLIAM HAD BEEN SEDUCED BY MORGAN LE FAY, SO IT WAS REALLY HER SORCERY THAT LED HIM TO REBEL AGAINST ARTHUR.
"EVEN THOUGH HE BROKE FREE OF MORGAN'S CONTROL, SIR WILLIAM WAS STILL HELD ACCOUNTABLE FOR HIS MISDEEDS.
"HIS PUNISHMENT WAS METED OUT BY MERLIN HIMSELF, WHO CURSED SIR WILLIAM TO BE FOREVER

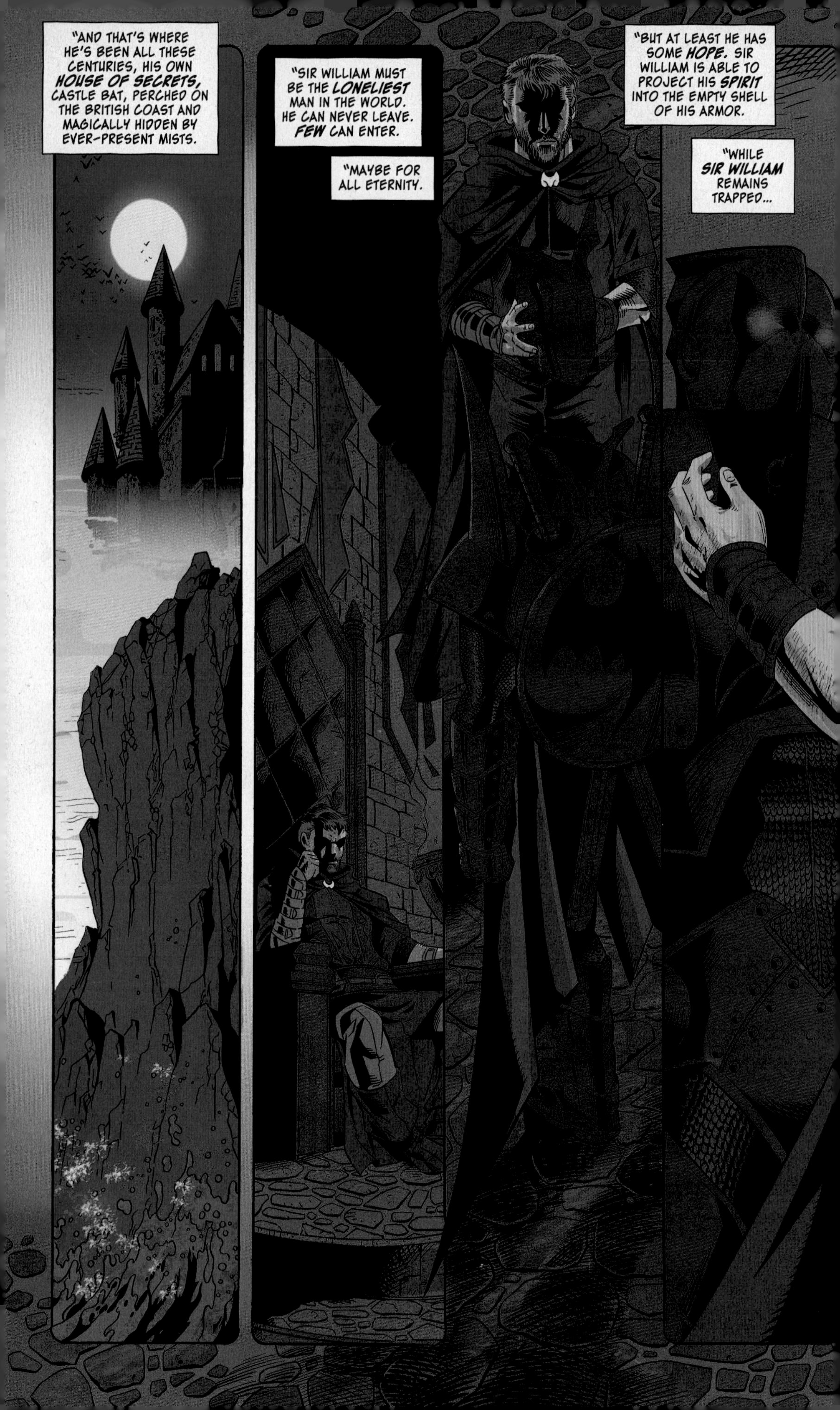
"AND THAT'S WHERE HE'S BEEN ALL THESE CENTURIES, HIS OWN HOUSE OF SECRETS, CASTLE BAT, PERCHED ON THE BRITISH COAST AND MAGICALLY HIDDEN BY EVER-PRESENT MISTS.
"SIR WILLIAM MUST BE THE LONELIEST MAN IN THE WORLD. HE CAN NEVER LEAVE. FEW CAN ENTER.
"MAYBE FOR ALL ETERNITY.
"BUT AT LEAST HE HAS SOME HOPE. SIR WILLIAM IS ABLE TO PROJECT HIS SPIRIT INTO THE EMPTY SHELL OF HIS ARMOR.
"WHILE SIR WILLIAM REMAINS TRAPPED...

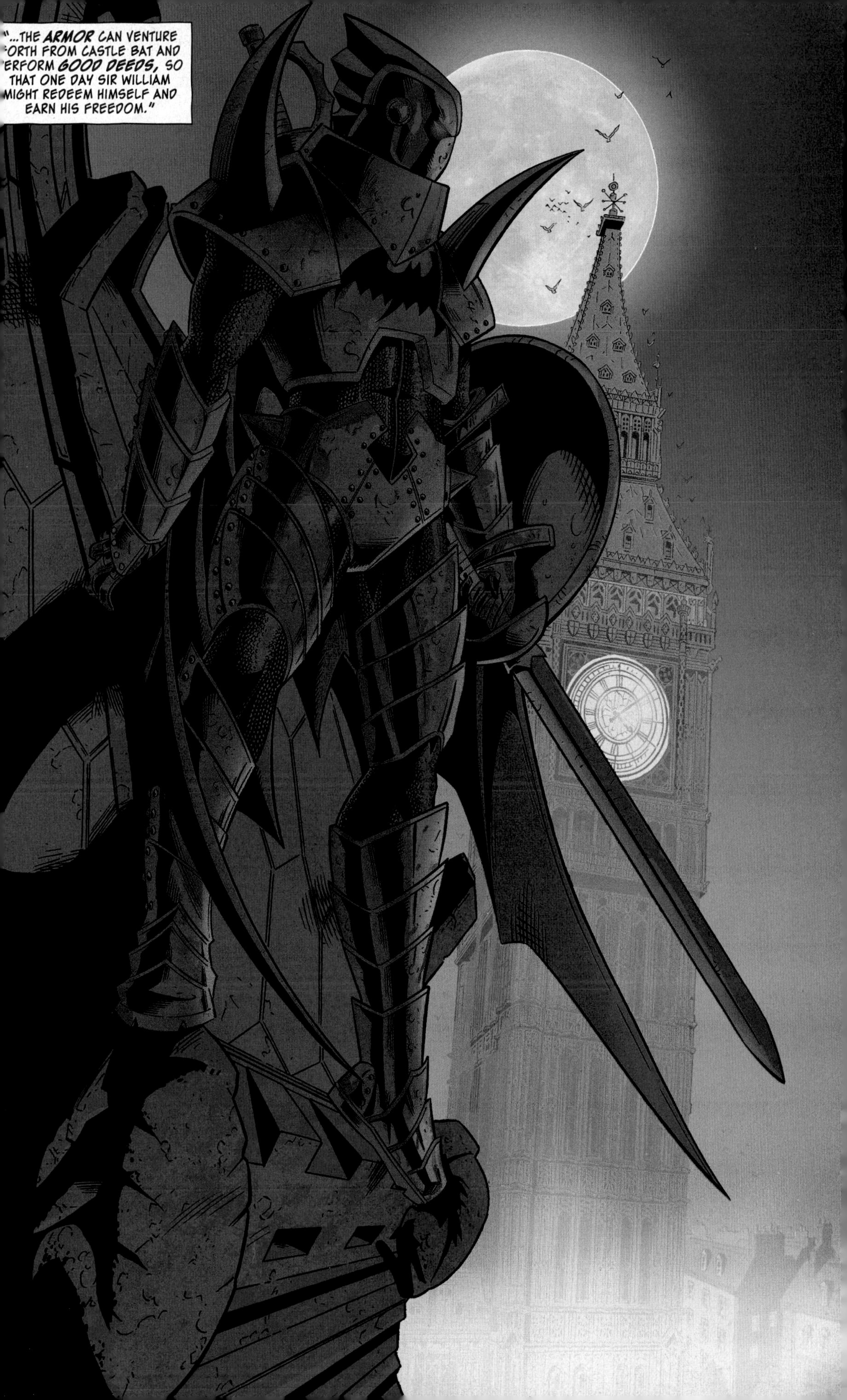
"...THE ARMOR CAN VENTURE
ORTH FROM CASTLE BAT AND
ERFORM GOOD DEEDS, SO
THAT ONE DAY SIR WILLIAM
MIGHT REDEEM HIMSELF AND
EARN HIS FREEDOM."

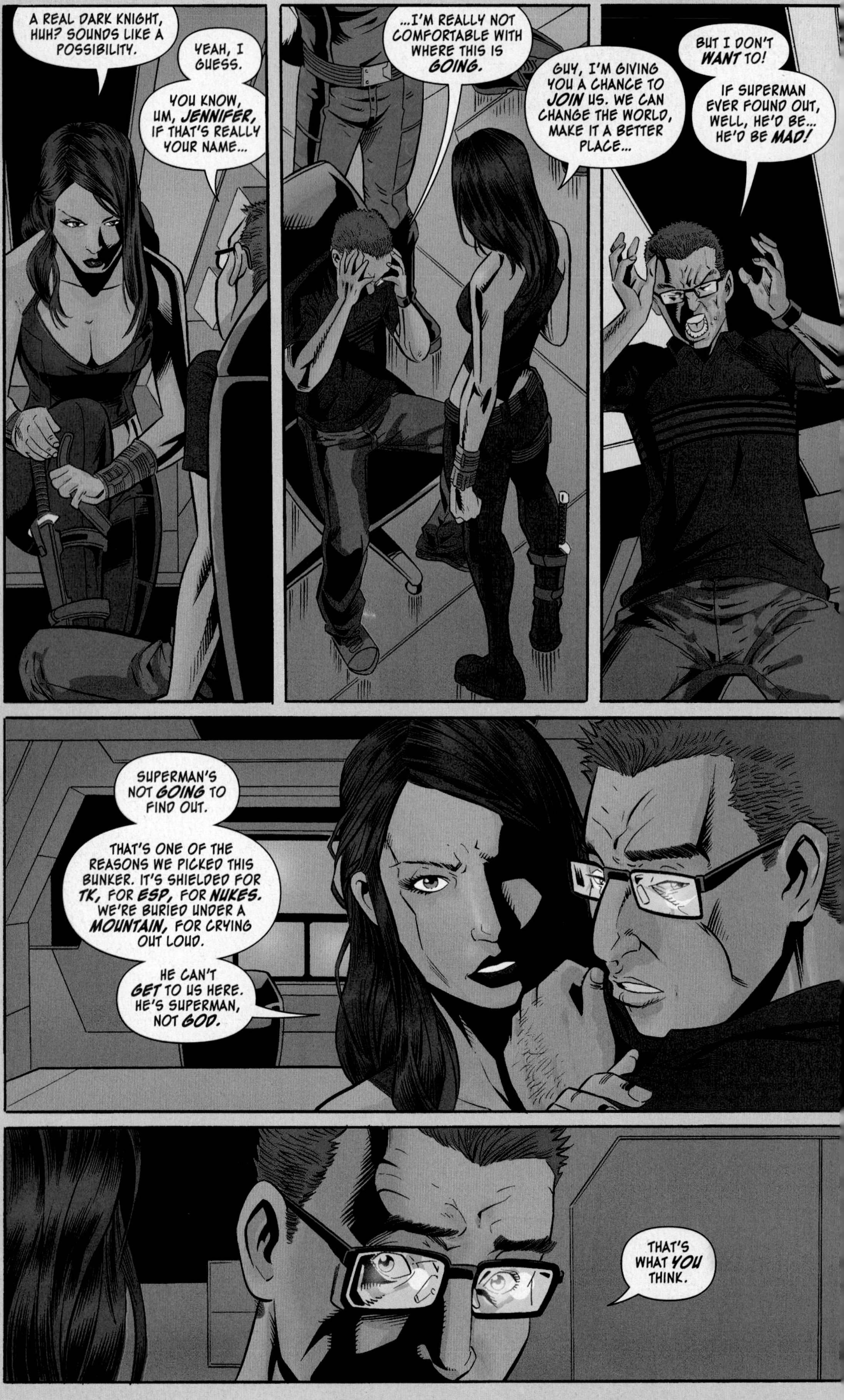
A REAL DARK KNIGHT, HUH? SOUNDS LIKE A POSSIBILITY.
YEAH, I GUESS.
YOU KNOW, UM, JENNIFER, IF THAT'S REALLY YOUR NAME...
...I'M REALLY NOT COMFORTABLE WITH WHERE THIS IS GOING.
GUY, I'M GIVING YOU A CHANCE TO JOIN US. WE CAN CHANGE THE WORLD, MAKE IT A BETTER PLACE...
BUT I DON'T WANT TO!
IF SUPERMAN EVER FOUND OUT, WELL, HE'D BE... HE'D BE MAD!
SUPERMAN'S NOT GOING TO FIND OUT.
THAT'S ONE OF THE REASONS WE PICKED THIS BUNKER. IT'S SHIELDED FOR TK, FOR ESP, FOR NUKES. WE'RE BURIED UNDER A MOUNTAIN, FOR CRYING OUT LOUD.
HE CAN'T GET TO US HERE. HE'S SUPERMAN, NOT GOD.
THAT'S WHAT YOU THINK.

HISTORY LESSON:

CHAPTER NINE

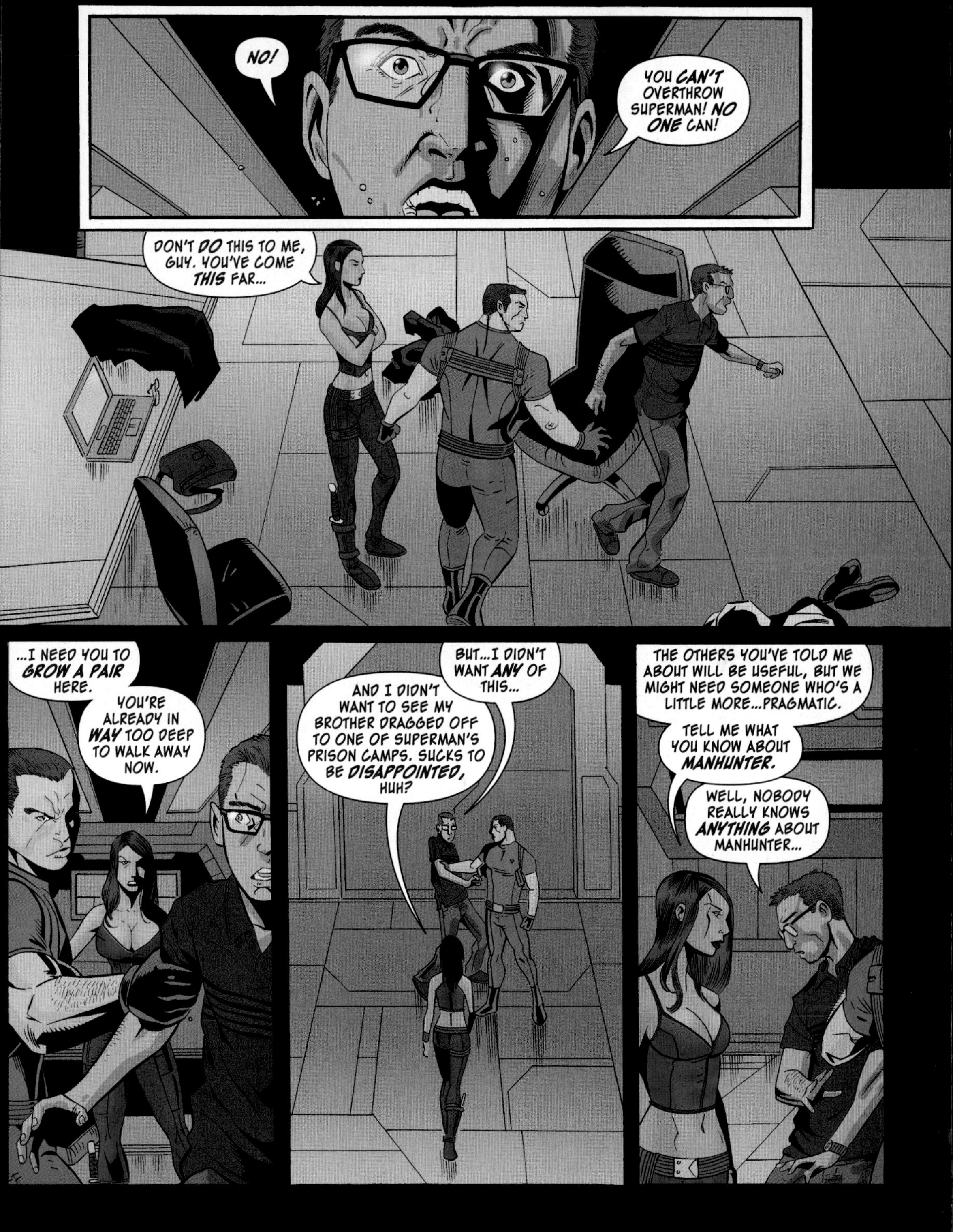

NO!
YOU CAN'T OVERTHROW SUPERMAN! NO ONE CAN!
DON'T DO THIS TO ME, GUY. YOU'VE COME THIS FAR...
...I NEED YOU TO GROW A PAIR HERE.
YOU'RE ALREADY IN WAY TOO DEEP TO WALK AWAY NOW.
BUT...I DIDN'T WANT ANY OF THIS...
AND I DIDN'T WANT TO SEE MY BROTHER DRAGGED OFF TO ONE OF SUPERMAN'S PRISON CAMPS. SUCKS TO BE DISAPPOINTED, HUH?
THE OTHERS YOU'VE TOLD ME ABOUT WILL BE USEFUL, BUT WE MIGHT NEED SOMEONE WHO'S A LITTLE MORE...PRAGMATIC.
TELL ME WHAT YOU KNOW ABOUT MANHUNTER.
WELL, NOBODY REALLY KNOWS ANYTHING ABOUT MANHUNTER...

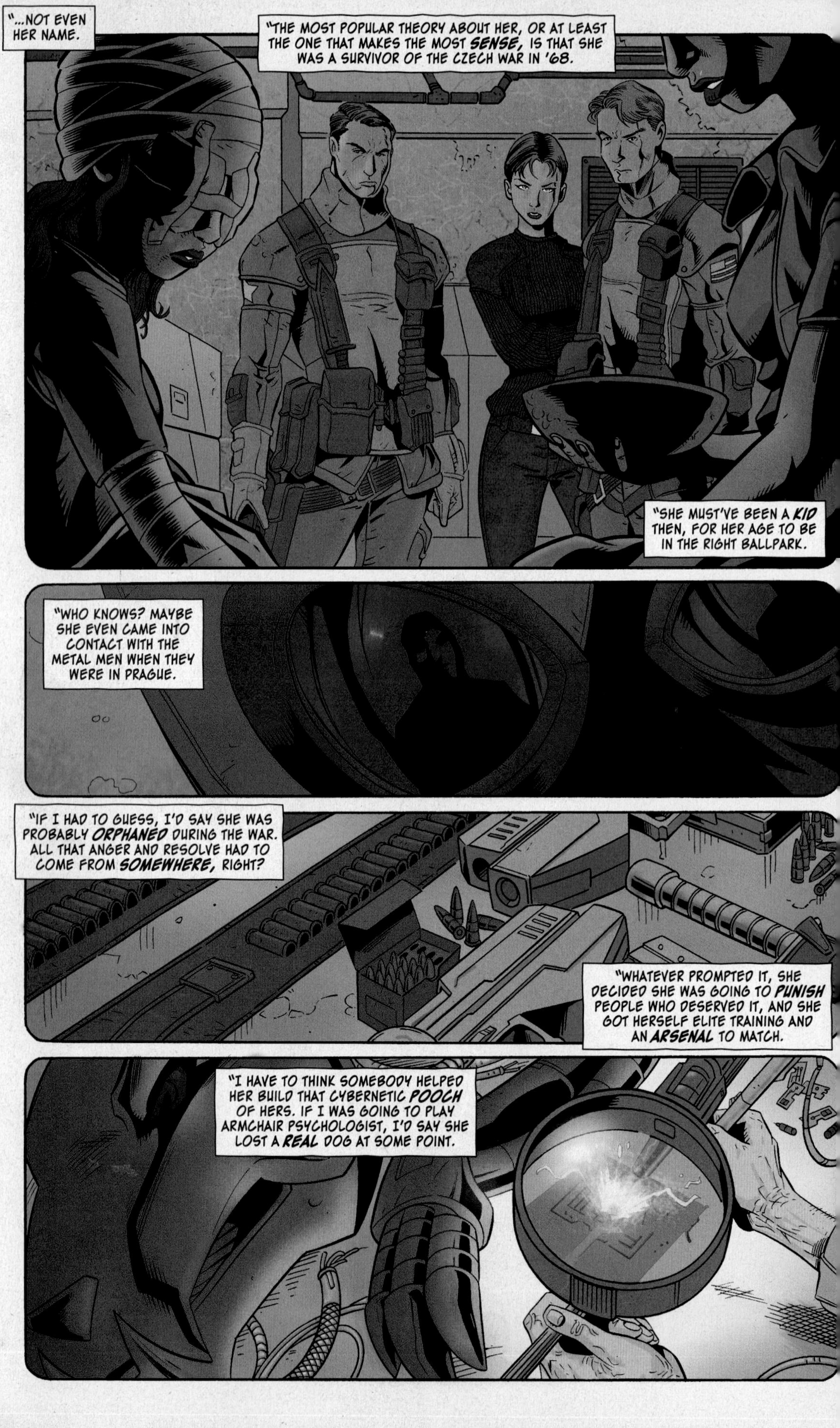
"...NOT EVEN HER NAME.
"THE MOST POPULAR THEORY ABOUT HER, OR AT LEAST THE ONE THAT MAKES THE MOST SENSE, IS THAT SHE WAS A SURVIVOR OF THE CZECH WAR IN '68.
"SHE MUST'VE BEEN A KID THEN, FOR HER AGE TO BE IN THE RIGHT BALLPARK.
"WHO KNOWS? MAYBE SHE EVEN CAME INTO CONTACT WITH THE METAL MEN WHEN THEY WERE IN PRAGUE.
"IF I HAD TO GUESS, I'D SAY SHE WAS PROBABLY ORPHANED DURING THE WAR. ALL THAT ANGER AND RESOLVE HAD TO COME FROM SOMEWHERE, RIGHT?
"WHATEVER PROMPTED IT, SHE DECIDED SHE WAS GOING TO PUNISH PEOPLE WHO DESERVED IT, AND SHE GOT HERSELF ELITE TRAINING AND AN ARSENAL TO MATCH.
"I HAVE TO THINK SOMEBODY HELPED HER BUILD THAT CYBERNETIC POOCH OF HERS. IF I WAS GOING TO PLAY ARMCHAIR PSYCHOLOGIST, I'D SAY SHE LOST A REAL DOG AT SOME POINT.

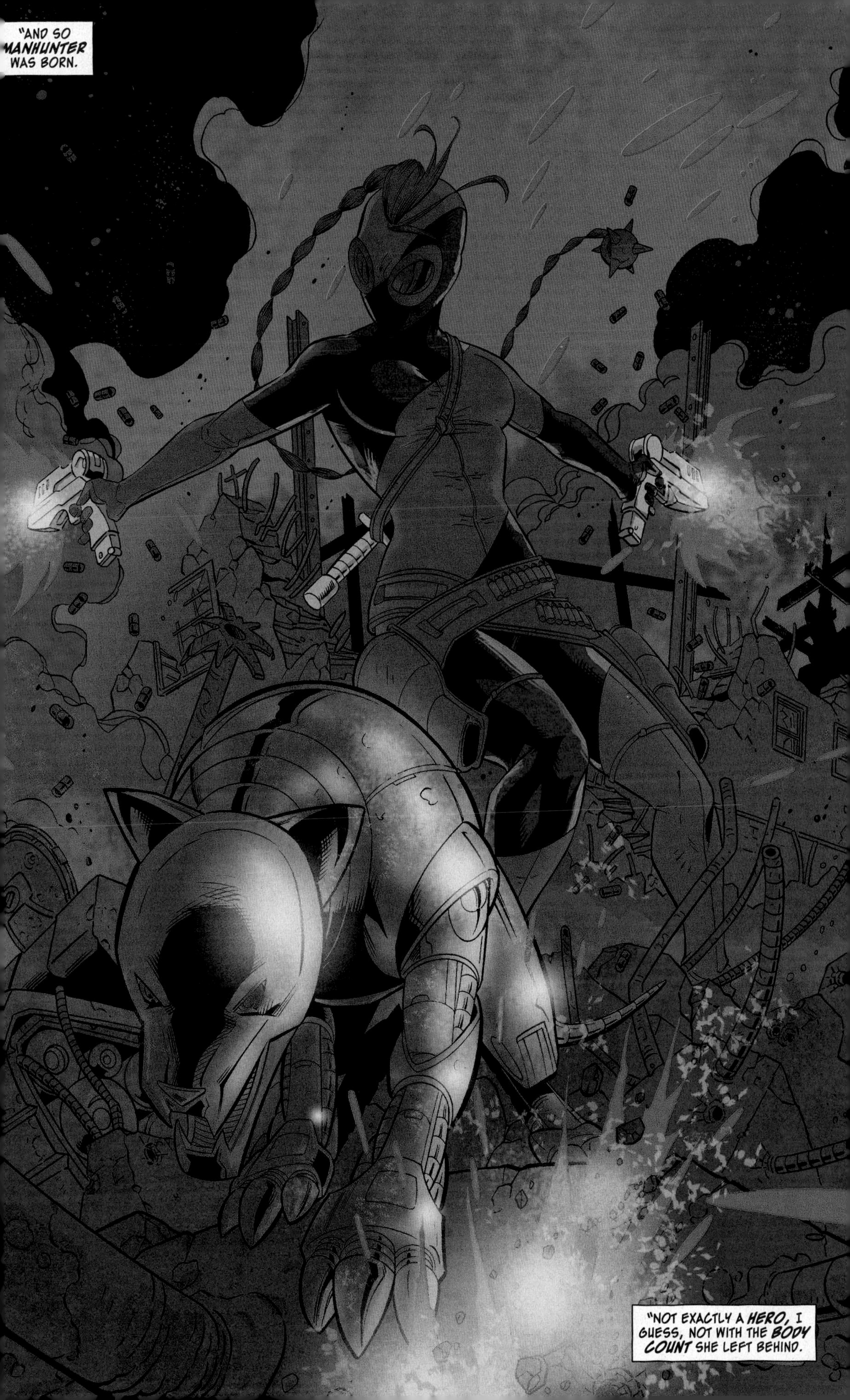
"AND SO MANHUNTER WAS BORN.
"NOT EXACTLY A HERO, I GUESS, NOT WITH THE BODY COUNT SHE LEFT BEHIND.

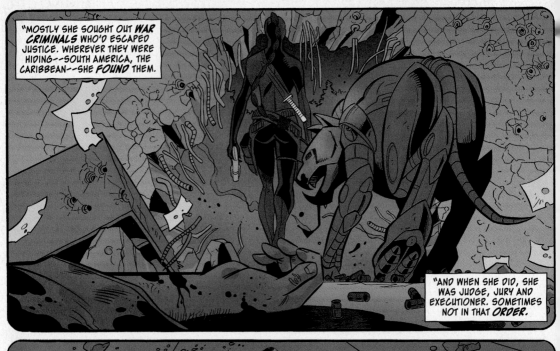

"MOSTLY SHE SOUGHT OUT *WAR CRIMINALS* WHO'D ESCAPED JUSTICE. WHEREVER THEY WERE HIDING--SOUTH AMERICA, THE CARIBBEAN--SHE *FOUND* THEM.

"AND WHEN SHE DID, SHE WAS JUDGE, JURY AND EXECUTIONER. SOMETIMES NOT IN THAT *ORDER*.

"I'M NOT SURE *HOW* SHE ENDED UP IN AMERICA, OR WHY SHE JOINED THE *SECRET SIX*.

"OF COURSE, SHE HAD TO BE A LITTLE LESS *LETHAL* ONCE SHE WAS ON THE TEAM.

"INDICATIONS ARE SHE DIDN'T CONFIDE IN ANY OF THEM. SHE SEEMED TO BE AS MUCH AN ENIGMA TO THEM AS SHE IS TO US.

"DESPITE THAT, SHE HUNG IN AND THE SIX STAYED TOGETHER UNTIL THEY WENT UP AGAINST SUPERMAN..."

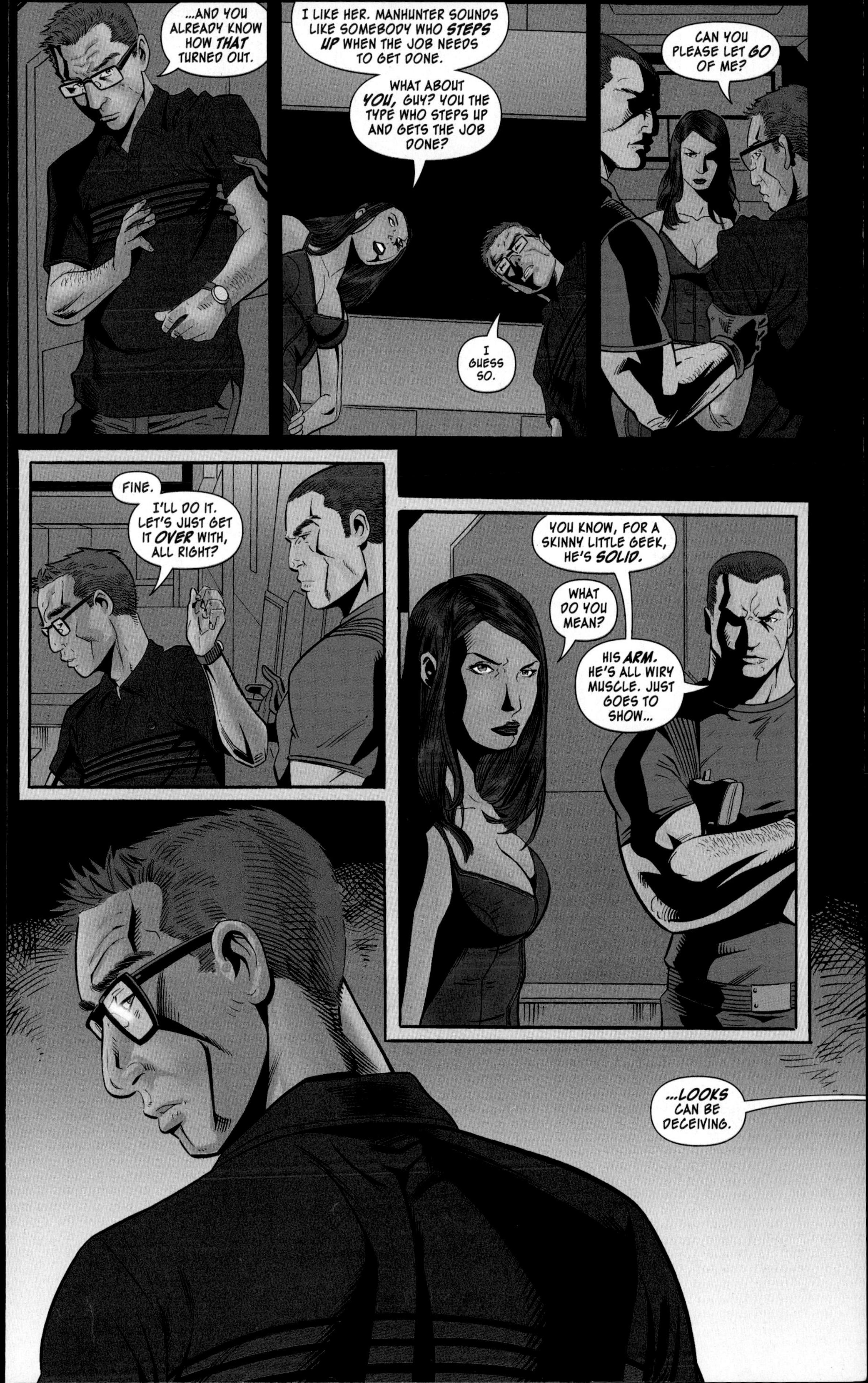
...AND YOU ALREADY KNOW HOW THAT TURNED OUT.
I LIKE HER. MANHUNTER SOUNDS LIKE SOMEBODY WHO STEPS UP WHEN THE JOB NEEDS TO GET DONE.
WHAT ABOUT YOU, GUY? YOU THE TYPE WHO STEPS UP AND GETS THE JOB DONE?
I GUESS SO.
CAN YOU PLEASE LET GO OF ME?
FINE.
I'LL DO IT. LET'S JUST GET IT OVER WITH, ALL RIGHT?
YOU KNOW, FOR A SKINNY LITTLE GEEK, HE'S SOLID.
WHAT DO YOU MEAN?
HIS ARM. HE'S ALL WIRY MUSCLE. JUST GOES TO SHOW...
...LOOKS CAN BE DECEIVING.

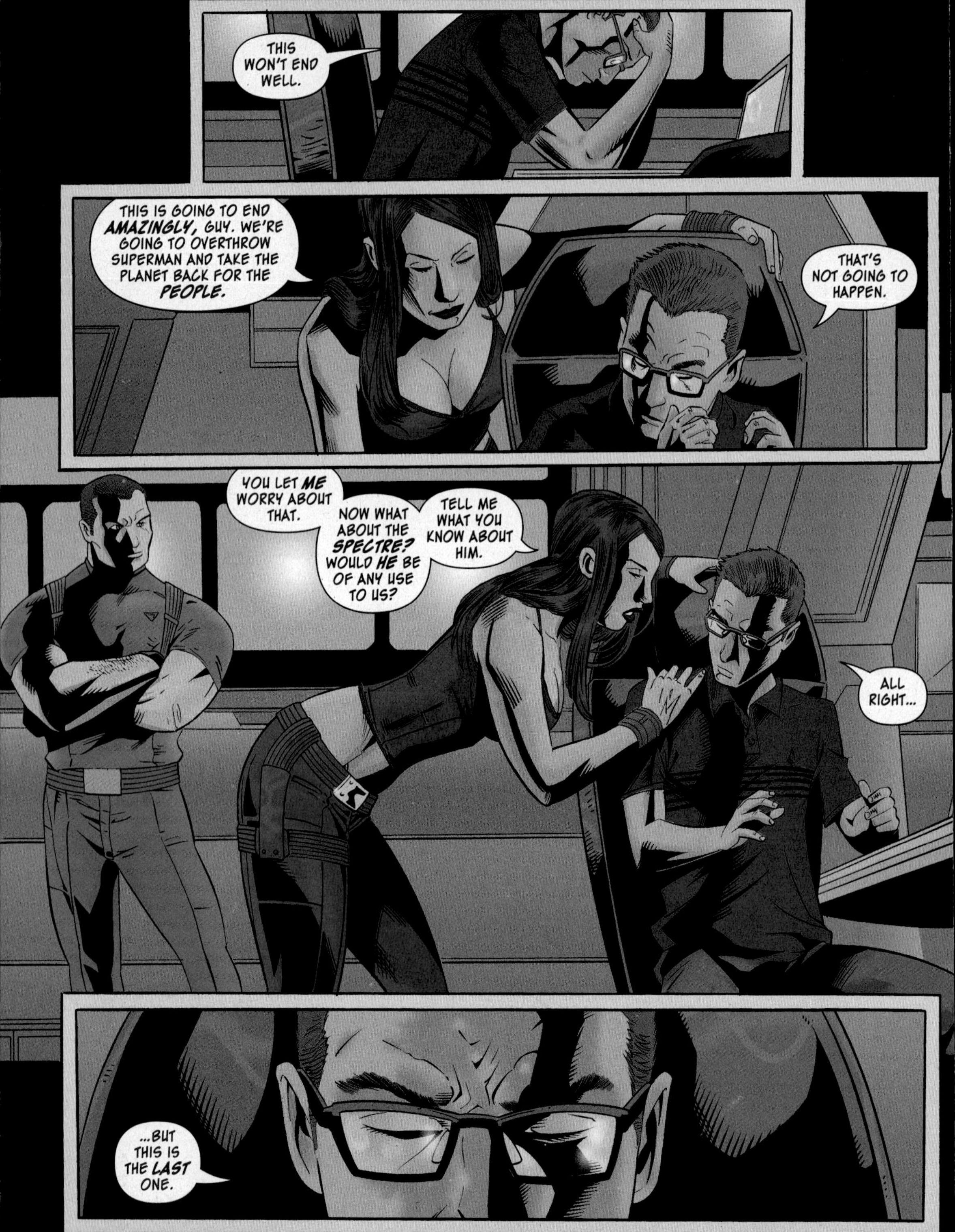
THIS WON'T END WELL.
THIS IS GOING TO END AMAZINGLY, GUY. WE'RE GOING TO OVERTHROW SUPERMAN AND TAKE THE PLANET BACK FOR THE PEOPLE.
THAT'S NOT GOING TO HAPPEN.
YOU LET ME WORRY ABOUT THAT.
NOW WHAT ABOUT THE SPECTRE? WOULD HE BE OF ANY USE TO US?
TELL ME WHAT YOU KNOW ABOUT HIM.
ALL RIGHT...
...BUT THIS IS THE LAST ONE.

HISTORY LESSON:

CHAPTER TEN

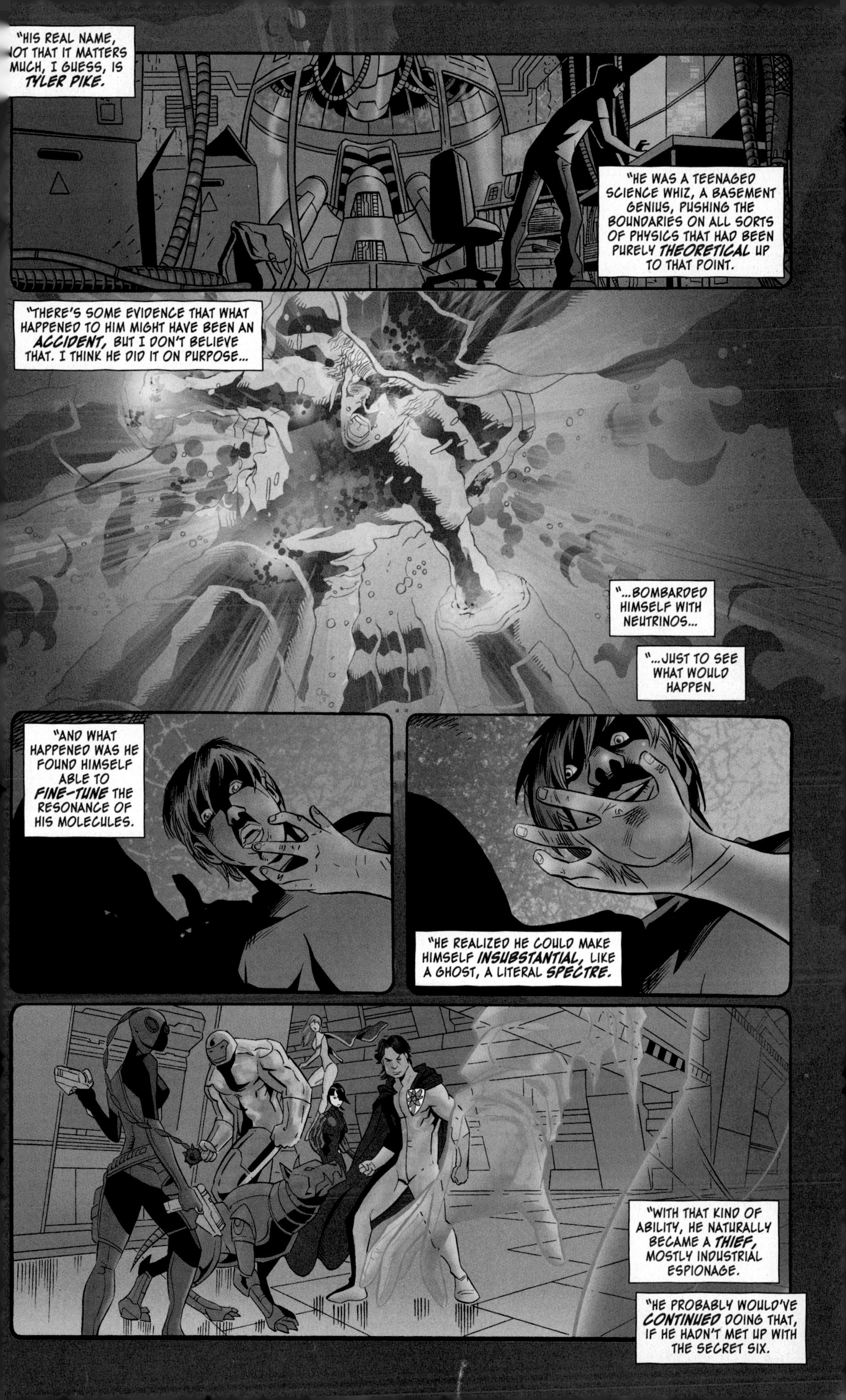
"HIS REAL NAME, NOT THAT IT MATTERS MUCH, I GUESS, IS TYLER PIKE.
"HE WAS A TEENAGED SCIENCE WHIZ, A BASEMENT GENIUS, PUSHING THE BOUNDARIES ON ALL SORTS OF PHYSICS THAT HAD BEEN PURELY THEORETICAL UP TO THAT POINT.
"THERE'S SOME EVIDENCE THAT WHAT HAPPENED TO HIM MIGHT HAVE BEEN AN ACCIDENT, BUT I DON'T BELIEVE THAT. I THINK HE DID IT ON PURPOSE...
"...BOMBARDED HIMSELF WITH NEUTRINOS...
"...JUST TO SEE WHAT WOULD HAPPEN.
"AND WHAT HAPPENED WAS HE FOUND HIMSELF ABLE TO FINE-TUNE THE RESONANCE OF HIS MOLECULES.
"HE REALIZED HE COULD MAKE HIMSELF INSUBSTANTIAL, LIKE A GHOST, A LITERAL SPECTRE.
"WITH THAT KIND OF ABILITY, HE NATURALLY BECAME A THIEF, MOSTLY INDUSTRIAL ESPIONAGE.
"HE PROBABLY WOULD'VE CONTINUED DOING THAT, IF HE HADN'T MET UP WITH THE SECRET SIX.

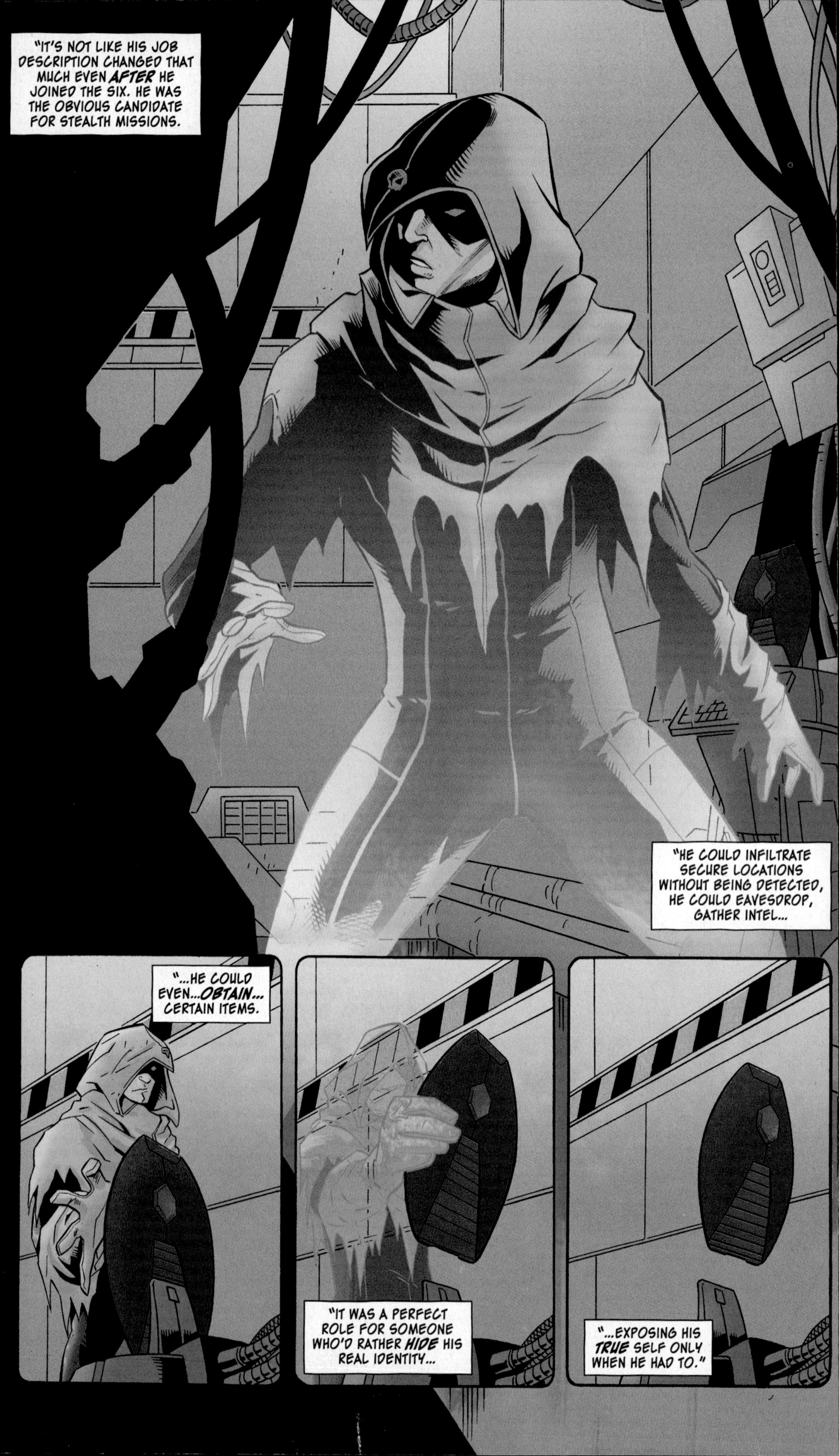
"IT'S NOT LIKE HIS JOB DESCRIPTION CHANGED THAT MUCH EVEN *AFTER* HE JOINED THE SIX. HE WAS THE OBVIOUS CANDIDATE FOR STEALTH MISSIONS.
"HE COULD INFILTRATE SECURE LOCATIONS WITHOUT BEING DETECTED, HE COULD EAVESDROP, GATHER INTEL...
"...HE COULD EVEN...*OBTAIN*... CERTAIN ITEMS.
"IT WAS A PERFECT ROLE FOR SOMEONE WHO'D RATHER *HIDE* HIS REAL IDENTITY...
"...EXPOSING HIS *TRUE* SELF ONLY WHEN HE HAD TO."

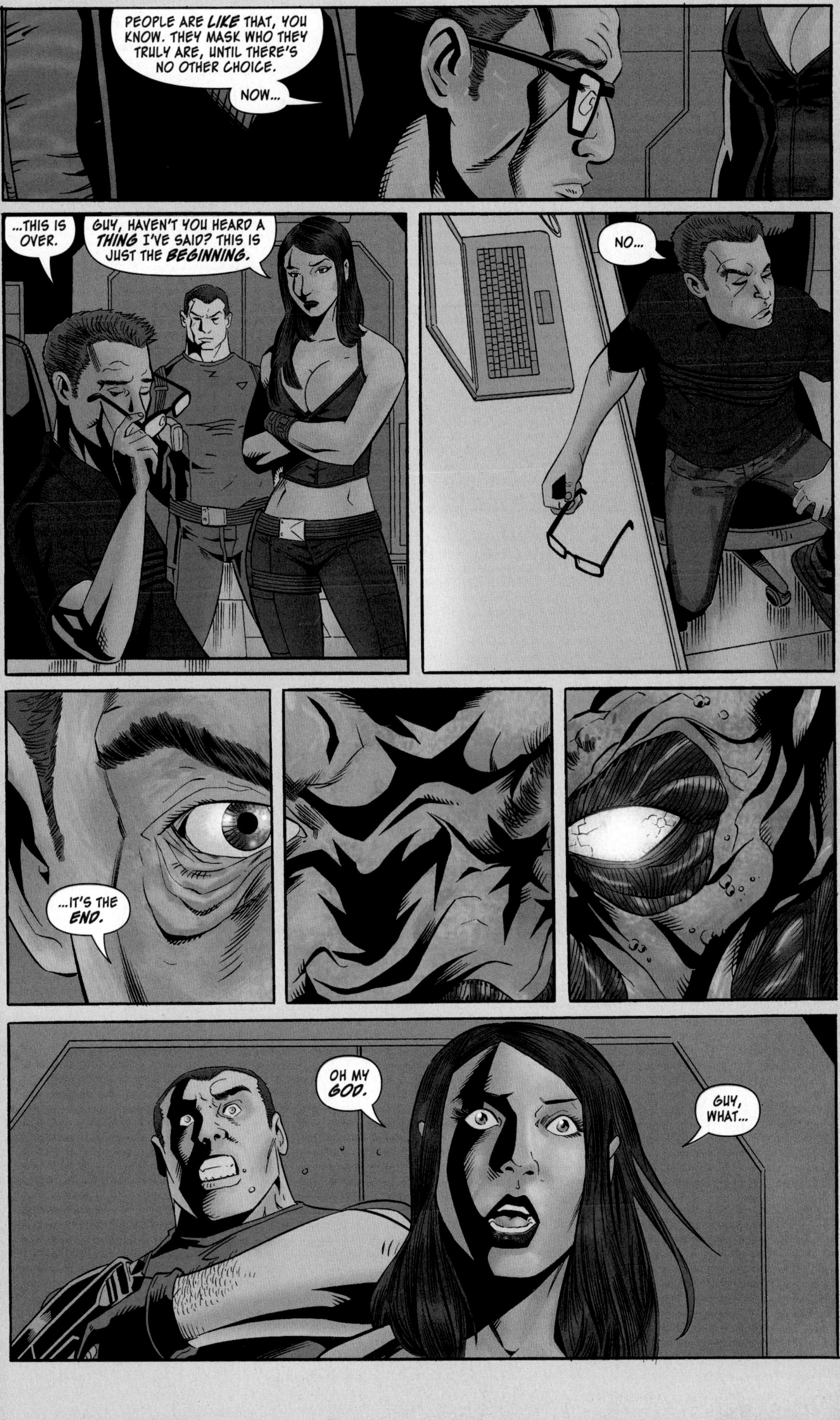
PEOPLE ARE LIKE THAT, YOU KNOW. THEY MASK WHO THEY TRULY ARE, UNTIL THERE'S NO OTHER CHOICE.
NOW...
...THIS IS OVER.
GUY, HAVEN'T YOU HEARD A THING I'VE SAID? THIS IS JUST THE BEGINNING.
NO...
...IT'S THE END.
OH MY GOD.
GUY, WHAT...

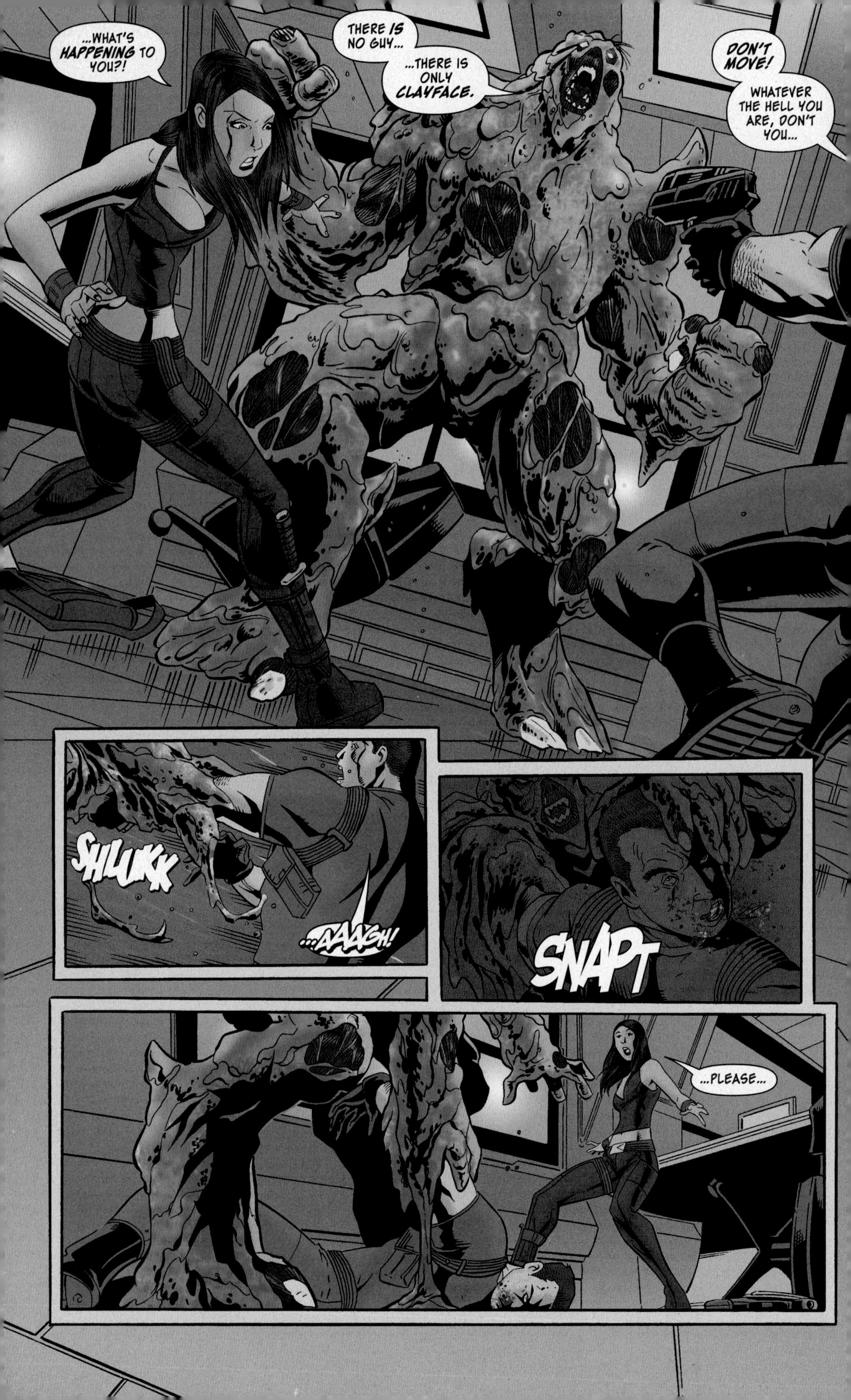
...WHAT'S HAPPENING TO YOU?!
THERE IS NO GUY...
...THERE IS ONLY CLAYFACE.
DON'T MOVE!
WHATEVER THE HELL YOU ARE, DON'T YOU...
SHLUKK
...AAAGH!
SNAPT
...PLEASE...

HISTORY LESSON:
CHAPTER ELEVEN

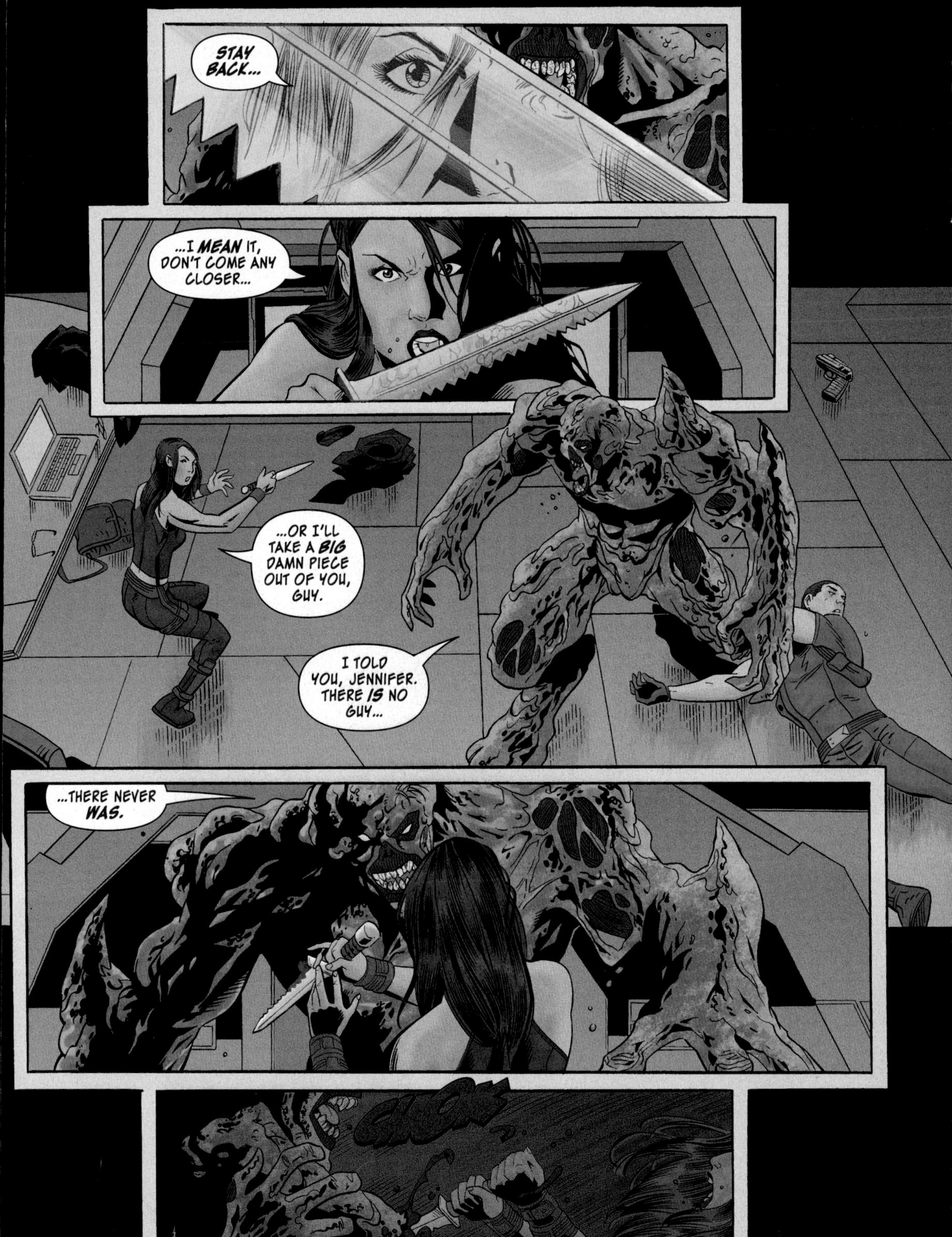

STAY BACK...
...I *MEAN* IT, DON'T COME ANY CLOSER...
...OR I'LL TAKE A *BIG* DAMN PIECE OUT OF YOU, GUY.
I TOLD YOU, JENNIFER. THERE *IS* NO GUY...
...THERE NEVER *WAS*.
CHOK

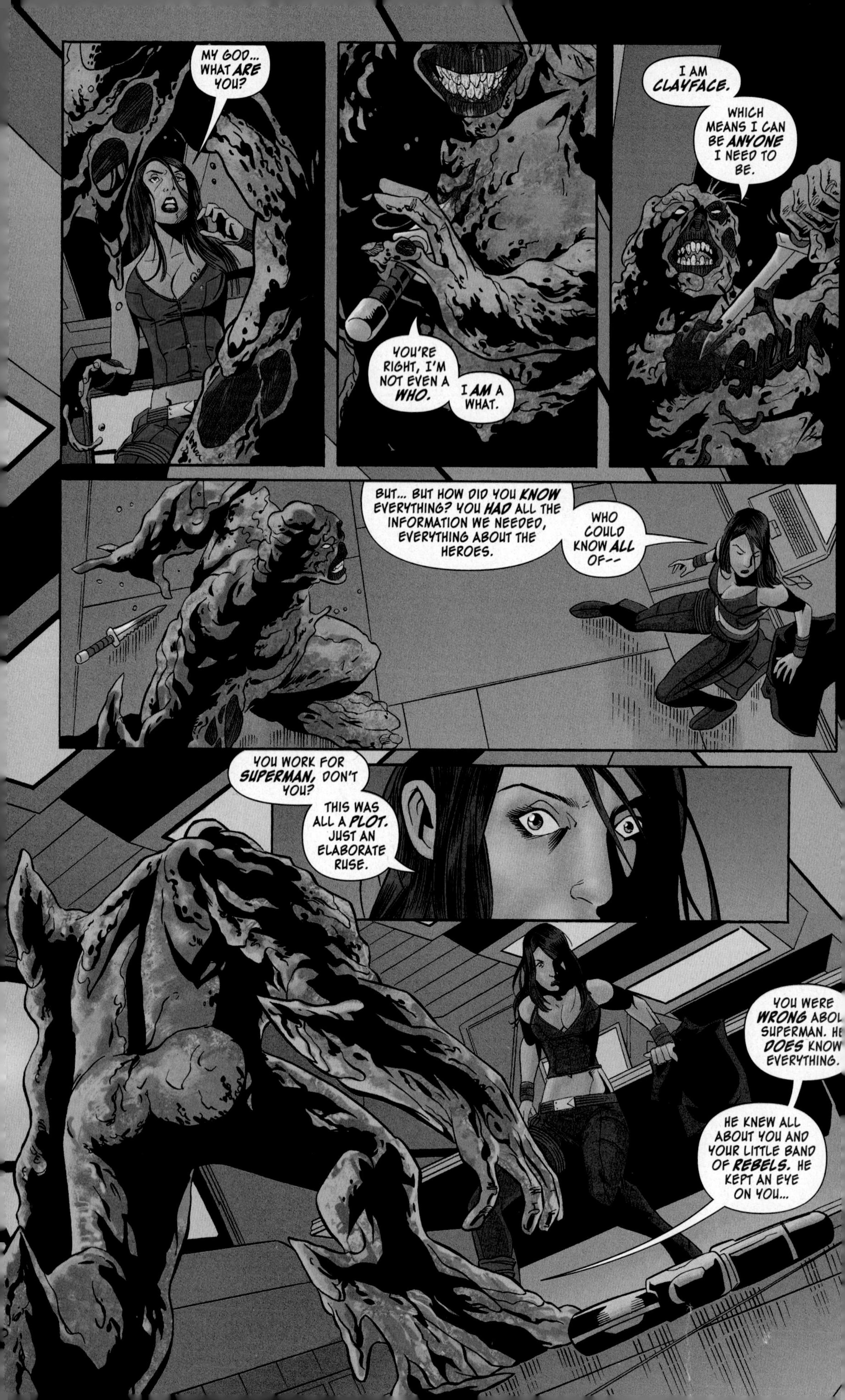
MY GOD... WHAT ARE YOU?
YOU'RE RIGHT, I'M NOT EVEN A WHO.
I AM A WHAT.
I AM CLAYFACE.
WHICH MEANS I CAN BE ANYONE I NEED TO BE.
SHLLK
BUT... BUT HOW DID YOU KNOW EVERYTHING? YOU HAD ALL THE INFORMATION WE NEEDED, EVERYTHING ABOUT THE HEROES.
WHO COULD KNOW ALL OF--
YOU WORK FOR SUPERMAN, DON'T YOU?
THIS WAS ALL A PLOT. JUST AN ELABORATE RUSE.
YOU WERE WRONG ABO SUPERMAN. H DOES KNOW EVERYTHING.
HE KNEW ALL ABOUT YOU AND YOUR LITTLE BAND OF REBELS. HE KEPT AN EYE ON YOU...

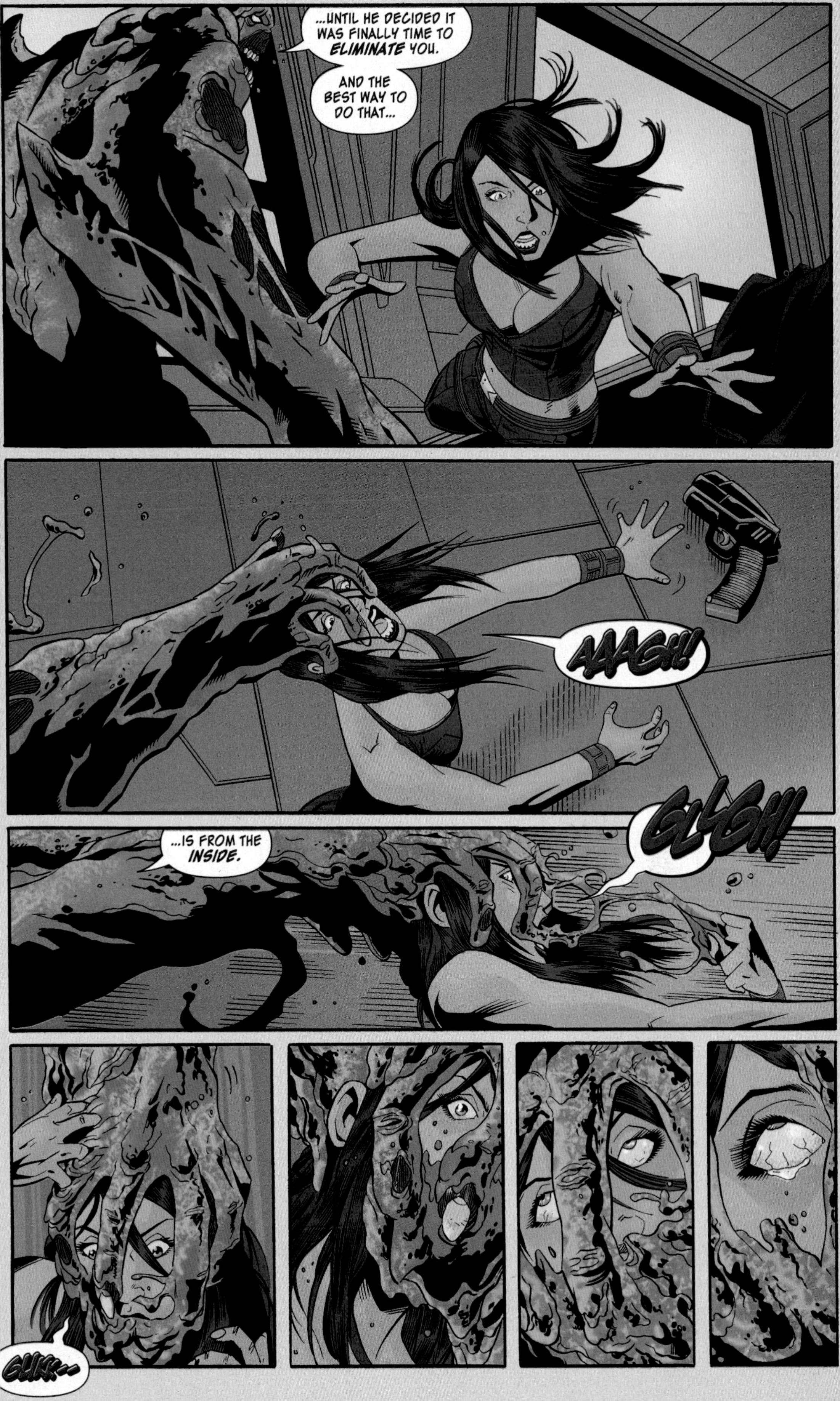
...UNTIL HE DECIDED IT WAS FINALLY TIME TO ELIMINATE YOU.
AND THE BEST WAY TO DO THAT...
AAAGH!
GLUGH!
...IS FROM THE INSIDE.
GLKK--

KVIK

IT'S
DONE.

GOOD.

MOVE ON
TO THE NEXT
PHASE.

FULL
SECURITY
PROTOCOLS
INSTITUTED.

I MUST TURN MY
ATTENTION TO A THREAT
FROM ANOTHER UNIVERSE...
ANOTHER EARTH. IF I'M
FORCED TO DEPART, YOU
WILL ASSUME CONTROL.

AS YOU WISH,
SUPERMAN.

KVIK

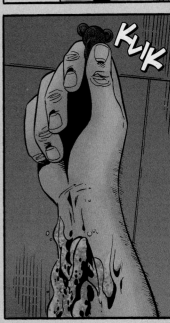

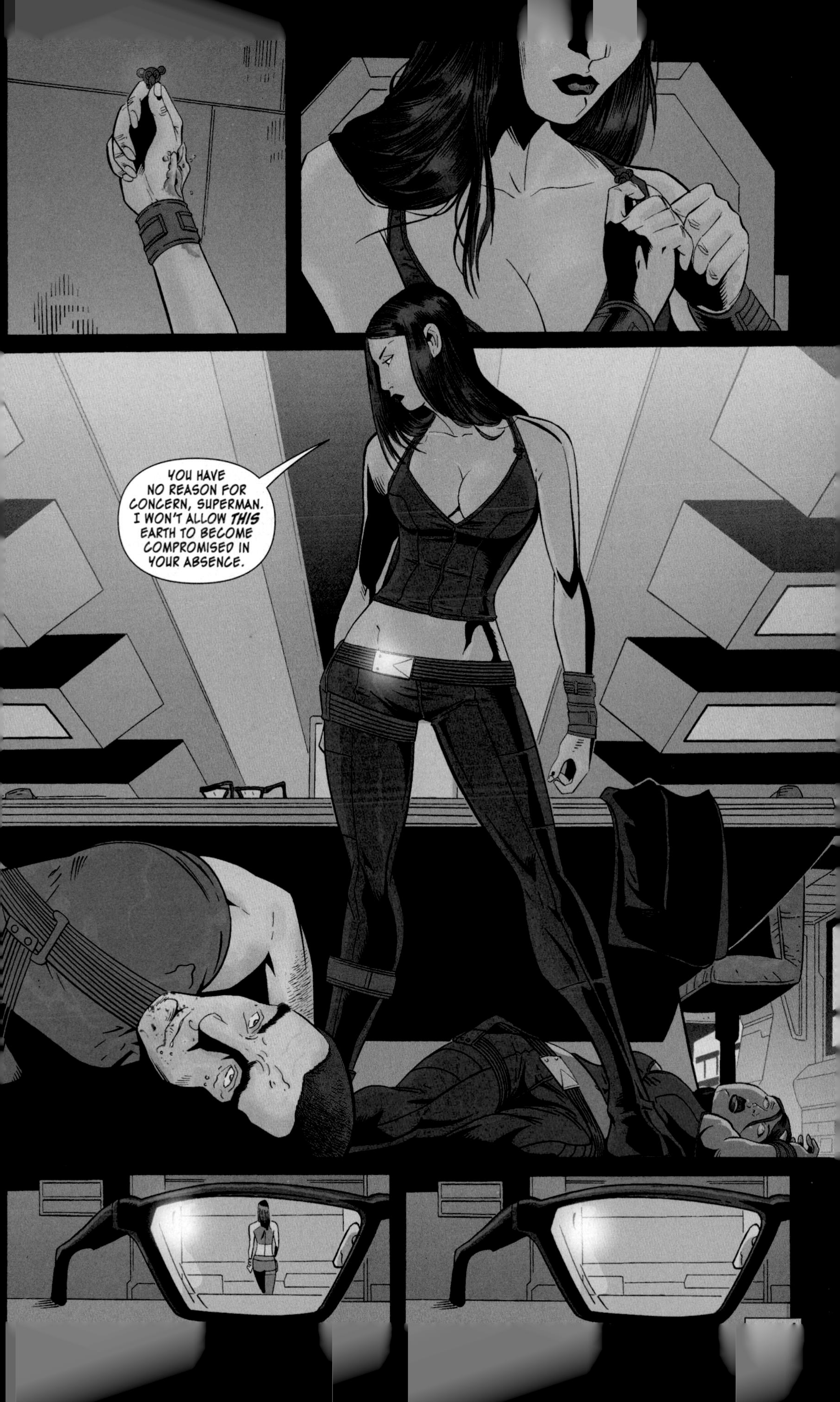
YOU HAVE NO REASON FOR CONCERN, SUPERMAN. I WON'T ALLOW *THIS* EARTH TO BECOME COMPROMISED IN YOUR ABSENCE.

TangentComics

Cover art by Andie Tong.

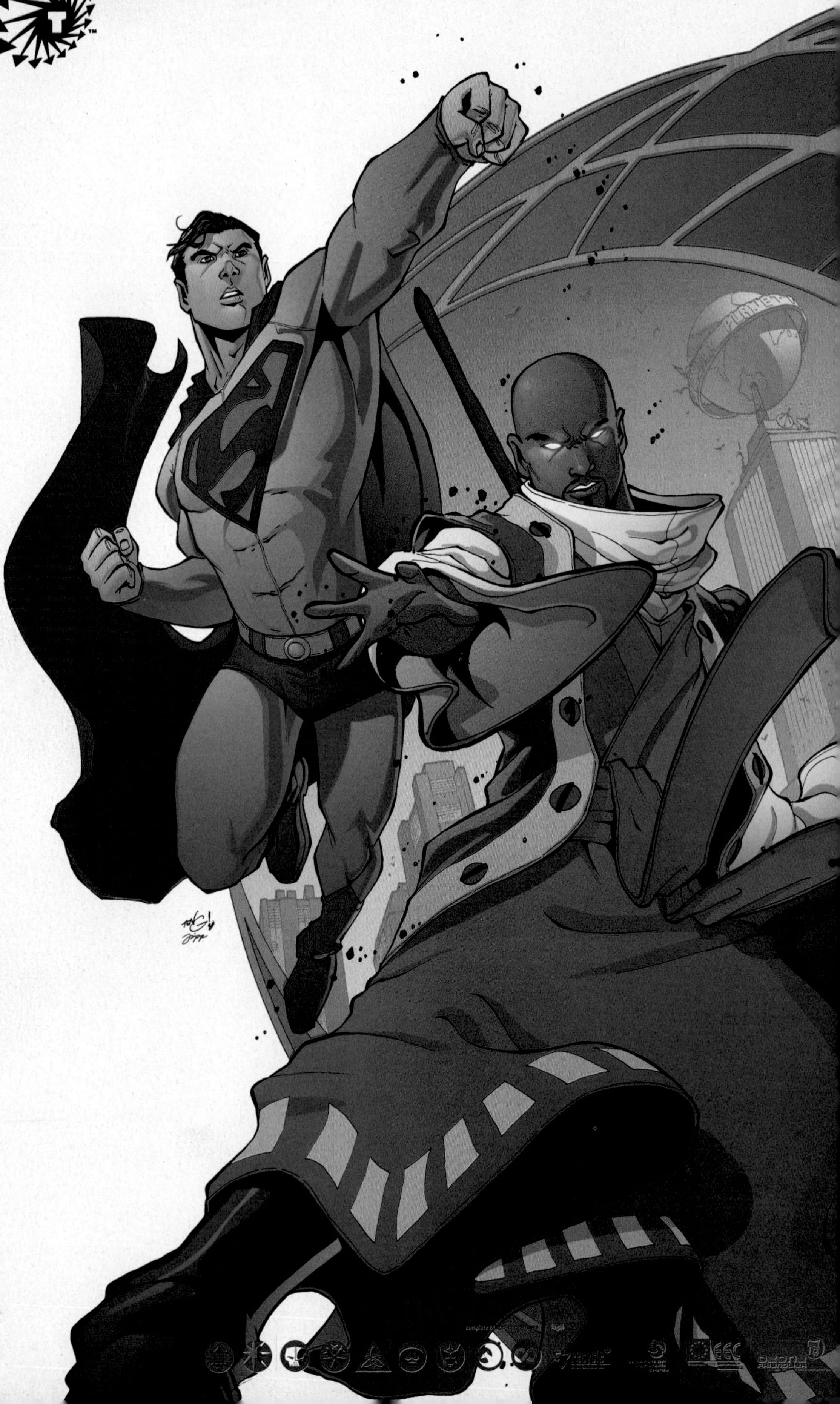

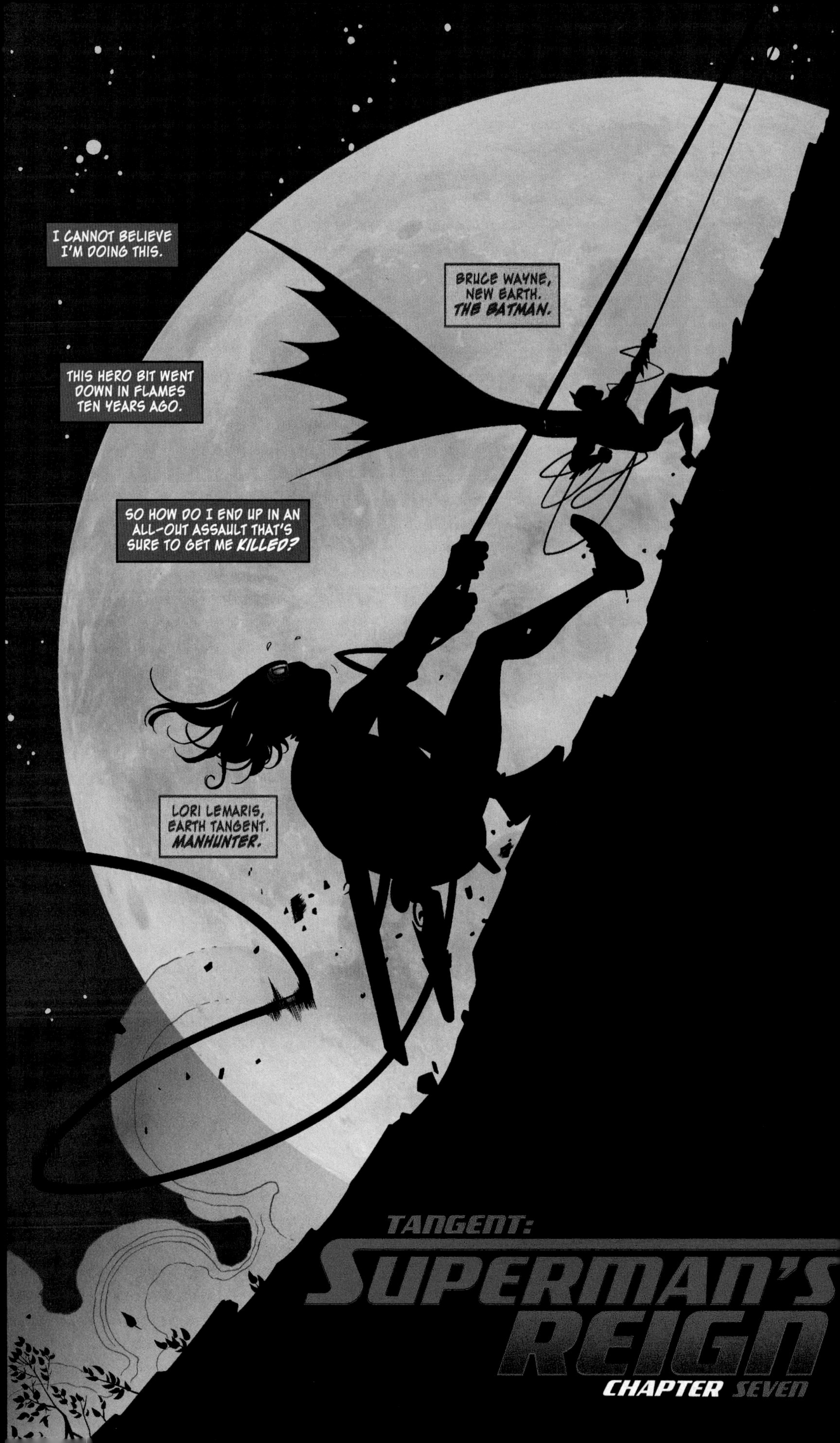
I CANNOT BELIEVE I'M DOING THIS.
BRUCE WAYNE, NEW EARTH. THE BATMAN.
THIS HERO BIT WENT DOWN IN FLAMES TEN YEARS AGO.
SO HOW DO I END UP IN AN ALL-OUT ASSAULT THAT'S SURE TO GET ME KILLED?
LORI LEMARIS, EARTH TANGENT. MANHUNTER.
TANGENT:
SUPERMAN'S REIGN
CHAPTER SEVEN

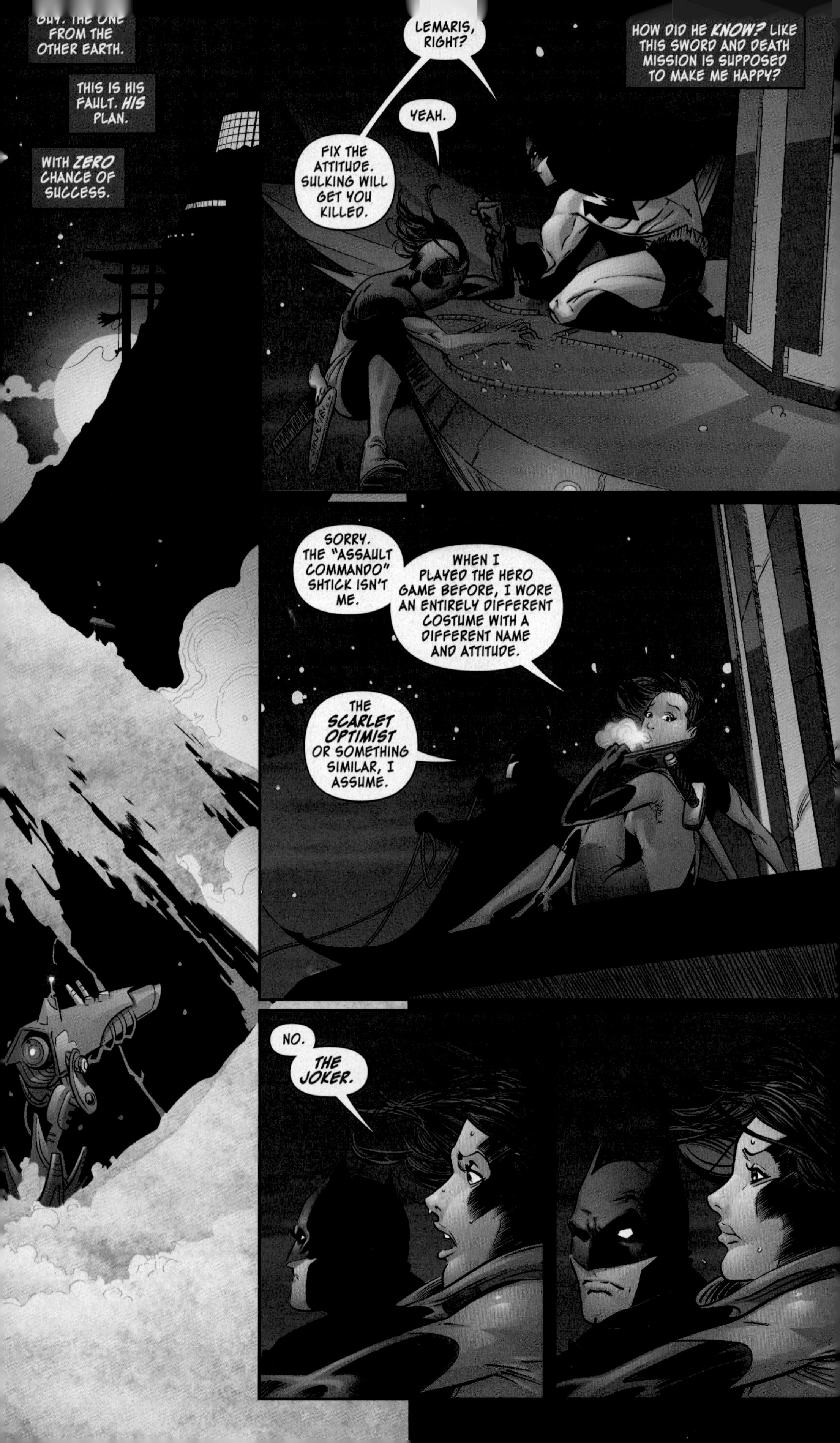

FROM THE OTHER EARTH.
THIS IS HIS FAULT. *HIS* PLAN.
WITH *ZERO* CHANCE OF SUCCESS.
LEMARIS, RIGHT?
YEAH.
FIX THE ATTITUDE. SULKING WILL GET YOU KILLED.
HOW DID HE *KNOW?* LIKE THIS SWORD AND DEATH MISSION IS SUPPOSED TO MAKE ME HAPPY?
SORRY. THE "ASSAULT COMMANDO" SHTICK ISN'T ME.
WHEN I PLAYED THE HERO GAME BEFORE, I WORE AN ENTIRELY DIFFERENT COSTUME WITH A DIFFERENT NAME AND ATTITUDE.
THE *SCARLET OPTIMIST* OR SOMETHING SIMILAR, I ASSUME.
NO. *THE JOKER.*

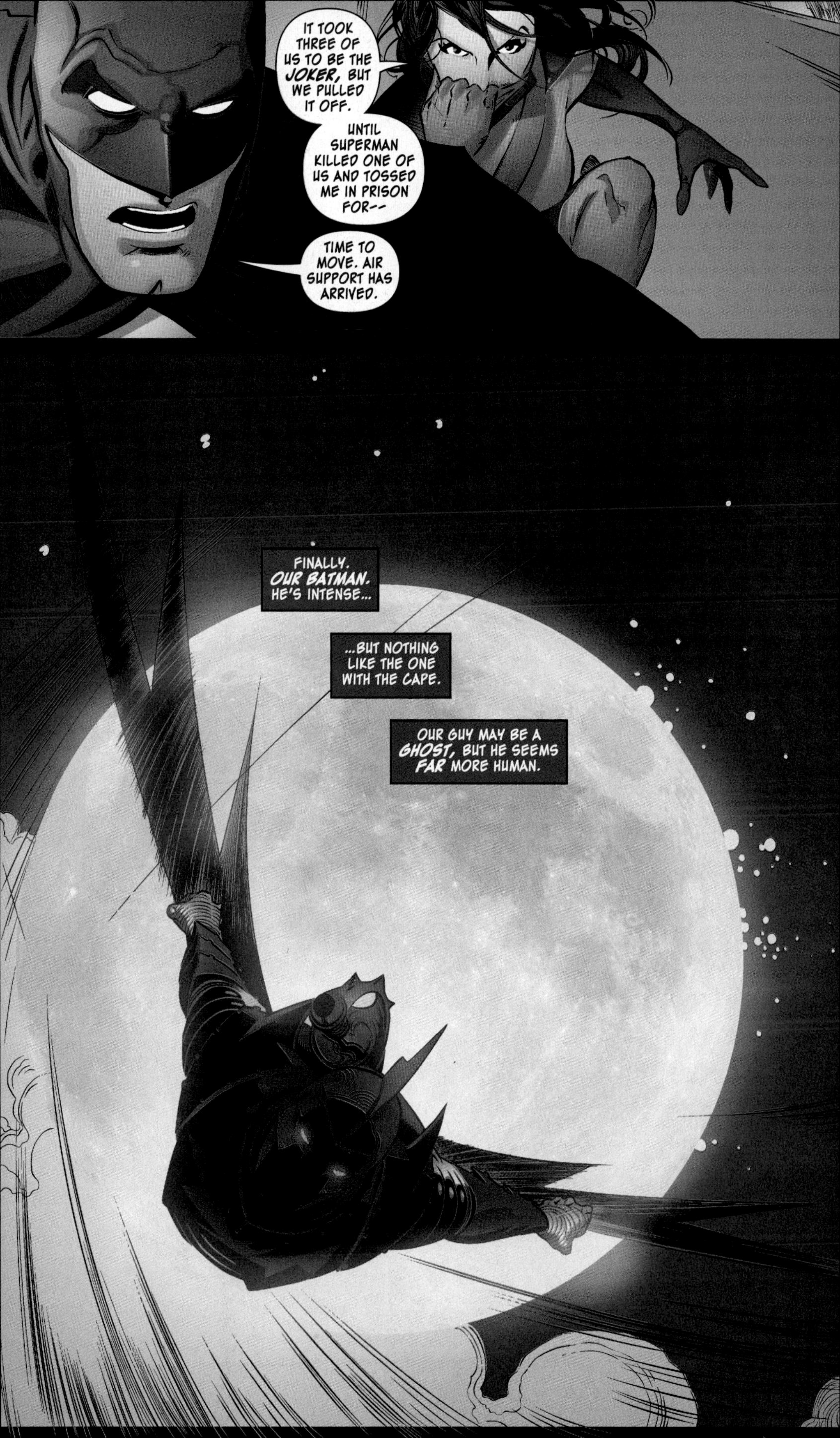
IT TOOK THREE OF US TO BE THE JOKER, BUT WE PULLED IT OFF.
UNTIL SUPERMAN KILLED ONE OF US AND TOSSED ME IN PRISON FOR--
TIME TO MOVE. AIR SUPPORT HAS ARRIVED.
FINALLY. OUR BATMAN. HE'S INTENSE...
...BUT NOTHING LIKE THE ONE WITH THE CAPE.
OUR GUY MAY BE A GHOST, BUT HE SEEMS FAR MORE HUMAN.

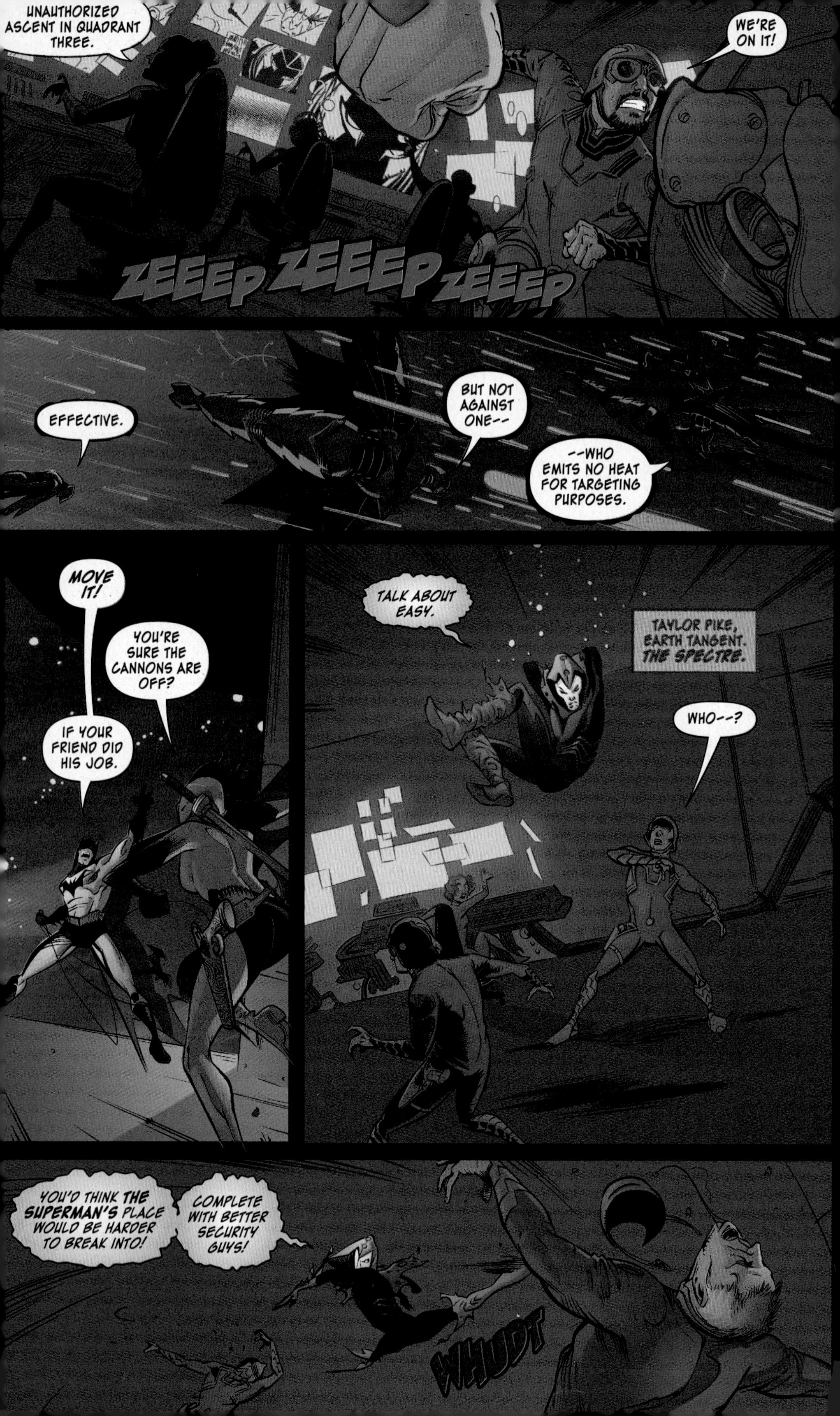
UNAUTHORIZED ASCENT IN QUADRANT THREE.
WE'RE ON IT!
ZEEEP ZEEEP ZEEEP
EFFECTIVE.
BUT NOT AGAINST ONE--
--WHO EMITS NO HEAT FOR TARGETING PURPOSES.
MOVE IT!
YOU'RE SURE THE CANNONS ARE OFF?
IF YOUR FRIEND DID HIS JOB.
TALK ABOUT EASY.
TAYLOR PIKE, EARTH TANGENT. THE SPECTRE.
WHO--?
YOU'D THINK THE SUPERMAN'S PLACE WOULD BE HARDER TO BREAK INTO!
COMPLETE WITH BETTER SECURITY GUYS!
WHUDT

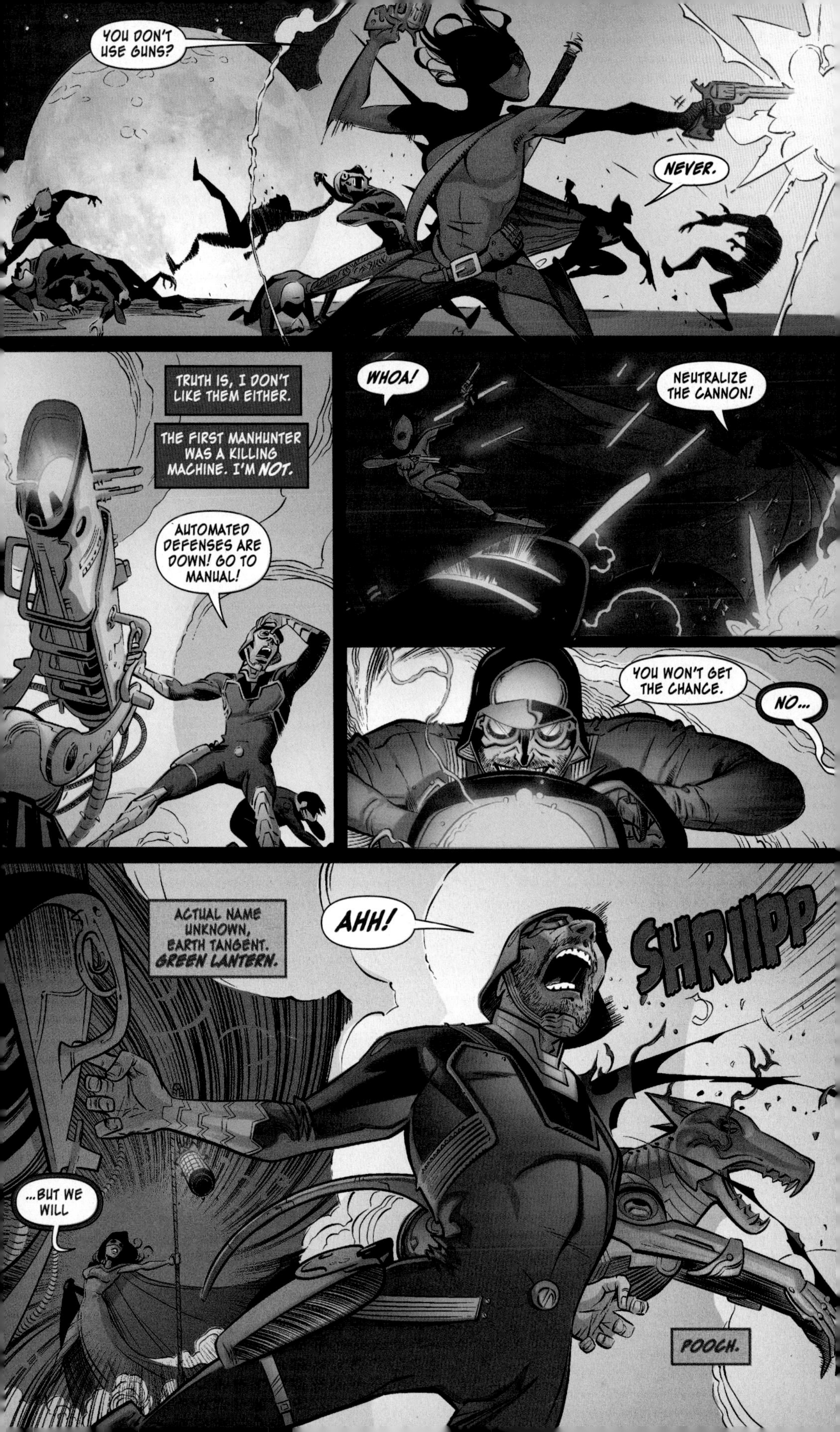
YOU DON'T USE GUNS?
NEVER.
TRUTH IS, I DON'T LIKE THEM EITHER.
THE FIRST MANHUNTER WAS A KILLING MACHINE. I'M NOT.
AUTOMATED DEFENSES ARE DOWN! GO TO MANUAL!
WHOA!
NEUTRALIZE THE CANNON!
YOU WON'T GET THE CHANCE.
NO...
ACTUAL NAME UNKNOWN, EARTH TANGENT. GREEN LANTERN.
AHH!
SHRIIPP
...BUT WE WILL
POOCH.

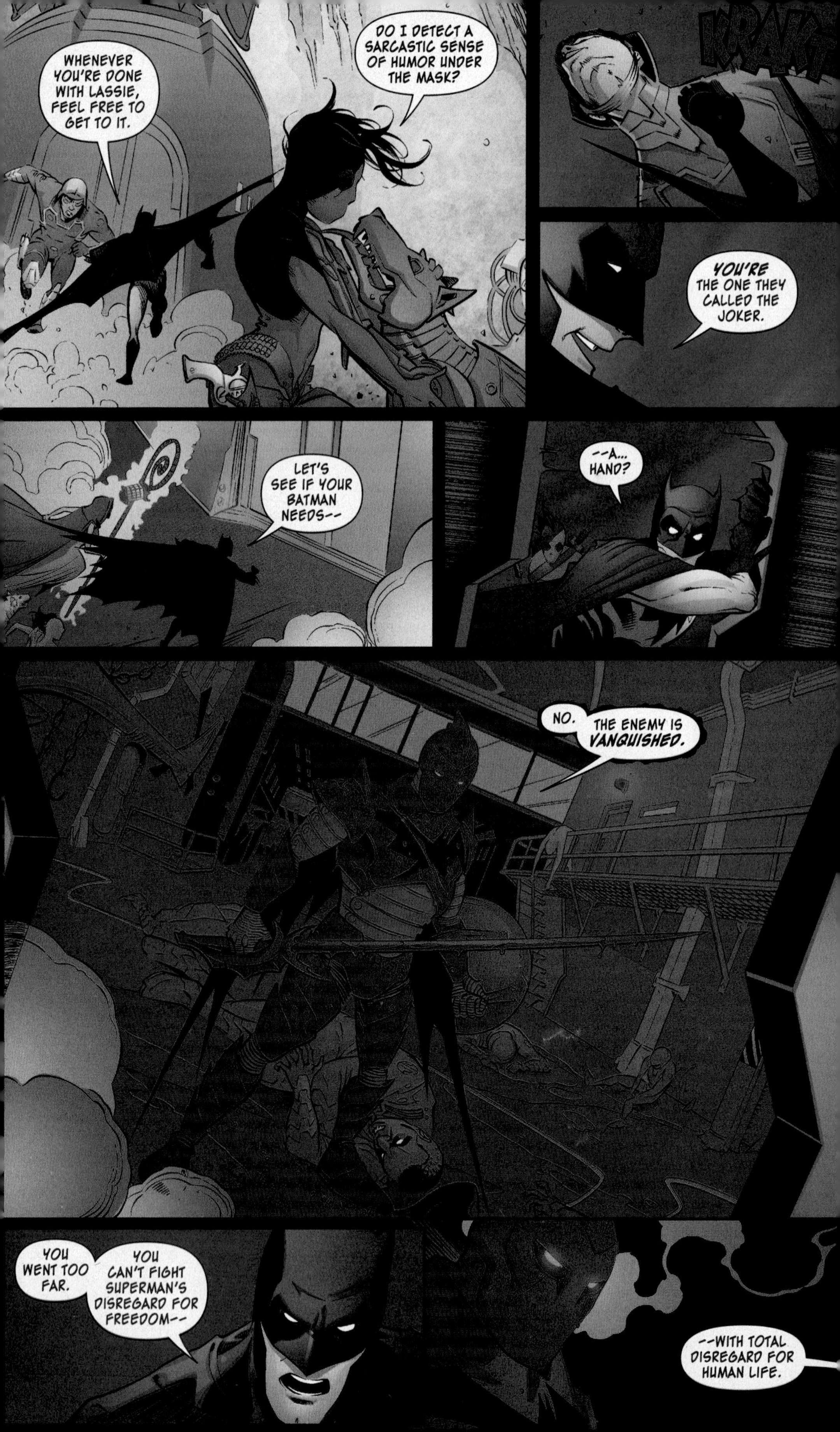
WHENEVER YOU'RE DONE WITH LASSIE, FEEL FREE TO GET TO IT.
DO I DETECT A SARCASTIC SENSE OF HUMOR UNDER THE MASK?
KRAK
YOU'RE THE ONE THEY CALLED THE JOKER.
LET'S SEE IF YOUR BATMAN NEEDS--
--A... HAND?
NO.
THE ENEMY IS VANQUISHED.
YOU WENT TOO FAR.
YOU CAN'T FIGHT SUPERMAN'S DISREGARD FOR FREEDOM--
--WITH TOTAL DISREGARD FOR HUMAN LIFE.

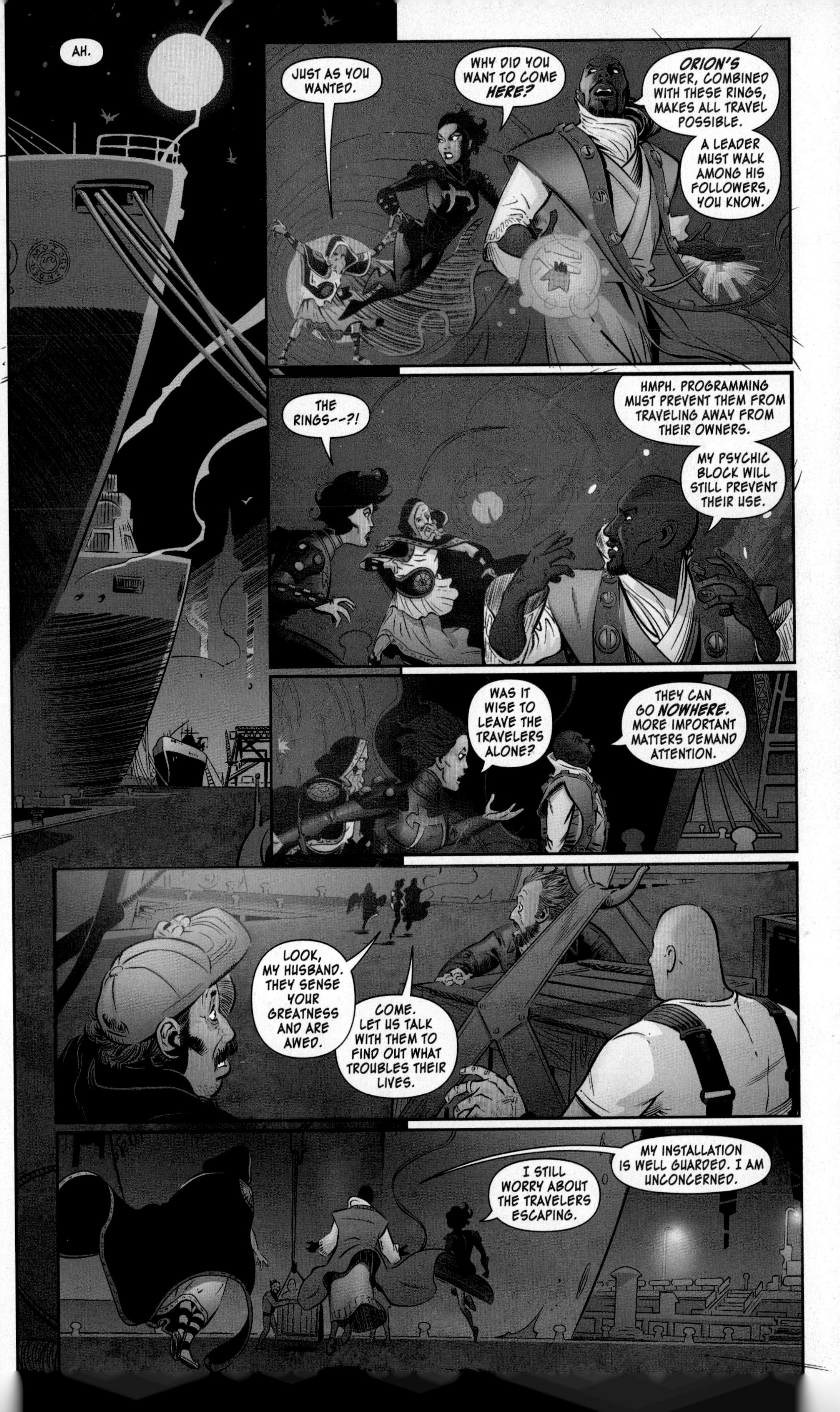
AH.
JUST AS YOU WANTED.
WHY DID YOU WANT TO COME HERE?
ORION'S POWER, COMBINED WITH THESE RINGS, MAKES ALL TRAVEL POSSIBLE.
A LEADER MUST WALK AMONG HIS FOLLOWERS, YOU KNOW.
THE RINGS--?!
HMPH. PROGRAMMING MUST PREVENT THEM FROM TRAVELING AWAY FROM THEIR OWNERS.
MY PSYCHIC BLOCK WILL STILL PREVENT THEIR USE.
WAS IT WISE TO LEAVE THE TRAVELERS ALONE?
THEY CAN GO NOWHERE. MORE IMPORTANT MATTERS DEMAND ATTENTION.
LOOK, MY HUSBAND. THEY SENSE YOUR GREATNESS AND ARE AWED.
COME. LET US TALK WITH THEM TO FIND OUT WHAT TROUBLES THEIR LIVES.
MY INSTALLATION IS WELL GUARDED. I AM UNCONCERNED.
I STILL WORRY ABOUT THE TRAVELERS ESCAPING.

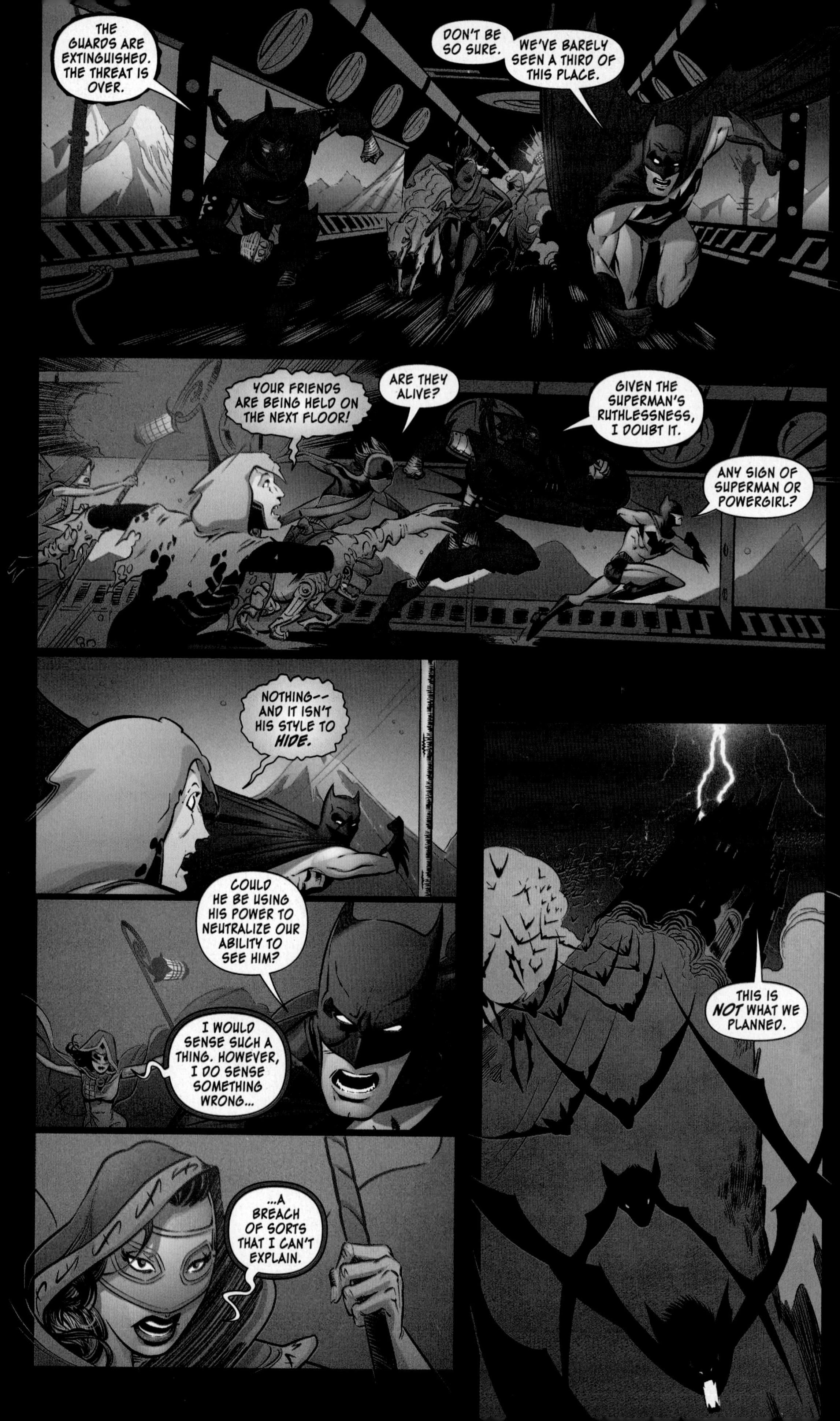
THE GUARDS ARE EXTINGUISHED. THE THREAT IS OVER.
DON'T BE SO SURE.
WE'VE BARELY SEEN A THIRD OF THIS PLACE.
YOUR FRIENDS ARE BEING HELD ON THE NEXT FLOOR!
ARE THEY ALIVE?
GIVEN THE SUPERMAN'S RUTHLESSNESS, I DOUBT IT.
ANY SIGN OF SUPERMAN OR POWERGIRL?
NOTHING-- AND IT ISN'T HIS STYLE TO HIDE.
COULD HE BE USING HIS POWER TO NEUTRALIZE OUR ABILITY TO SEE HIM?
I WOULD SENSE SUCH A THING. HOWEVER, I DO SENSE SOMETHING WRONG...
...A BREACH OF SORTS THAT I CAN'T EXPLAIN.
THIS IS NOT WHAT WE PLANNED.

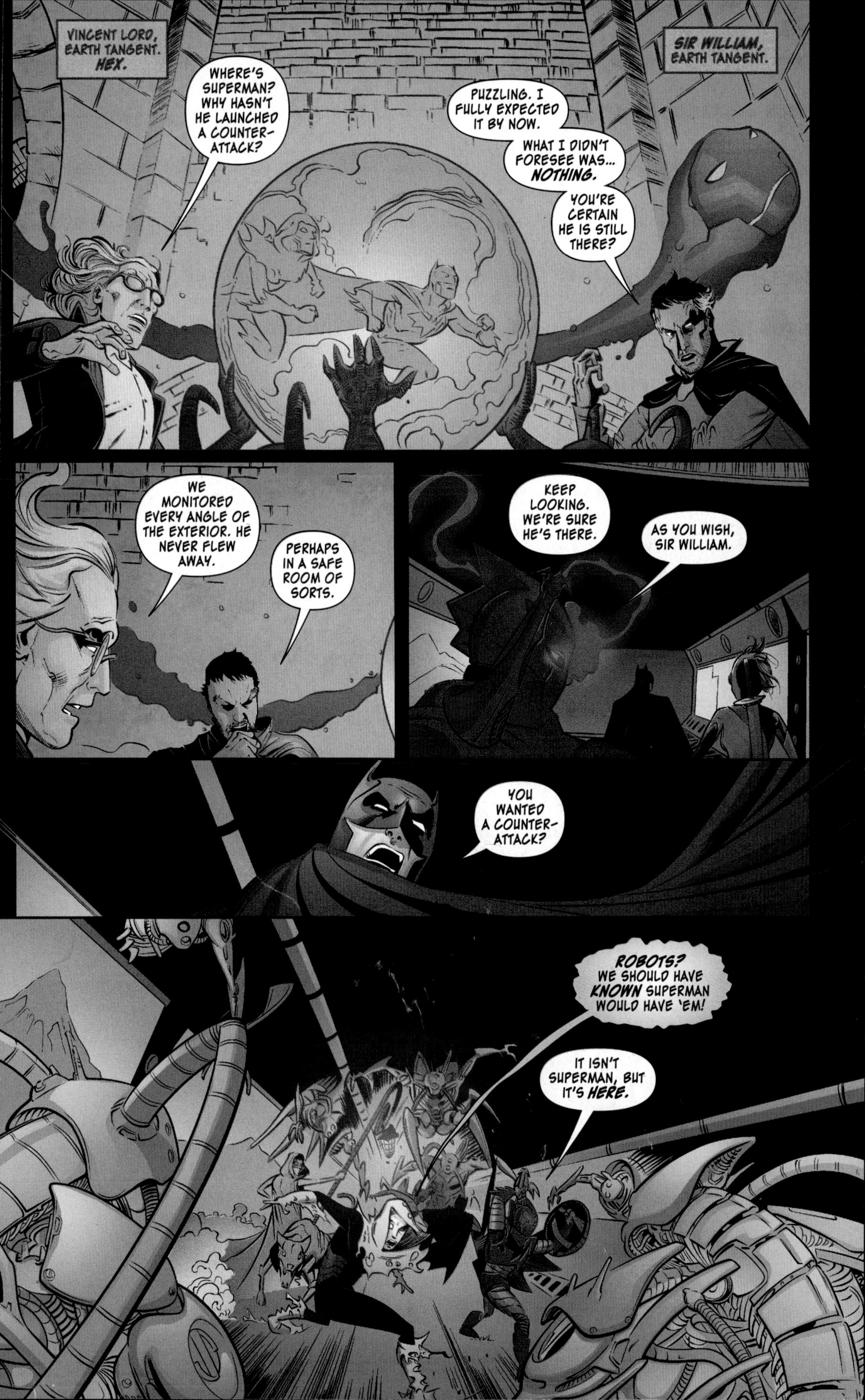
VINCENT LORD, EARTH TANGENT. HEX.
WHERE'S SUPERMAN? WHY HASN'T HE LAUNCHED A COUNTER-ATTACK?
SIR WILLIAM, EARTH TANGENT.
PUZZLING. I FULLY EXPECTED IT BY NOW.
WHAT I DIDN'T FORESEE WAS... NOTHING.
YOU'RE CERTAIN HE IS STILL THERE?
WE MONITORED EVERY ANGLE OF THE EXTERIOR. HE NEVER FLEW AWAY.
PERHAPS IN A SAFE ROOM OF SORTS.
KEEP LOOKING. WE'RE SURE HE'S THERE.
AS YOU WISH, SIR WILLIAM.
YOU WANTED A COUNTER-ATTACK?
ROBOTS? WE SHOULD HAVE KNOWN SUPERMAN WOULD HAVE 'EM!
IT ISN'T SUPERMAN, BUT IT'S HERE.

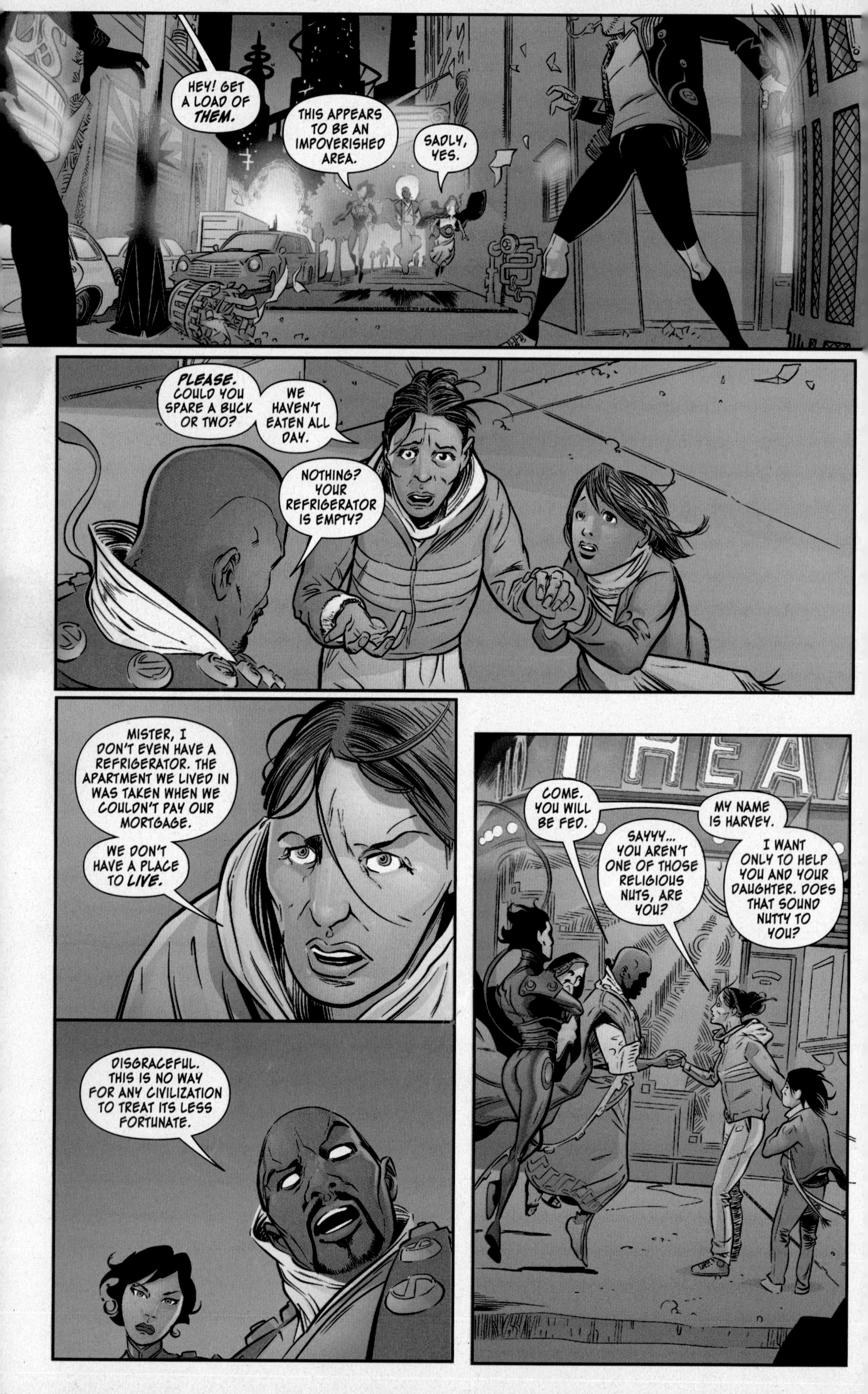
HEY! GET A LOAD OF *THEM.*
THIS APPEARS TO BE AN IMPOVERISHED AREA.
SADLY, YES.
PLEASE. COULD YOU SPARE A BUCK OR TWO?
WE HAVEN'T EATEN ALL DAY.
NOTHING? YOUR REFRIGERATOR IS EMPTY?
MISTER, I DON'T EVEN HAVE A REFRIGERATOR. THE APARTMENT WE LIVED IN WAS TAKEN WHEN WE COULDN'T PAY OUR MORTGAGE.
WE DON'T HAVE A PLACE TO *LIVE.*
DISGRACEFUL. THIS IS NO WAY FOR ANY CIVILIZATION TO TREAT ITS LESS FORTUNATE.
COME. YOU WILL BE FED.
MY NAME IS HARVEY.
SAYYY... YOU AREN'T ONE OF THOSE RELIGIOUS NUTS, ARE YOU?
I WANT ONLY TO HELP YOU AND YOUR DAUGHTER. DOES THAT SOUND NUTTY TO YOU?

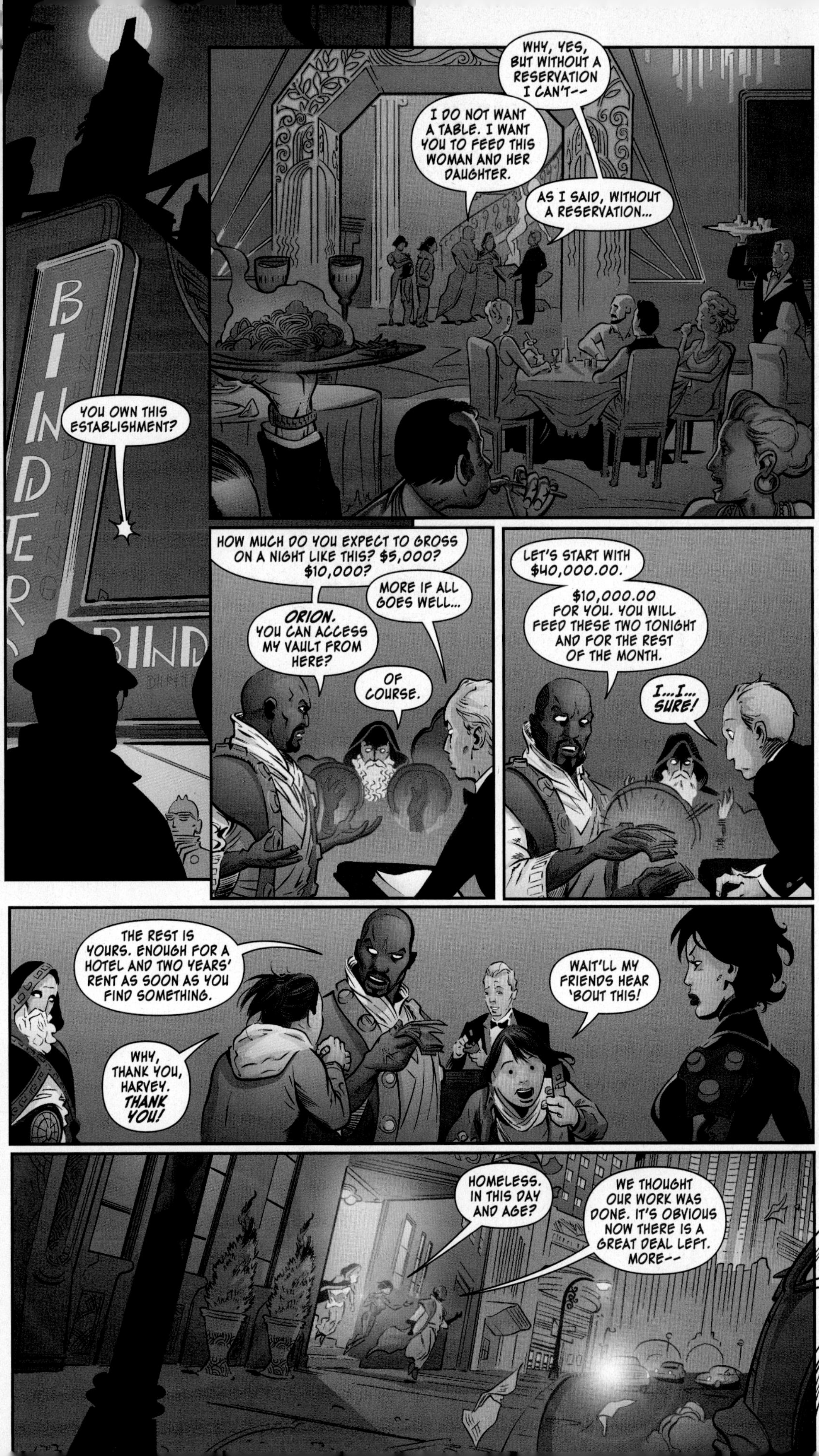
BINDERS
BINDERS
YOU OWN THIS ESTABLISHMENT?
WHY, YES, BUT WITHOUT A RESERVATION I CAN'T--
I DO NOT WANT A TABLE. I WANT YOU TO FEED THIS WOMAN AND HER DAUGHTER.
AS I SAID, WITHOUT A RESERVATION...
HOW MUCH DO YOU EXPECT TO GROSS ON A NIGHT LIKE THIS? $5,000? $10,000?
MORE IF ALL GOES WELL...
ORION. YOU CAN ACCESS MY VAULT FROM HERE?
OF COURSE.
LET'S START WITH $40,000.00.
$10,000.00 FOR YOU. YOU WILL FEED THESE TWO TONIGHT AND FOR THE REST OF THE MONTH.
I...I... SURE!
THE REST IS YOURS. ENOUGH FOR A HOTEL AND TWO YEARS' RENT AS SOON AS YOU FIND SOMETHING.
WHY, THANK YOU, HARVEY. THANK YOU!
WAIT'LL MY FRIENDS HEAR 'BOUT THIS!
HOMELESS. IN THIS DAY AND AGE?
WE THOUGHT OUR WORK WAS DONE. IT'S OBVIOUS NOW THERE IS A GREAT DEAL LEFT. MORE--

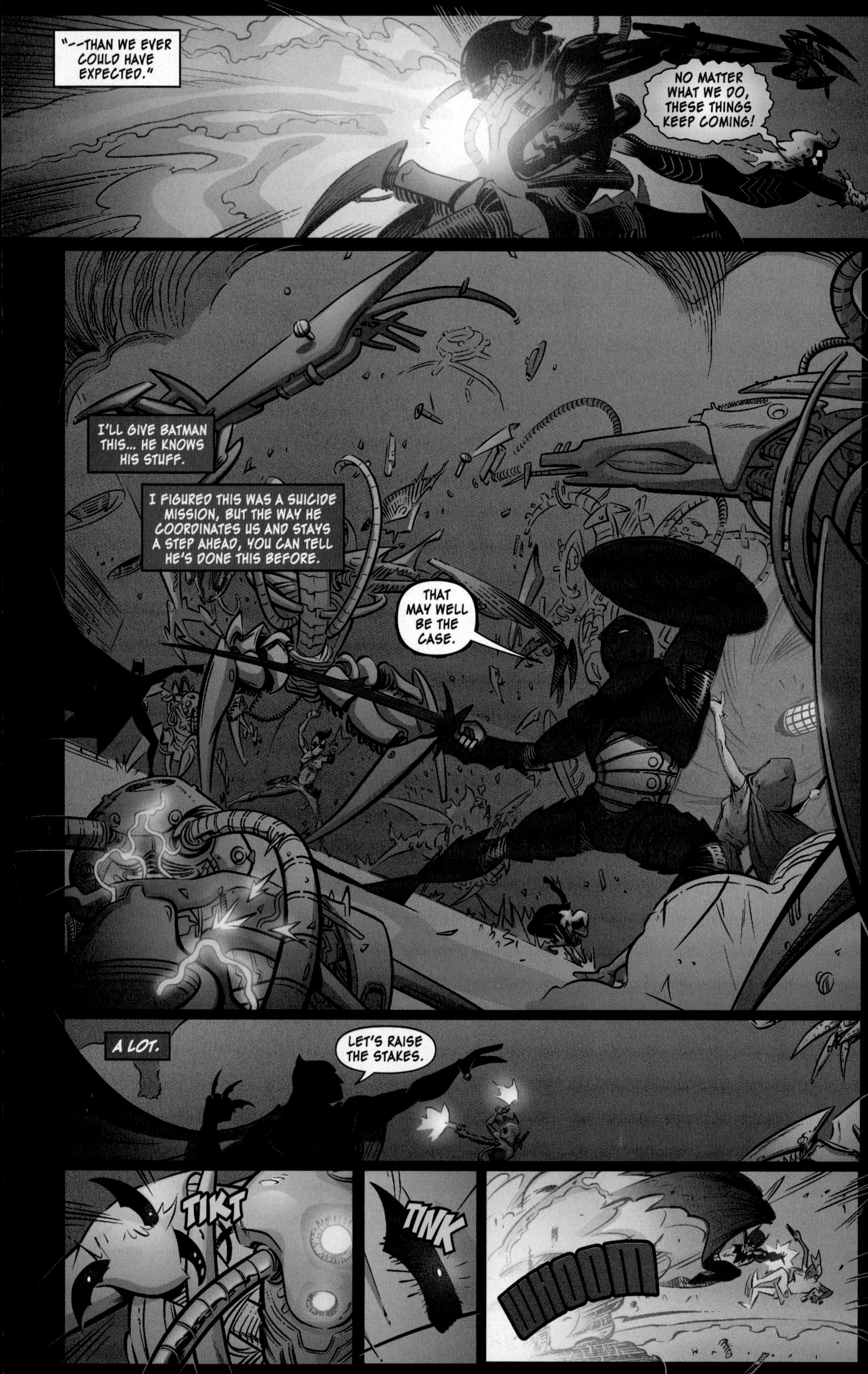
"--THAN WE EVER COULD HAVE EXPECTED."
NO MATTER WHAT WE DO, THESE THINGS KEEP COMING!
I'LL GIVE BATMAN THIS... HE KNOWS HIS STUFF.
I FIGURED THIS WAS A SUICIDE MISSION, BUT THE WAY HE COORDINATES US AND STAYS A STEP AHEAD, YOU CAN TELL HE'S DONE THIS BEFORE.
THAT MAY WELL BE THE CASE.
A LOT.
LET'S RAISE THE STAKES.
TIKT
TINK
WHOOM

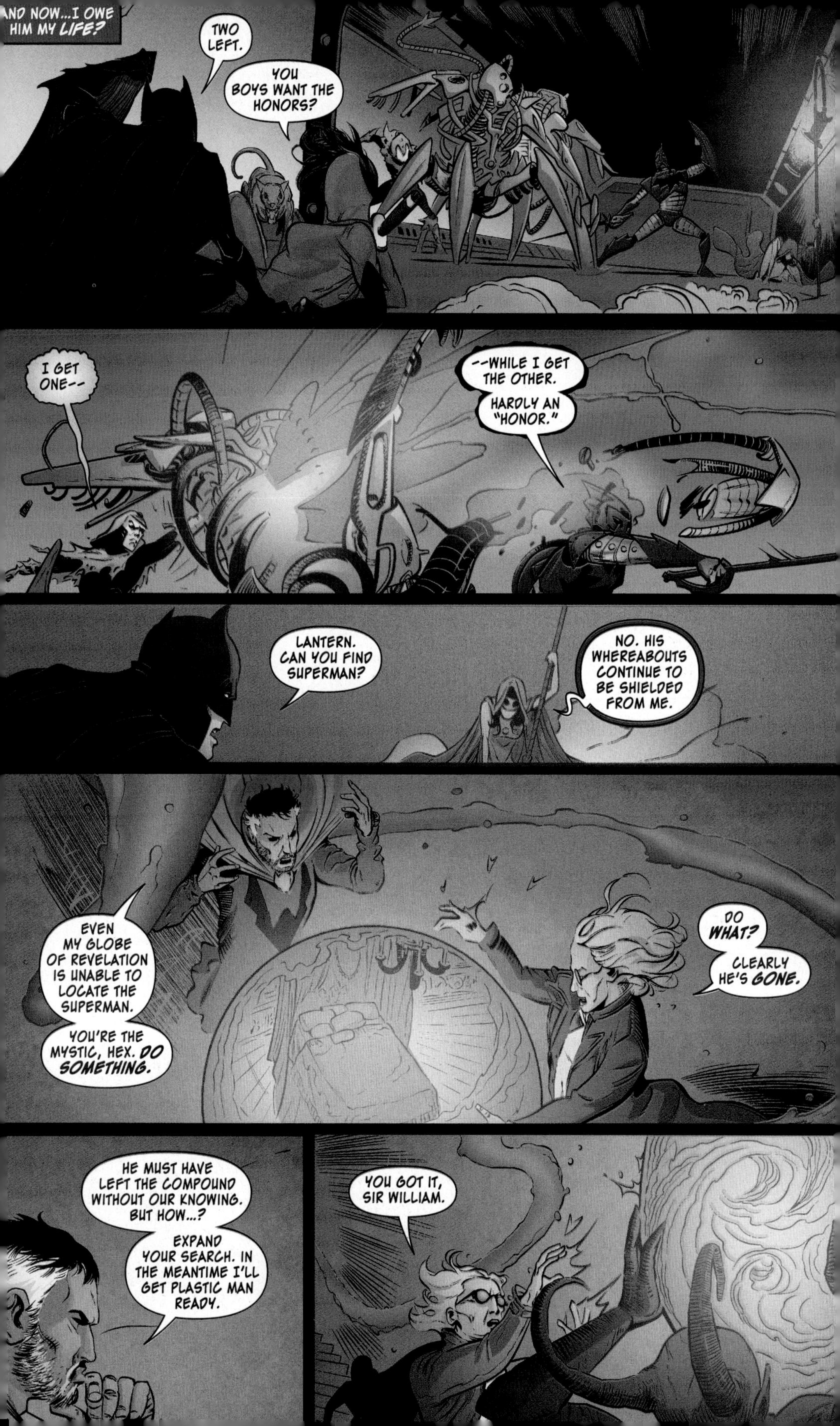
AND NOW...I OWE HIM MY *LIFE?*
TWO LEFT.
YOU BOYS WANT THE HONORS?
I GET ONE--
--WHILE I GET THE OTHER.
HARDLY AN "HONOR."
LANTERN. CAN YOU FIND SUPERMAN?
NO. HIS WHEREABOUTS CONTINUE TO BE SHIELDED FROM ME.
EVEN MY GLOBE OF REVELATION IS UNABLE TO LOCATE THE SUPERMAN.
YOU'RE THE MYSTIC, HEX. ***DO SOMETHING.***
DO ***WHAT?***
CLEARLY HE'S ***GONE.***
HE MUST HAVE LEFT THE COMPOUND WITHOUT OUR KNOWING. BUT HOW...?
EXPAND YOUR SEARCH. IN THE MEANTIME I'LL GET PLASTIC MAN READY.
YOU GOT IT, SIR WILLIAM.

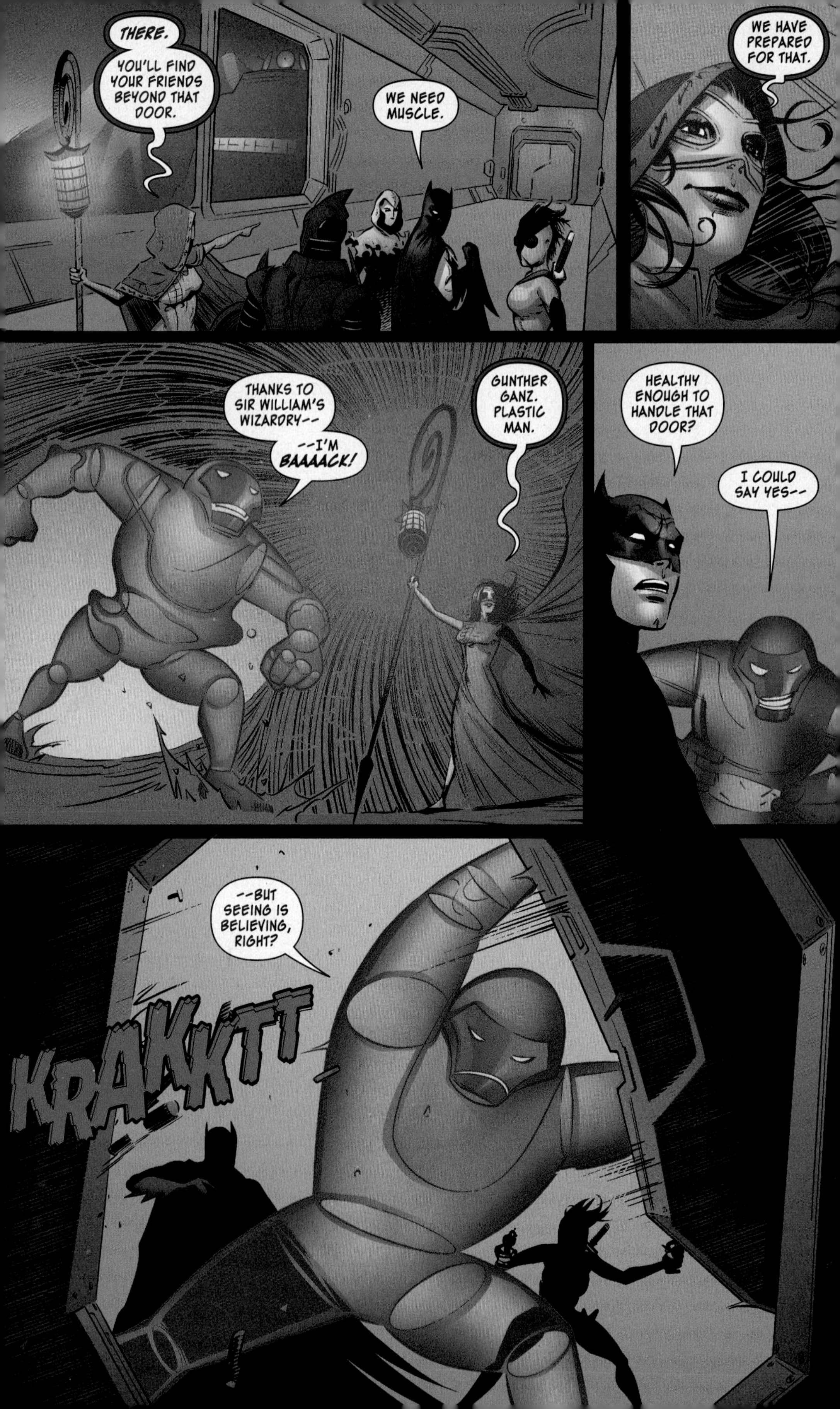
THERE.
YOU'LL FIND YOUR FRIENDS BEYOND THAT DOOR.
WE NEED MUSCLE.
WE HAVE PREPARED FOR THAT.
THANKS TO SIR WILLIAM'S WIZARDRY--
--I'M BAAAACK!
GUNTHER GANZ. PLASTIC MAN.
HEALTHY ENOUGH TO HANDLE THAT DOOR?
I COULD SAY YES--
--BUT SEEING IS BELIEVING, RIGHT?
KRAKKTT

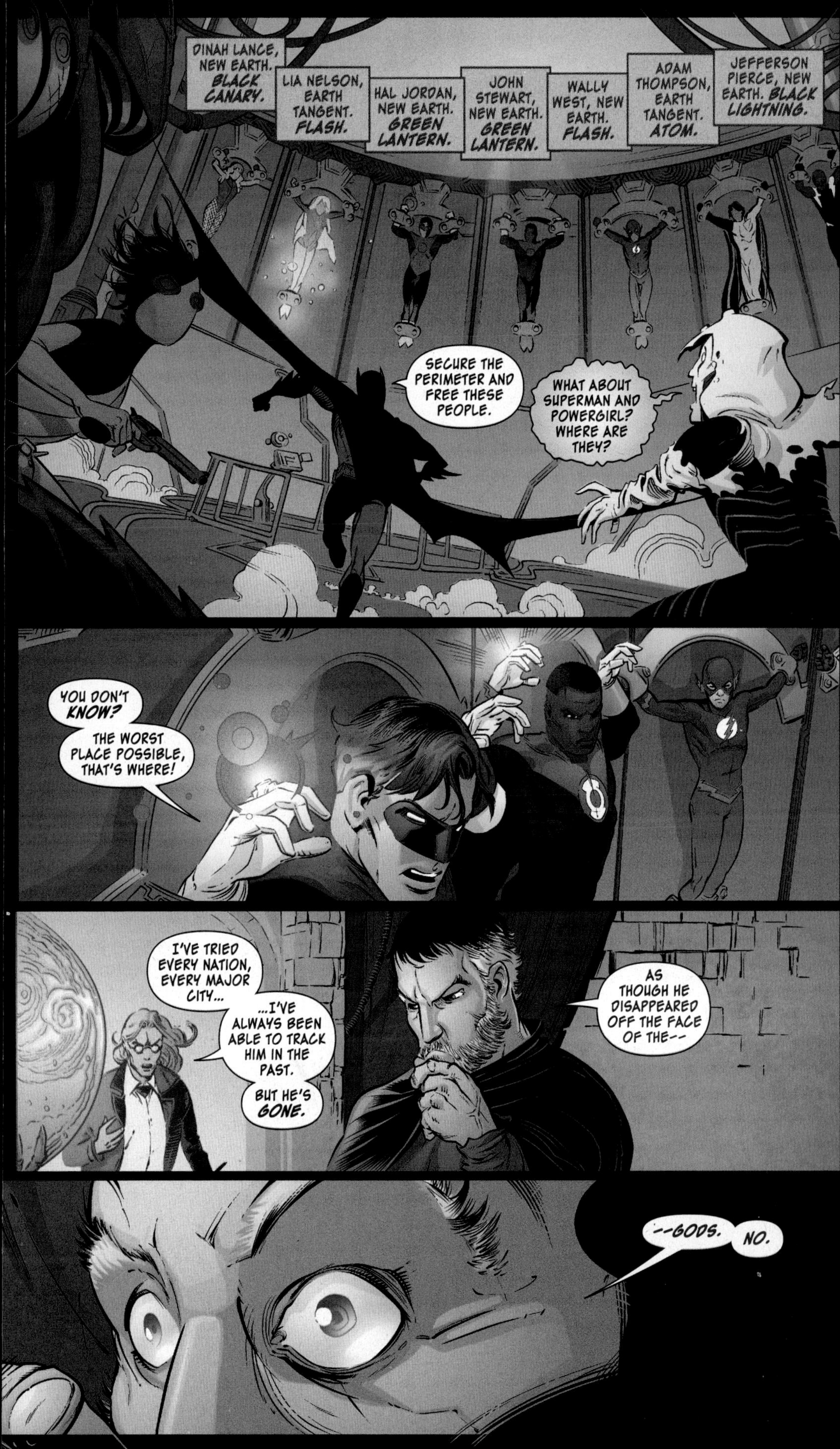
DINAH LANCE, NEW EARTH. BLACK CANARY.
LIA NELSON, EARTH TANGENT. FLASH.
HAL JORDAN, NEW EARTH. GREEN LANTERN.
JOHN STEWART, NEW EARTH. GREEN LANTERN.
WALLY WEST, NEW EARTH. FLASH.
ADAM THOMPSON, EARTH TANGENT. ATOM.
JEFFERSON PIERCE, NEW EARTH. BLACK LIGHTNING.
SECURE THE PERIMETER AND FREE THESE PEOPLE.
WHAT ABOUT SUPERMAN AND POWERGIRL? WHERE ARE THEY?
YOU DON'T KNOW?
THE WORST PLACE POSSIBLE, THAT'S WHERE!
I'VE TRIED EVERY NATION, EVERY MAJOR CITY...
...I'VE ALWAYS BEEN ABLE TO TRACK HIM IN THE PAST.
BUT HE'S GONE.
AS THOUGH HE DISAPPEARED OFF THE FACE OF THE--
--GODS.
NO.

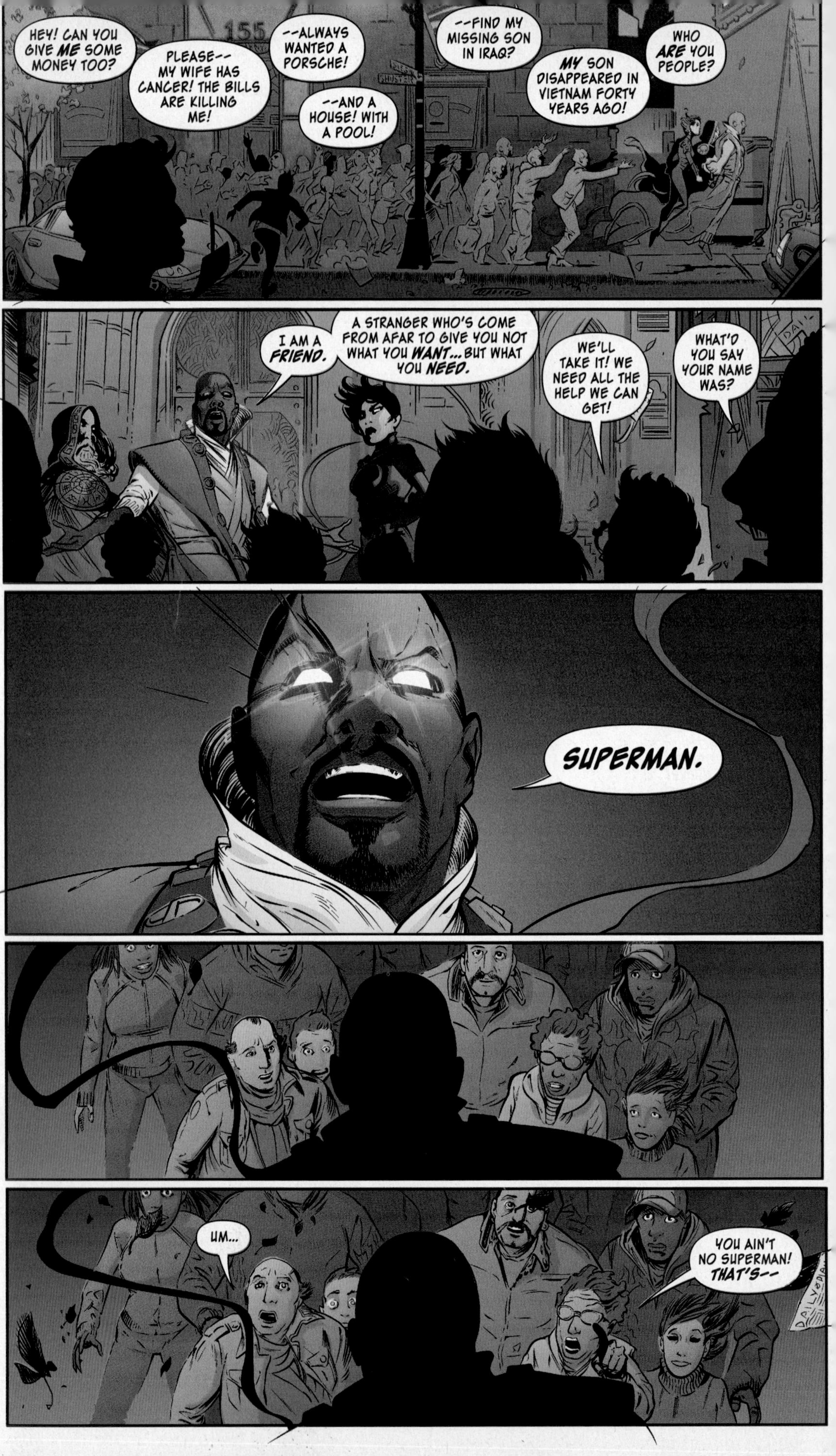
HEY! CAN YOU GIVE ME SOME MONEY TOO?
PLEASE-- MY WIFE HAS CANCER! THE BILLS ARE KILLING ME!
--ALWAYS WANTED A PORSCHE!
--AND A HOUSE! WITH A POOL!
--FIND MY MISSING SON IN IRAQ?
MY SON DISAPPEARED IN VIETNAM FORTY YEARS AGO!
WHO ARE YOU PEOPLE?
I AM A FRIEND.
A STRANGER WHO'S COME FROM AFAR TO GIVE YOU NOT WHAT YOU WANT... BUT WHAT YOU NEED.
WE'LL TAKE IT! WE NEED ALL THE HELP WE CAN GET!
WHAT'D YOU SAY YOUR NAME WAS?
SUPERMAN.
UM...
YOU AIN'T NO SUPERMAN! THAT'S--

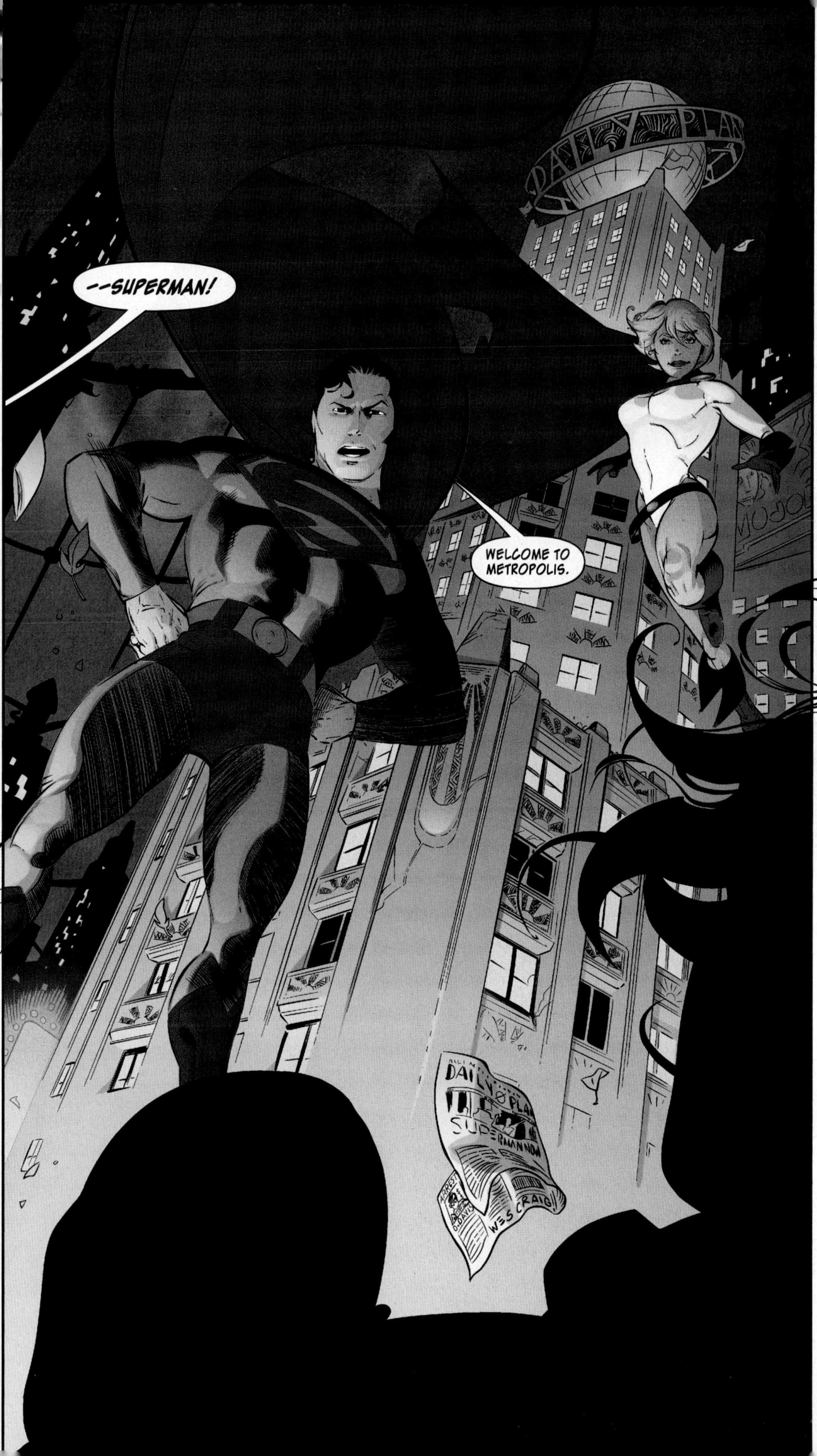
--SUPERMAN!
WELCOME TO METROPOLIS.

Cover art by Matt Haley.

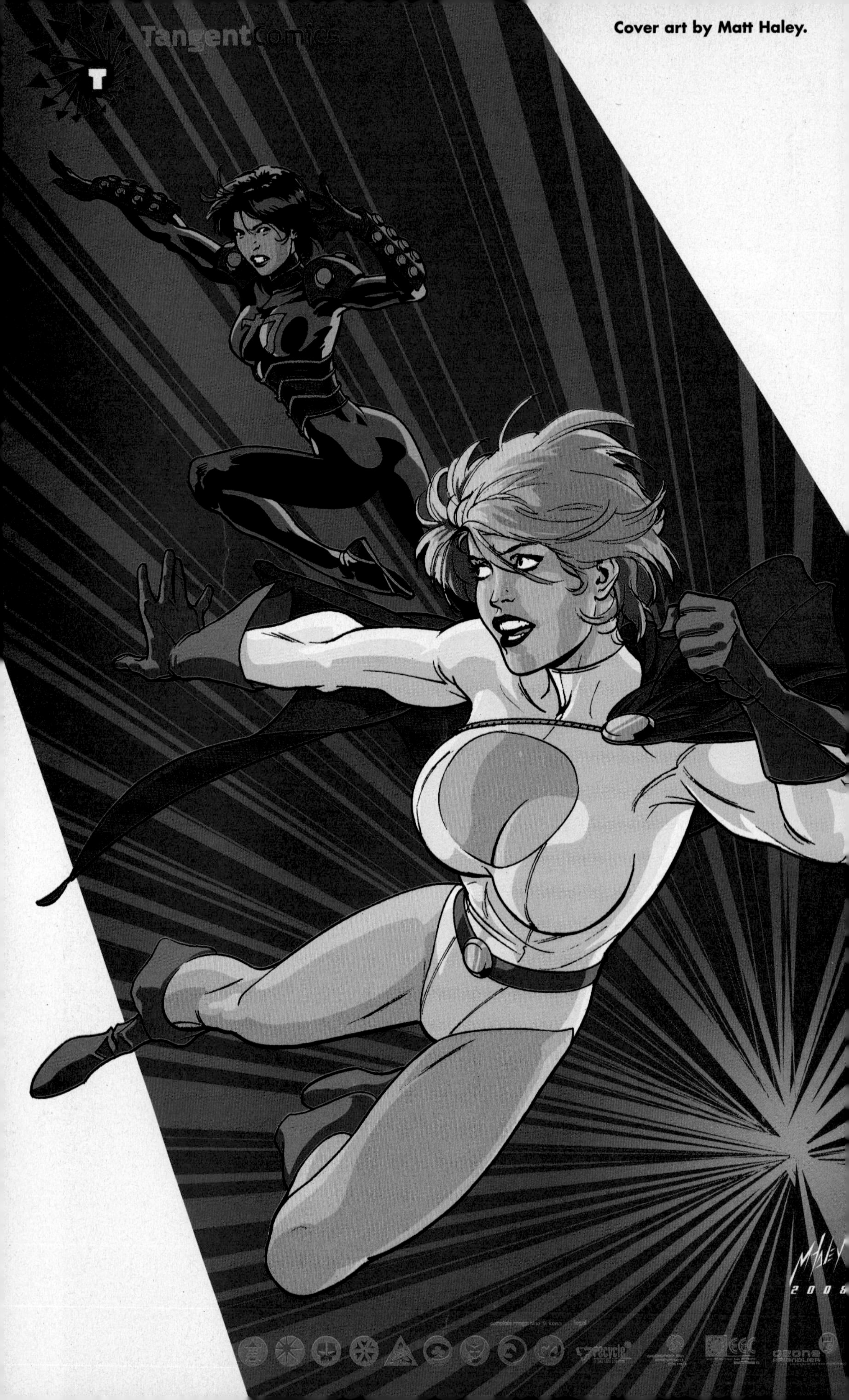
Tangent Comics
T
M HALEY
2008

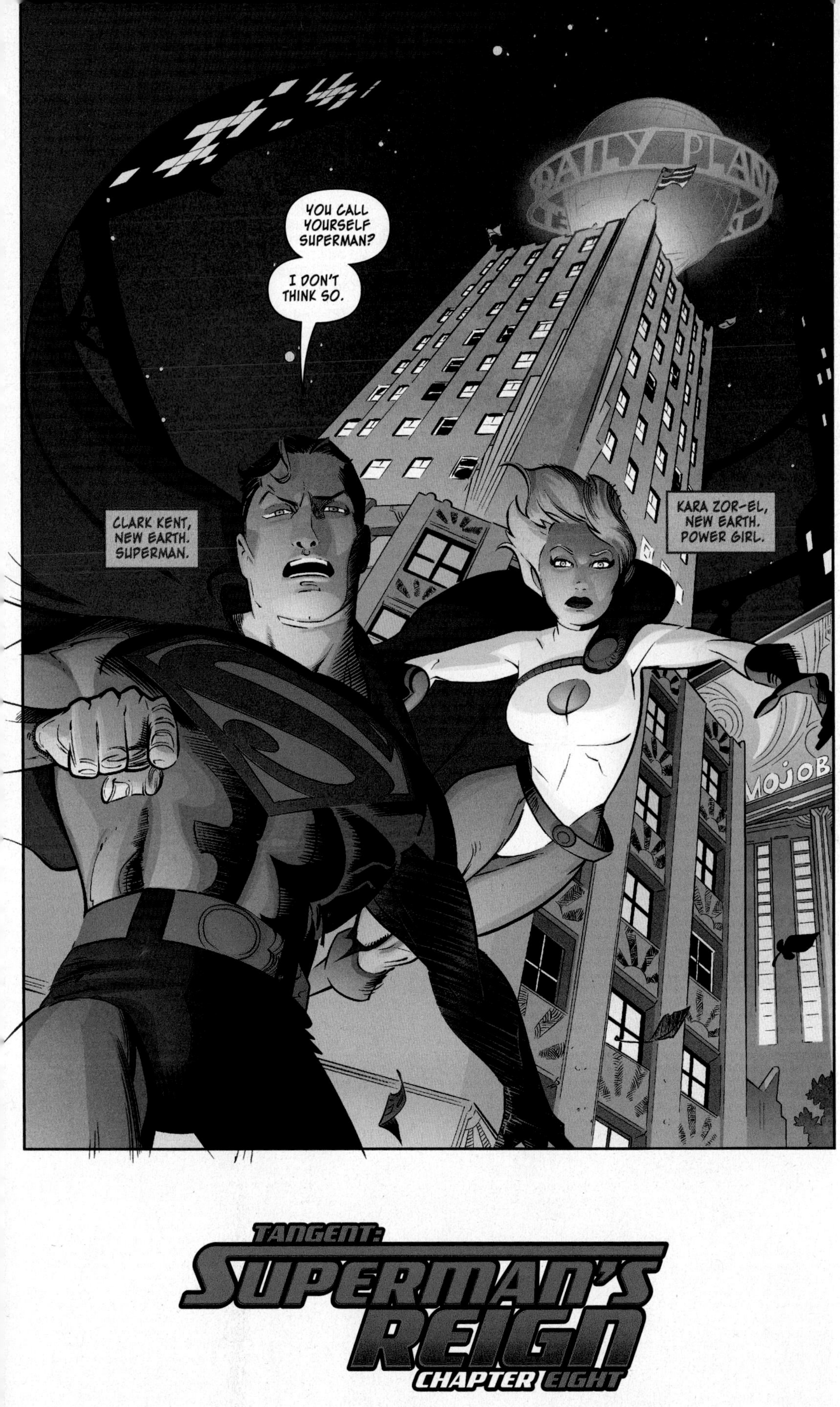
YOU CALL YOURSELF SUPERMAN?
I DON'T THINK SO.
CLARK KENT, NEW EARTH. SUPERMAN.
KARA ZOR-EL, NEW EARTH. POWER GIRL.

TANGENT: SUPERMAN'S REIGN

CHAPTER EIGHT

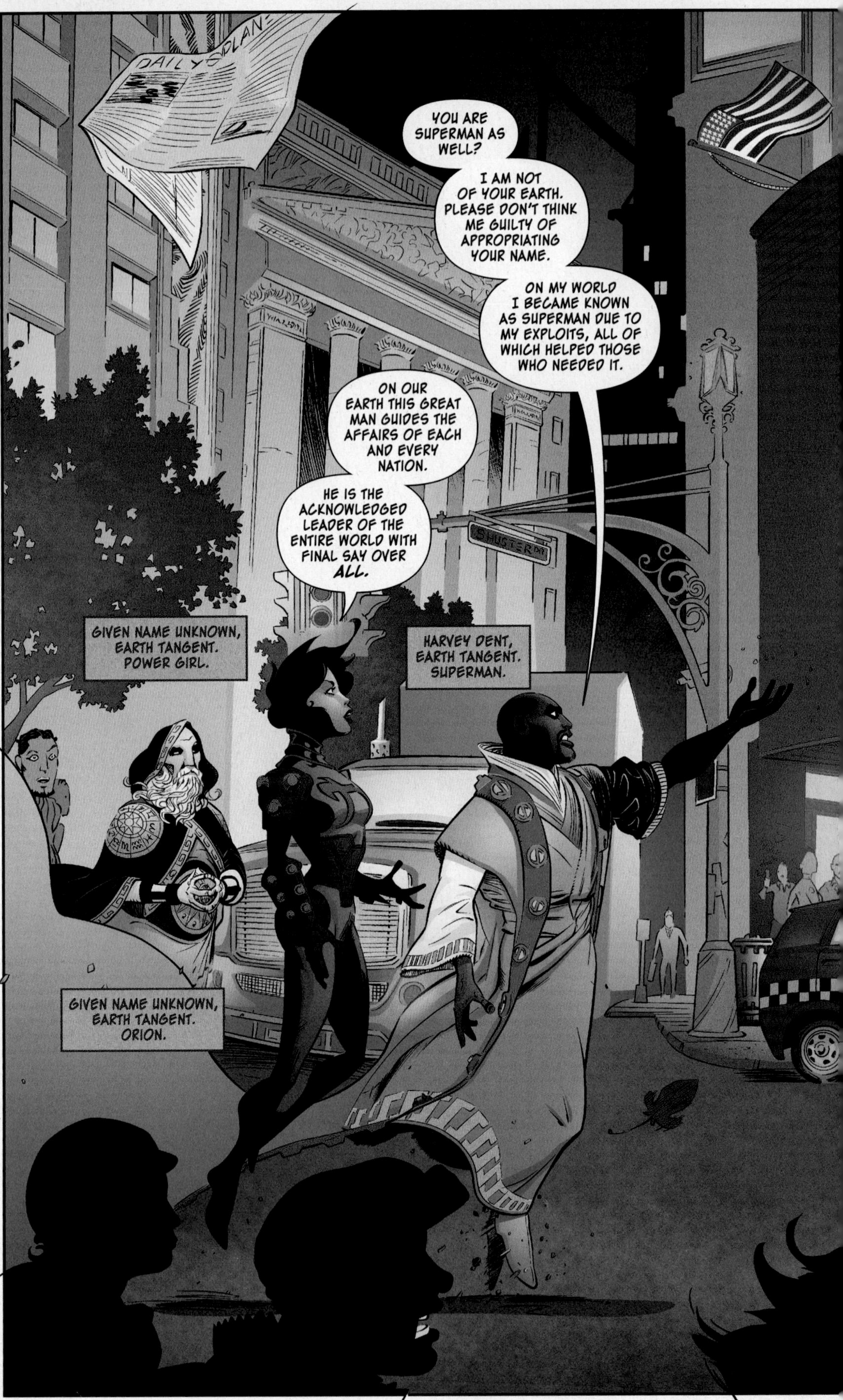

DAILY PLANET
YOU ARE SUPERMAN AS WELL?
I AM NOT OF YOUR EARTH. PLEASE DON'T THINK ME GUILTY OF APPROPRIATING YOUR NAME.
ON MY WORLD I BECAME KNOWN AS SUPERMAN DUE TO MY EXPLOITS, ALL OF WHICH HELPED THOSE WHO NEEDED IT.
ON OUR EARTH THIS GREAT MAN GUIDES THE AFFAIRS OF EACH AND EVERY NATION.
HE IS THE ACKNOWLEDGED LEADER OF THE ENTIRE WORLD WITH FINAL SAY OVER ALL.
SHUSTER DR.
GIVEN NAME UNKNOWN, EARTH TANGENT. POWER GIRL.
HARVEY DENT, EARTH TANGENT. SUPERMAN.
GIVEN NAME UNKNOWN, EARTH TANGENT. ORION.

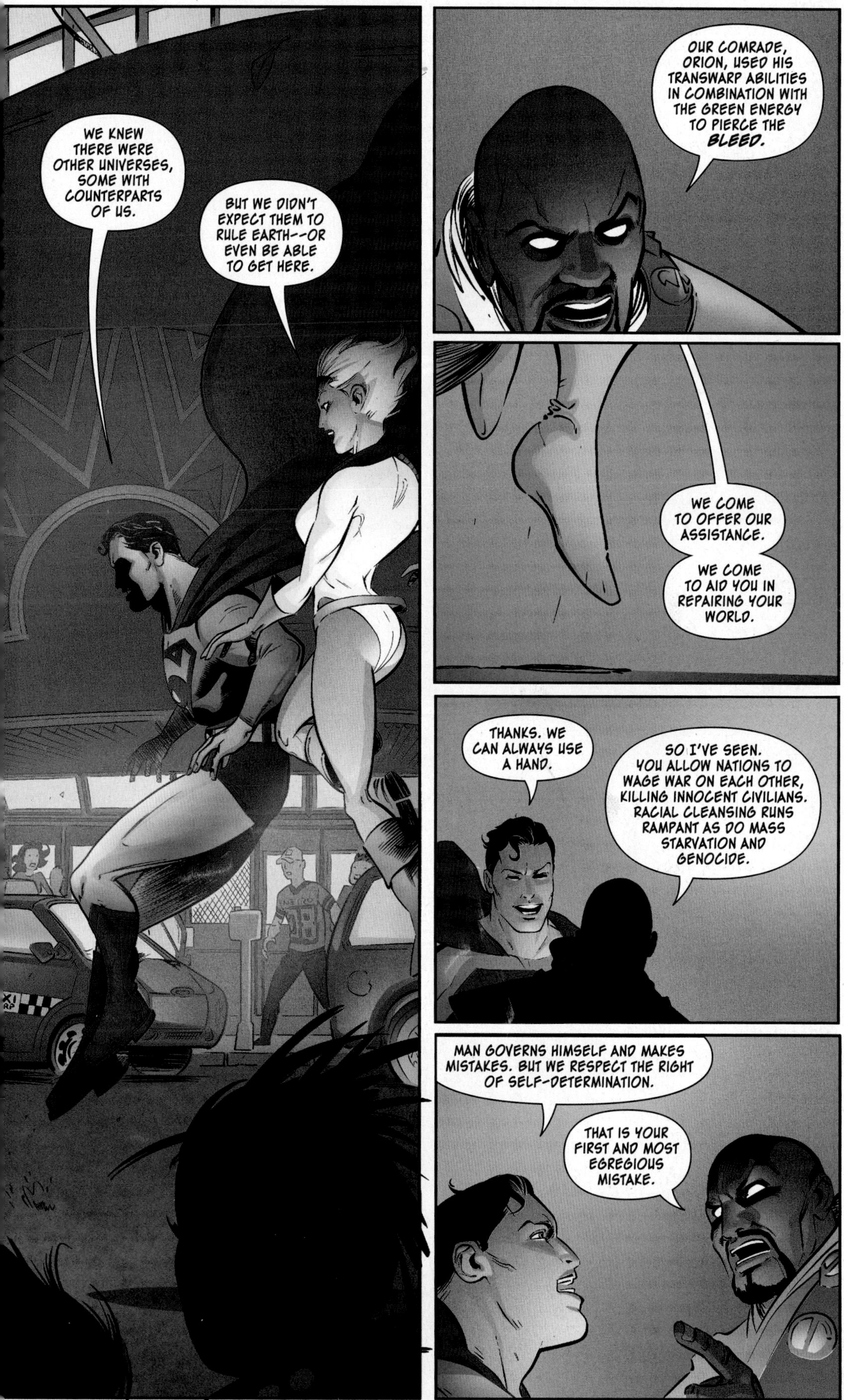
WE KNEW THERE WERE OTHER UNIVERSES, SOME WITH COUNTERPARTS OF US.
BUT WE DIDN'T EXPECT THEM TO RULE EARTH--OR EVEN BE ABLE TO GET HERE.
OUR COMRADE, ORION, USED HIS TRANSWARP ABILITIES IN COMBINATION WITH THE GREEN ENERGY TO PIERCE THE BLEED.
WE COME TO OFFER OUR ASSISTANCE.
WE COME TO AID YOU IN REPAIRING YOUR WORLD.
THANKS. WE CAN ALWAYS USE A HAND.
SO I'VE SEEN. YOU ALLOW NATIONS TO WAGE WAR ON EACH OTHER, KILLING INNOCENT CIVILIANS. RACIAL CLEANSING RUNS RAMPANT AS DO MASS STARVATION AND GENOCIDE.
MAN GOVERNS HIMSELF AND MAKES MISTAKES. BUT WE RESPECT THE RIGHT OF SELF-DETERMINATION.
THAT IS YOUR FIRST AND MOST EGREGIOUS MISTAKE.

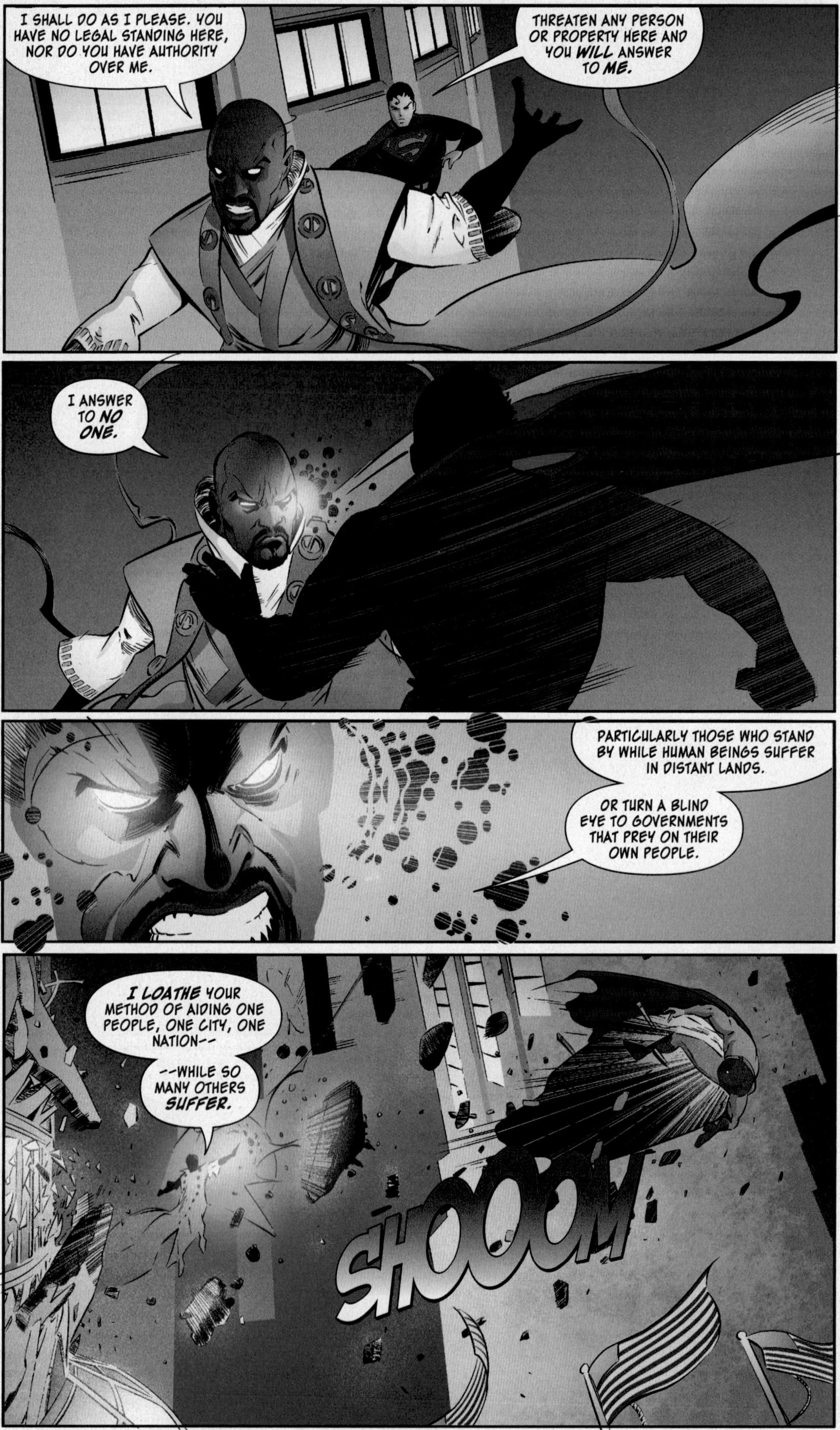
I SHALL DO AS I PLEASE. YOU HAVE NO LEGAL STANDING HERE, NOR DO YOU HAVE AUTHORITY OVER ME.
THREATEN ANY PERSON OR PROPERTY HERE AND YOU WILL ANSWER TO ME.
I ANSWER TO NO ONE.
PARTICULARLY THOSE WHO STAND BY WHILE HUMAN BEINGS SUFFER IN DISTANT LANDS.
OR TURN A BLIND EYE TO GOVERNMENTS THAT PREY ON THEIR OWN PEOPLE.
I LOATHE YOUR METHOD OF AIDING ONE PEOPLE, ONE CITY, ONE NATION--
--WHILE SO MANY OTHERS SUFFER.
SHOOOM

CAN'T SAY I'M A BIG FAN OF YOUR METHODS EITHER, MISTER.

I HAVE NO DESIRE TO WASTE TIME FIGHTING WITH YOU.

YOU NEED SOMETHING ELSE TO OCCUPY YOUR TIME.

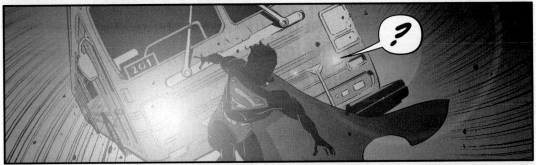

?

KRAMMM

THIS CITY DOES NOT OFFER WHAT WE NEED.

I IMAGINE THE UNITED NATIONS IS THERE JUST AS IT IS ON OUR WORLD.

NEW YORK?

NEVERTHELESS, I THINK WASHINGTON IS A BETTER DESTINATION FOR WHAT WE HOPE TO ACCOMPLISH.

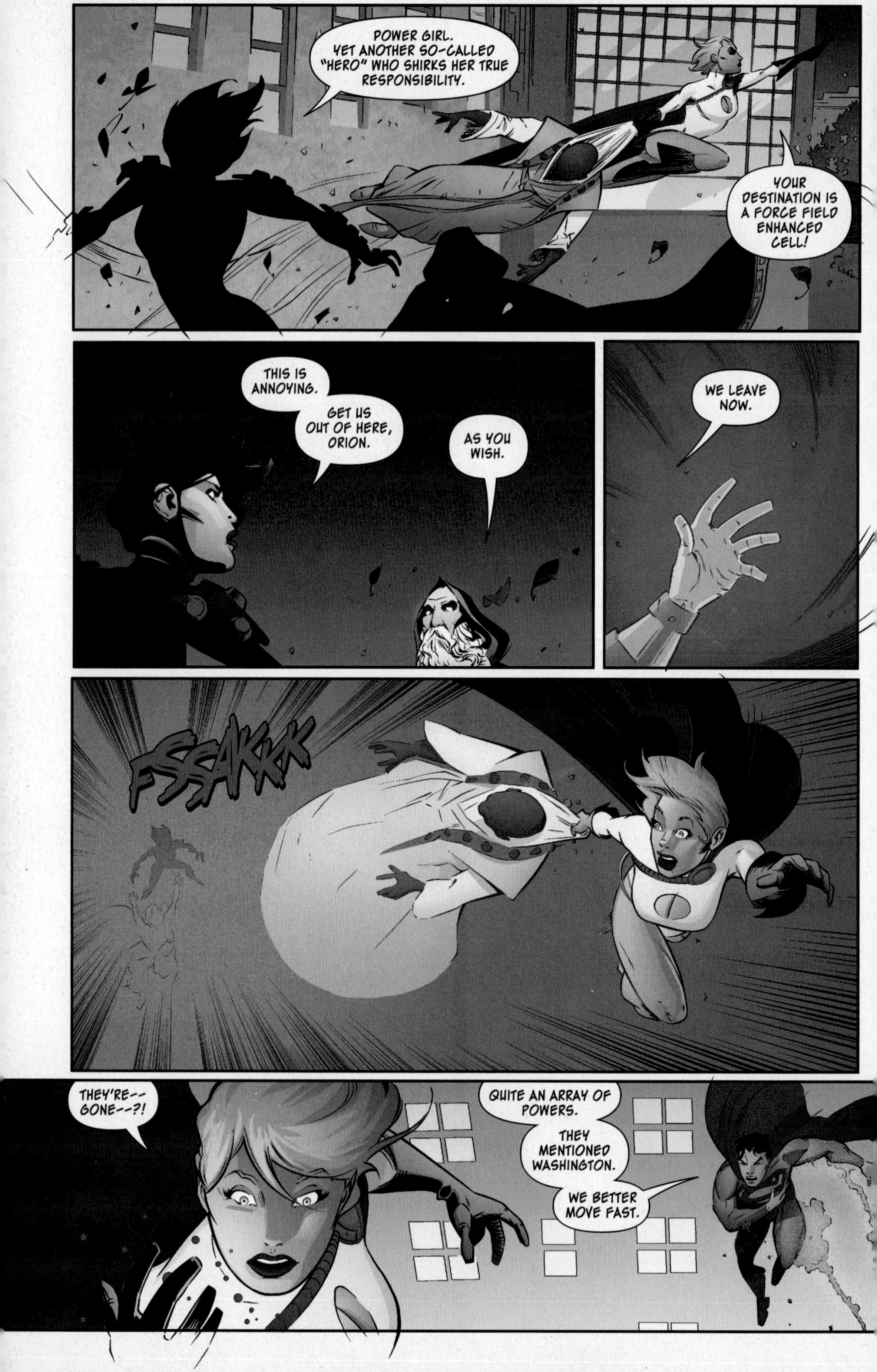
POWER GIRL. YET ANOTHER SO-CALLED "HERO" WHO SHIRKS HER TRUE RESPONSIBILITY.
YOUR DESTINATION IS A FORCE FIELD ENHANCED CELL!
THIS IS ANNOYING.
GET US OUT OF HERE, ORION.
AS YOU WISH.
WE LEAVE NOW.
FSSAKKK
THEY'RE-- GONE--?!
QUITE AN ARRAY OF POWERS.
THEY MENTIONED WASHINGTON.
WE BETTER MOVE FAST.

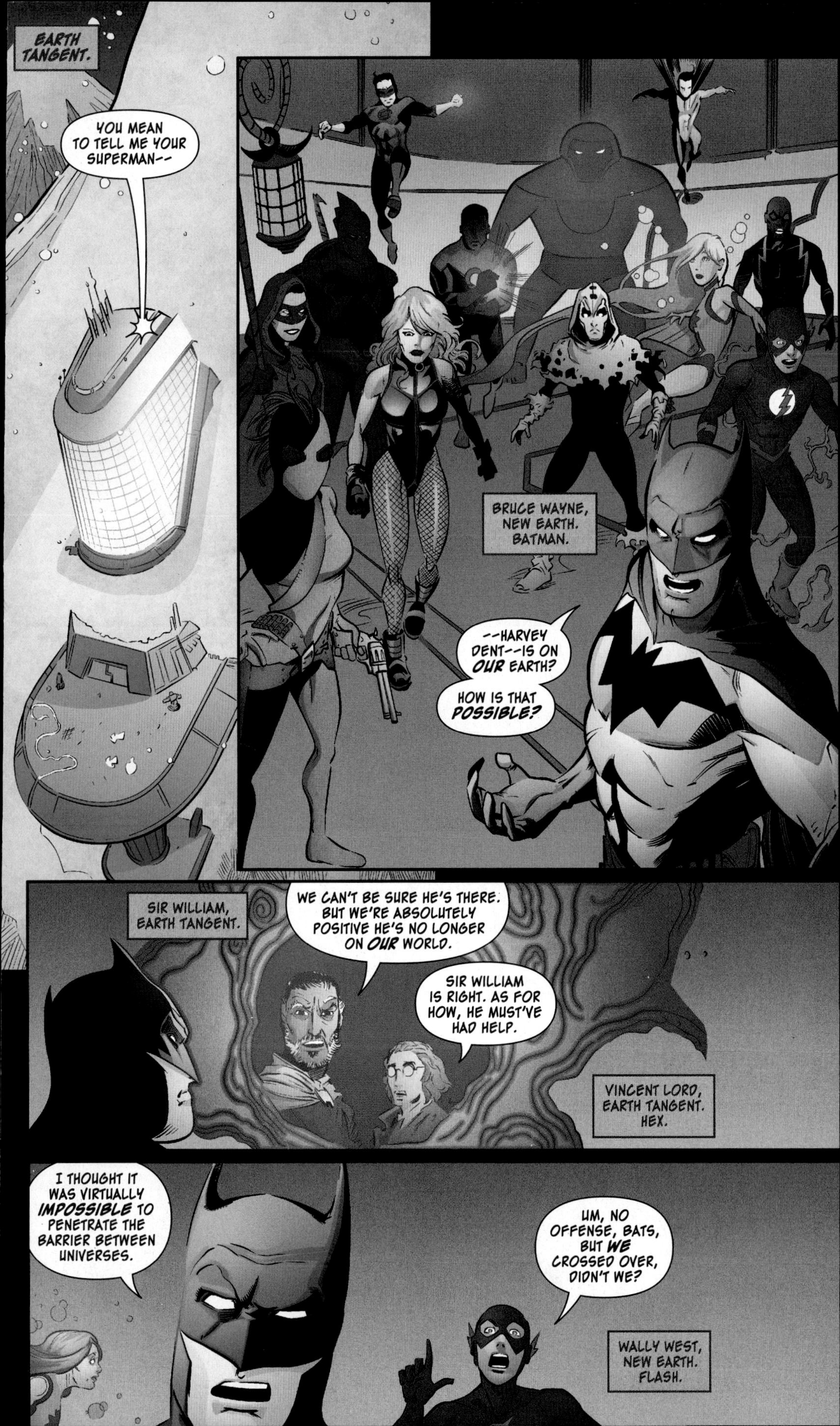
EARTH TANGENT.
YOU MEAN TO TELL ME YOUR SUPERMAN--
BRUCE WAYNE, NEW EARTH. BATMAN.
--HARVEY DENT--IS ON *OUR* EARTH?
HOW IS THAT *POSSIBLE?*
SIR WILLIAM, EARTH TANGENT.
WE CAN'T BE SURE HE'S THERE. BUT WE'RE ABSOLUTELY POSITIVE HE'S NO LONGER ON *OUR* WORLD.
SIR WILLIAM IS RIGHT. AS FOR HOW, HE MUST'VE HAD HELP.
VINCENT LORD, EARTH TANGENT. HEX.
I THOUGHT IT WAS VIRTUALLY *IMPOSSIBLE* TO PENETRATE THE BARRIER BETWEEN UNIVERSES.
UM, NO OFFENSE, BATS, BUT *WE* CROSSED OVER, DIDN'T WE?
WALLY WEST, NEW EARTH. FLASH.

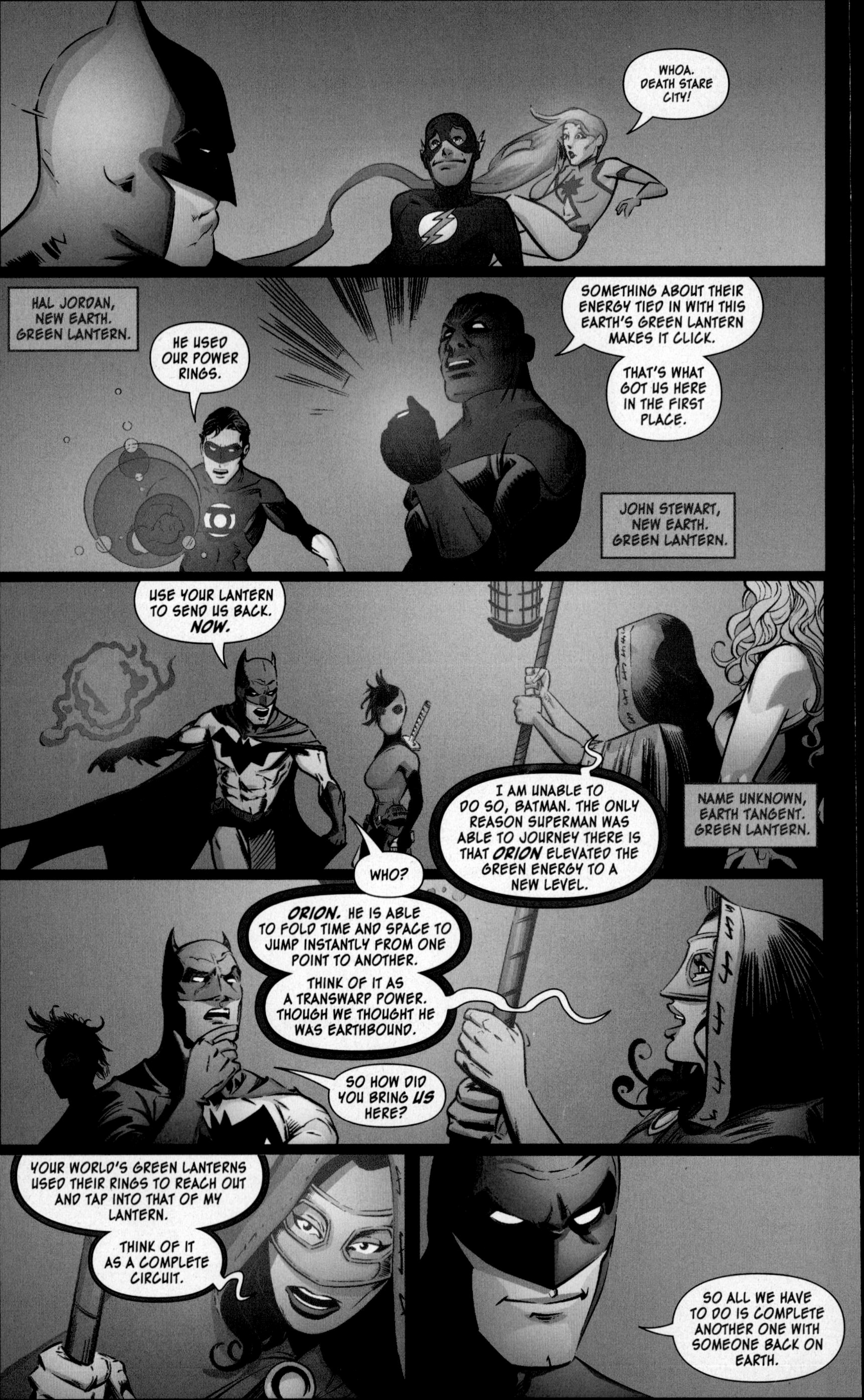

WHOA. DEATH STARE CITY!
HAL JORDAN, NEW EARTH. GREEN LANTERN.
HE USED OUR POWER RINGS.
SOMETHING ABOUT THEIR ENERGY TIED IN WITH THIS EARTH'S GREEN LANTERN MAKES IT CLICK.
THAT'S WHAT GOT US HERE IN THE FIRST PLACE.
JOHN STEWART, NEW EARTH. GREEN LANTERN.
USE YOUR LANTERN TO SEND US BACK. NOW.
I AM UNABLE TO DO SO, BATMAN. THE ONLY REASON SUPERMAN WAS ABLE TO JOURNEY THERE IS THAT ORION ELEVATED THE GREEN ENERGY TO A NEW LEVEL.
NAME UNKNOWN, EARTH TANGENT. GREEN LANTERN.
WHO?
ORION. HE IS ABLE TO FOLD TIME AND SPACE TO JUMP INSTANTLY FROM ONE POINT TO ANOTHER.
THINK OF IT AS A TRANSWARP POWER. THOUGH WE THOUGHT HE WAS EARTHBOUND.
SO HOW DID YOU BRING US HERE?
YOUR WORLD'S GREEN LANTERNS USED THEIR RINGS TO REACH OUT AND TAP INTO THAT OF MY LANTERN.
THINK OF IT AS A COMPLETE CIRCUIT.
SO ALL WE HAVE TO DO IS COMPLETE ANOTHER ONE WITH SOMEONE BACK ON EARTH.

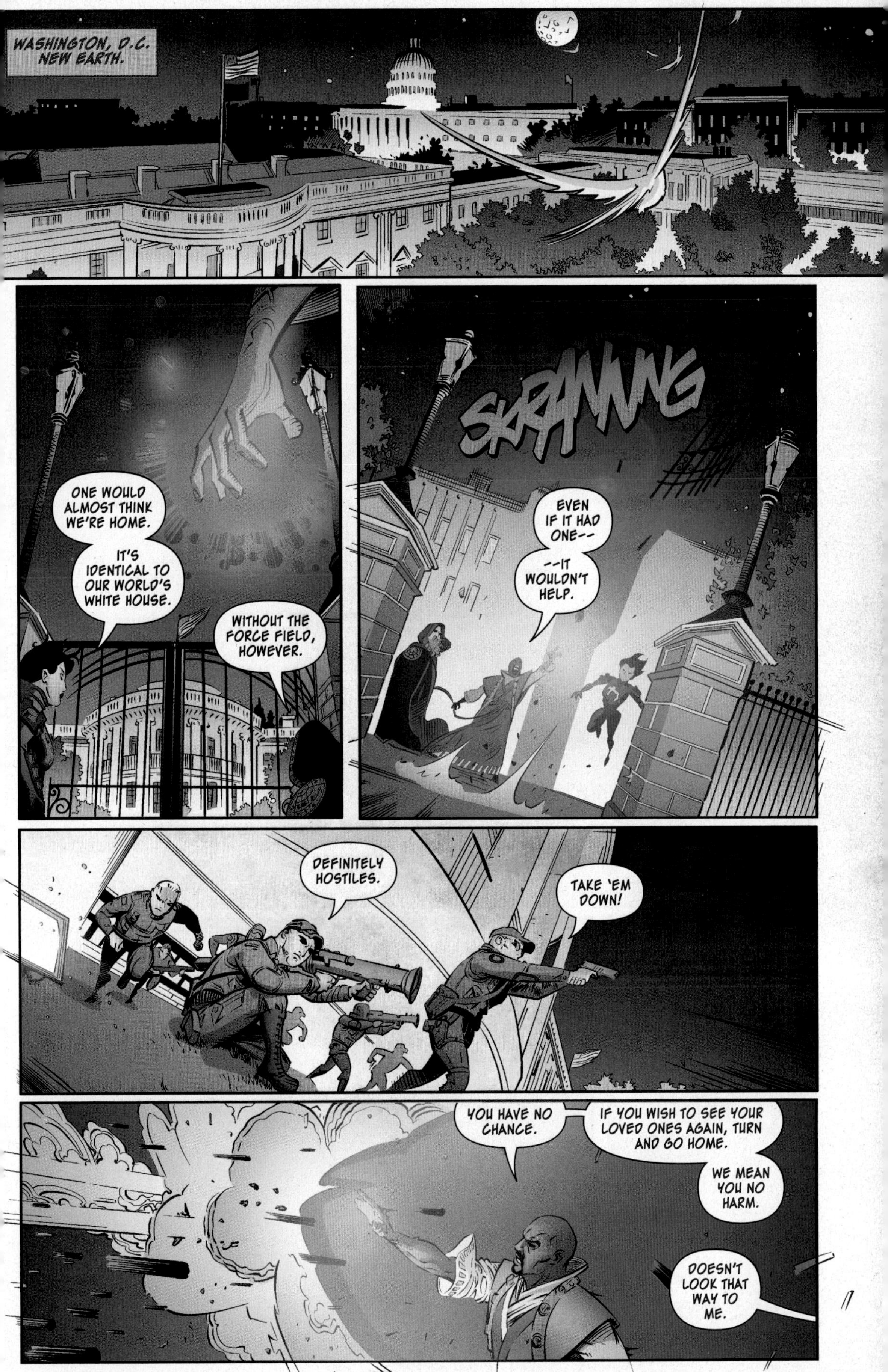
WASHINGTON, D.C. NEW EARTH.
ONE WOULD ALMOST THINK WE'RE HOME.
IT'S IDENTICAL TO OUR WORLD'S WHITE HOUSE.
WITHOUT THE FORCE FIELD, HOWEVER.
SKRANNNG
EVEN IF IT HAD ONE--
--IT WOULDN'T HELP.
DEFINITELY HOSTILES.
TAKE 'EM DOWN!
YOU HAVE NO CHANCE.
IF YOU WISH TO SEE YOUR LOVED ONES AGAIN, TURN AND GO HOME.
WE MEAN YOU NO HARM.
DOESN'T LOOK THAT WAY TO ME.

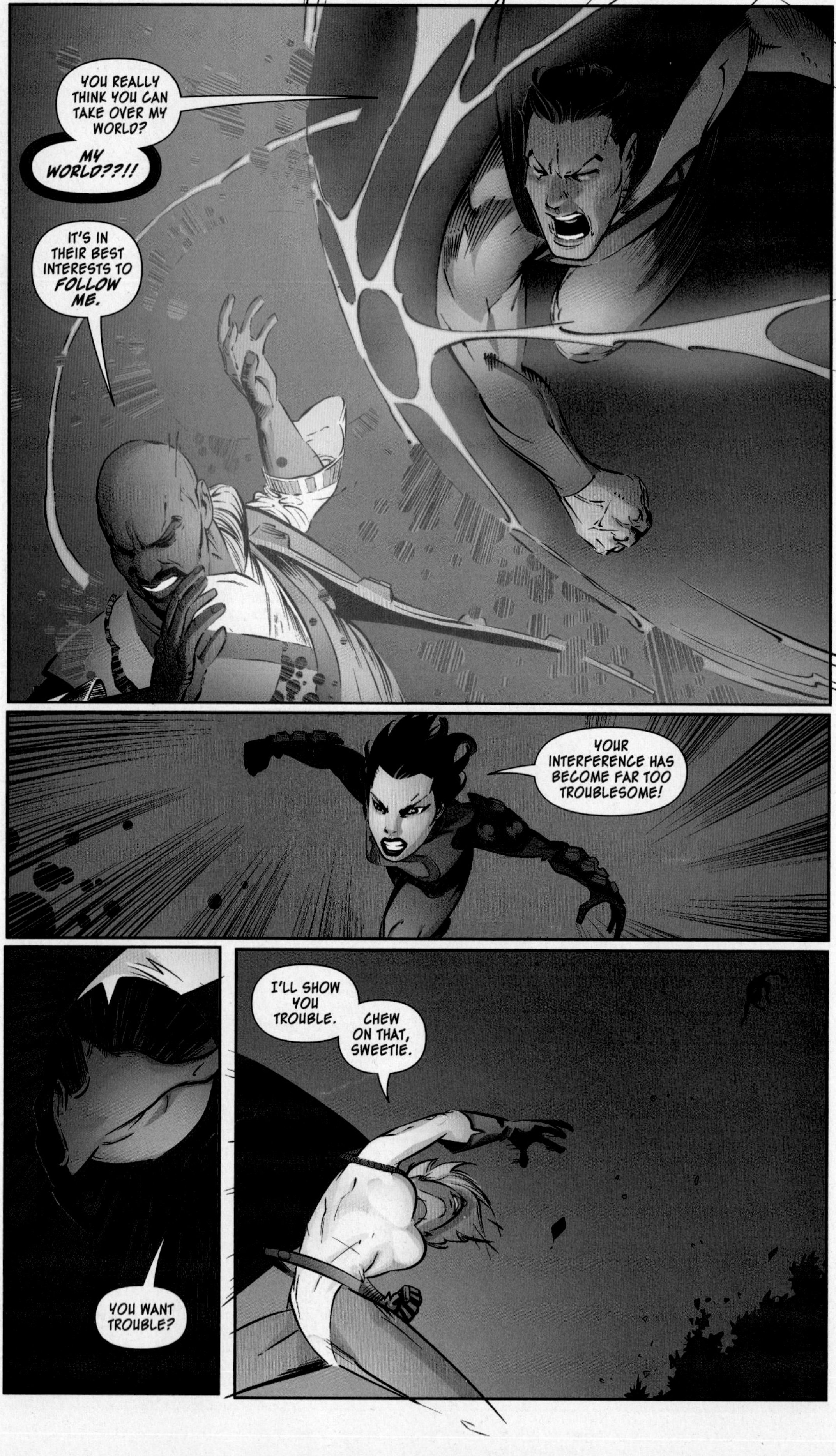
YOU REALLY THINK YOU CAN TAKE OVER MY WORLD?
MY WORLD??!!
IT'S IN THEIR BEST INTERESTS TO FOLLOW ME.
YOUR INTERFERENCE HAS BECOME FAR TOO TROUBLESOME!
YOU WANT TROUBLE?
I'LL SHOW YOU TROUBLE.
CHEW ON THAT, SWEETIE.

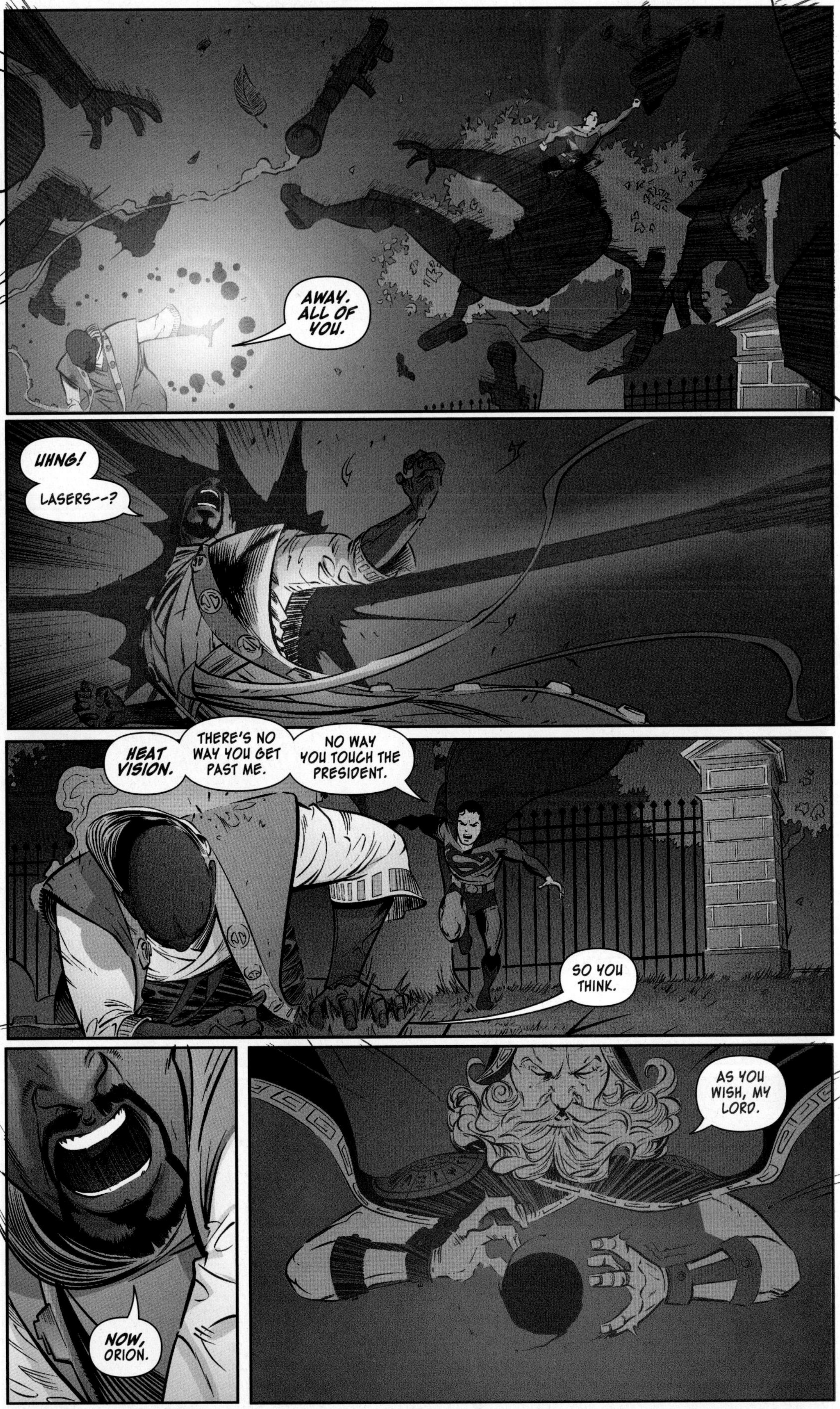
AWAY. ALL OF YOU.
UHNG!
LASERS--?
HEAT VISION.
THERE'S NO WAY YOU GET PAST ME.
NO WAY YOU TOUCH THE PRESIDENT.
SO YOU THINK.
NOW, ORION.
AS YOU WISH, MY LORD.

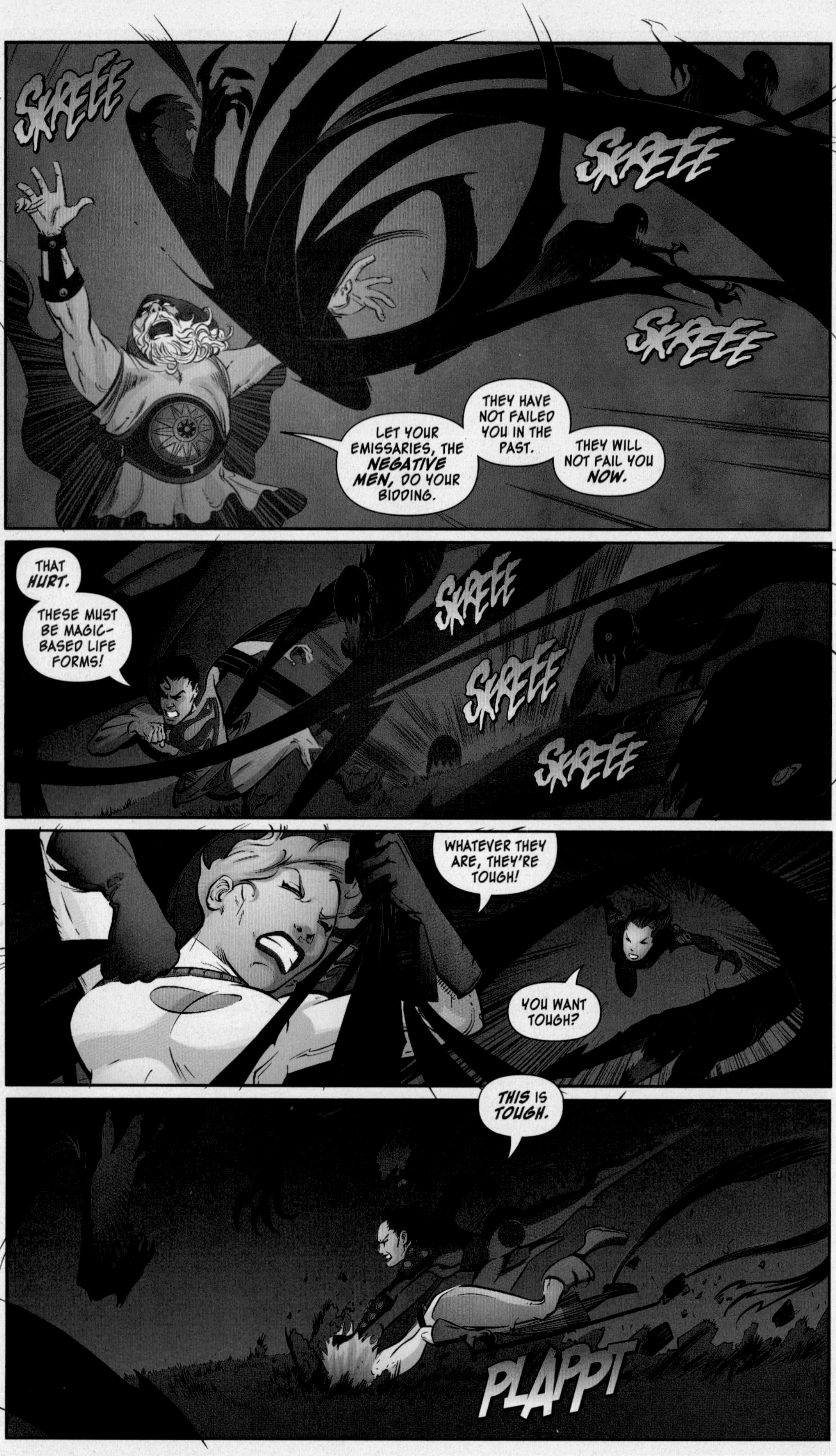
SKREEE
SKREEE
SKREEE
LET YOUR EMISSARIES, THE NEGATIVE MEN, DO YOUR BIDDING.
THEY HAVE NOT FAILED YOU IN THE PAST.
THEY WILL NOT FAIL YOU NOW.
THAT HURT.
THESE MUST BE MAGIC-BASED LIFE FORMS!
SKREEE
SKREEE
SKREEE
WHATEVER THEY ARE, THEY'RE TOUGH!
YOU WANT TOUGH?
THIS IS TOUGH.
PLAPPT

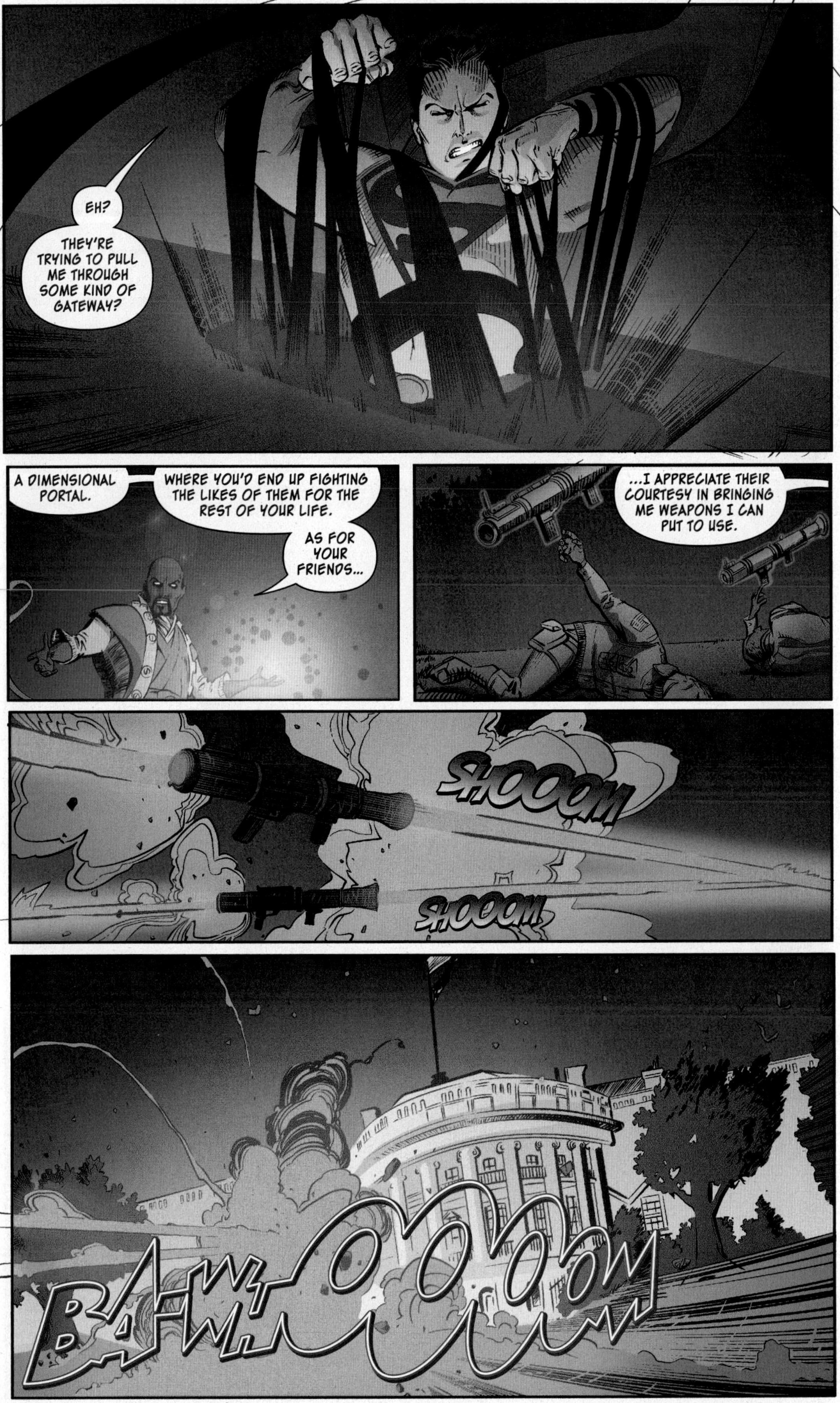
EH?
THEY'RE TRYING TO PULL ME THROUGH SOME KIND OF GATEWAY?
A DIMENSIONAL PORTAL.
WHERE YOU'D END UP FIGHTING THE LIKES OF THEM FOR THE REST OF YOUR LIFE.
AS FOR YOUR FRIENDS...
...I APPRECIATE THEIR COURTESY IN BRINGING ME WEAPONS I CAN PUT TO USE.
SHOOOM
SHOOOM
BAHHHOOOOM

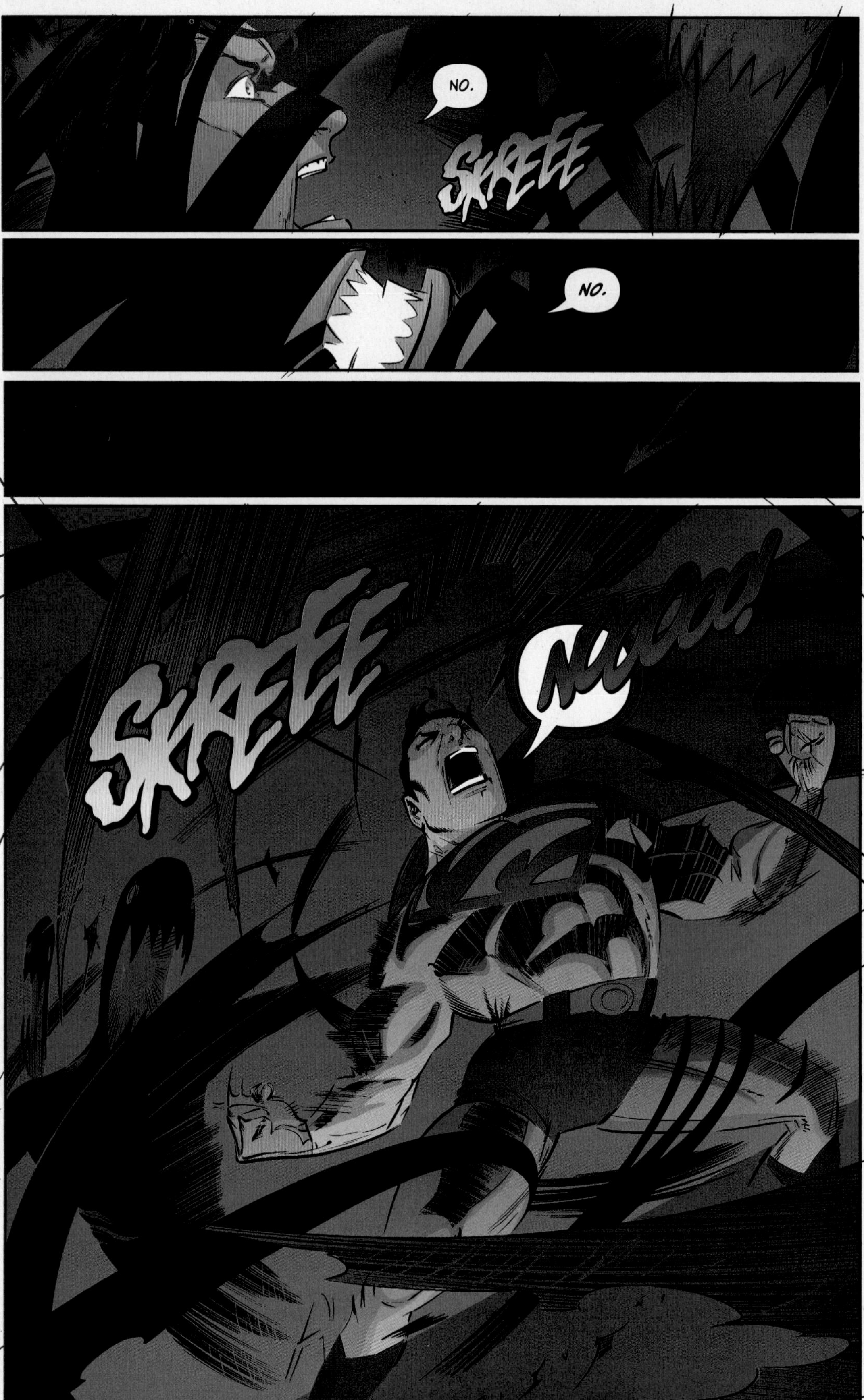
NO.
SKREEE
NO.
SKREEE
NOOOO!

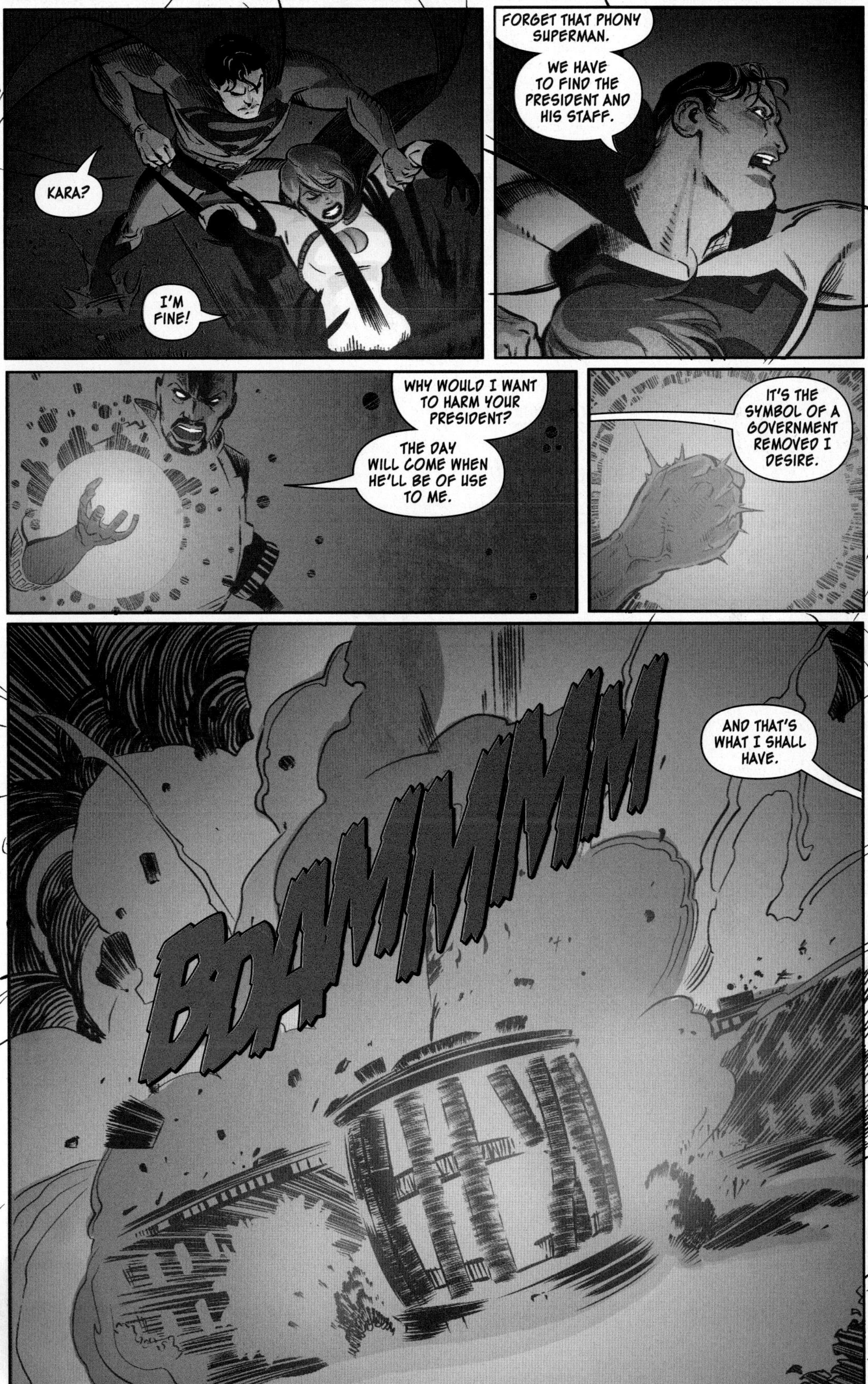
KARA?
I'M FINE!
FORGET THAT PHONY SUPERMAN.
WE HAVE TO FIND THE PRESIDENT AND HIS STAFF.
WHY WOULD I WANT TO HARM YOUR PRESIDENT?
THE DAY WILL COME WHEN HE'LL BE OF USE TO ME.
IT'S THE SYMBOL OF A GOVERNMENT REMOVED I DESIRE.
AND THAT'S WHAT I SHALL HAVE.
BDAMMMMM

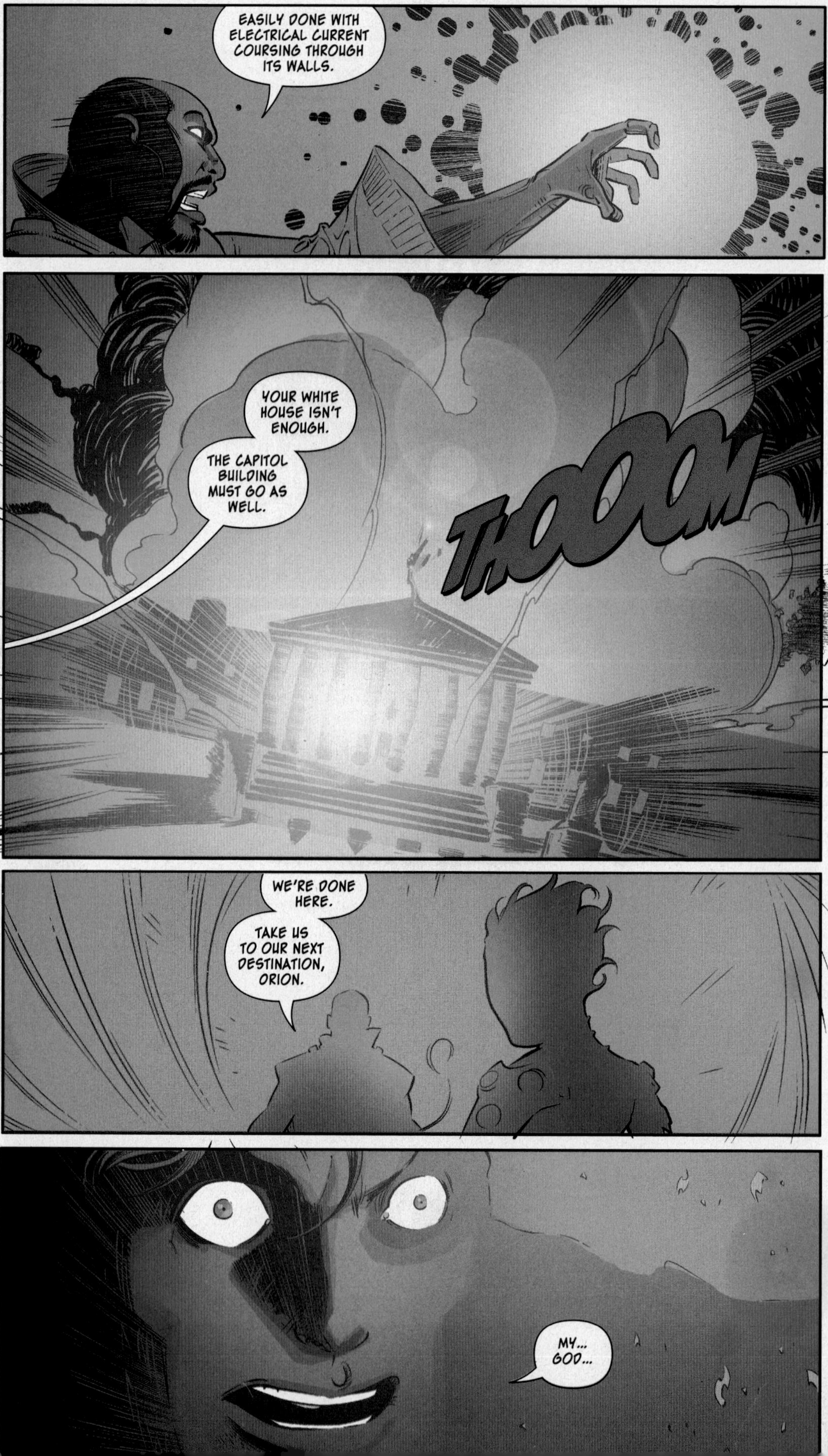
EASILY DONE WITH ELECTRICAL CURRENT COURSING THROUGH ITS WALLS.
YOUR WHITE HOUSE ISN'T ENOUGH.
THE CAPITOL BUILDING MUST GO AS WELL.
THOOOM
WE'RE DONE HERE.
TAKE US TO OUR NEXT DESTINATION, ORION.
MY... GOD...

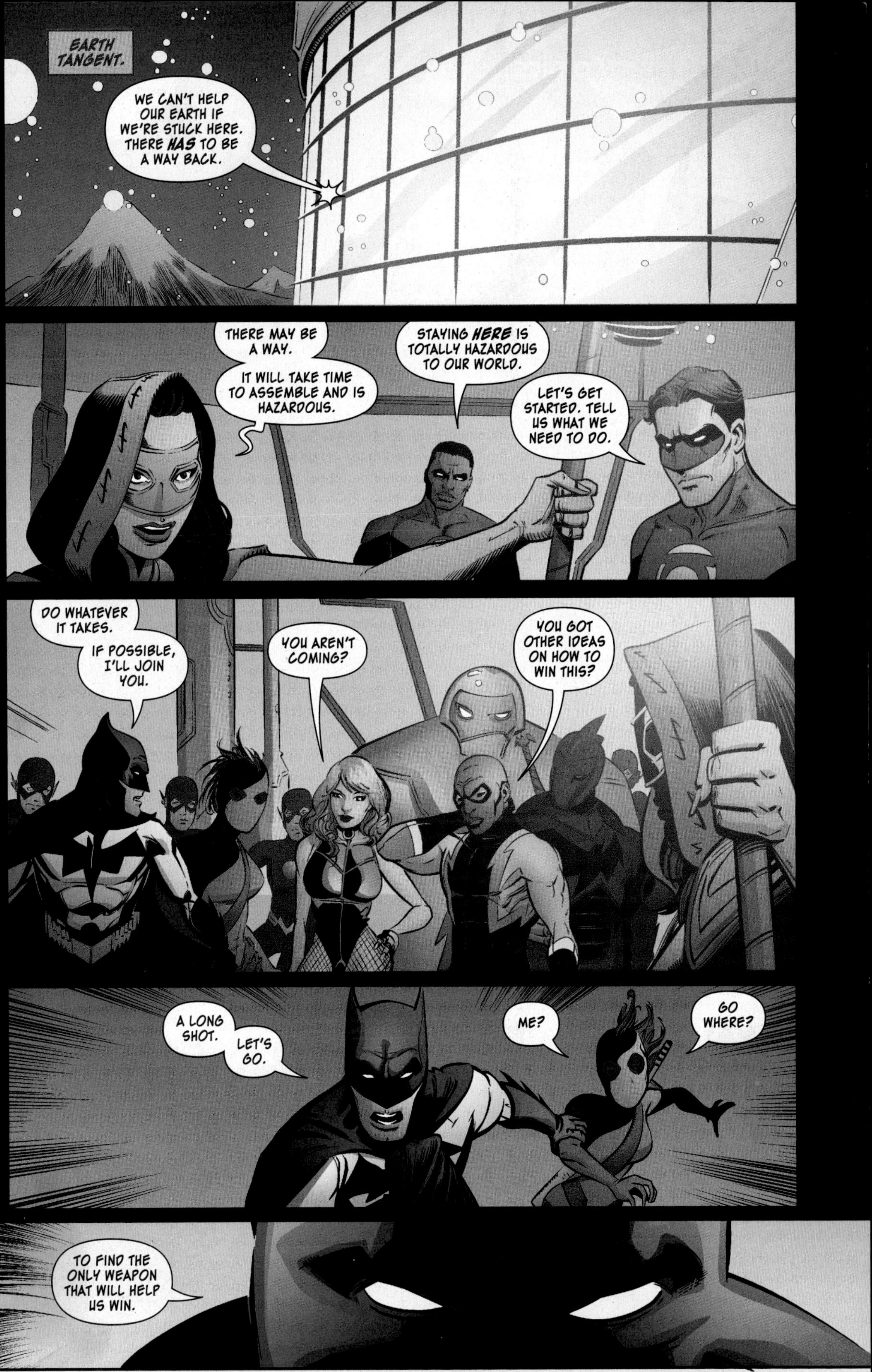
EARTH TANGENT.
WE CAN'T HELP OUR EARTH IF WE'RE STUCK HERE. THERE HAS TO BE A WAY BACK.
THERE MAY BE A WAY.
IT WILL TAKE TIME TO ASSEMBLE AND IS HAZARDOUS.
STAYING HERE IS TOTALLY HAZARDOUS TO OUR WORLD.
LET'S GET STARTED. TELL US WHAT WE NEED TO DO.
DO WHATEVER IT TAKES.
IF POSSIBLE, I'LL JOIN YOU.
YOU AREN'T COMING?
YOU GOT OTHER IDEAS ON HOW TO WIN THIS?
A LONG SHOT.
LET'S GO.
ME?
GO WHERE?
TO FIND THE ONLY WEAPON THAT WILL HELP US WIN.

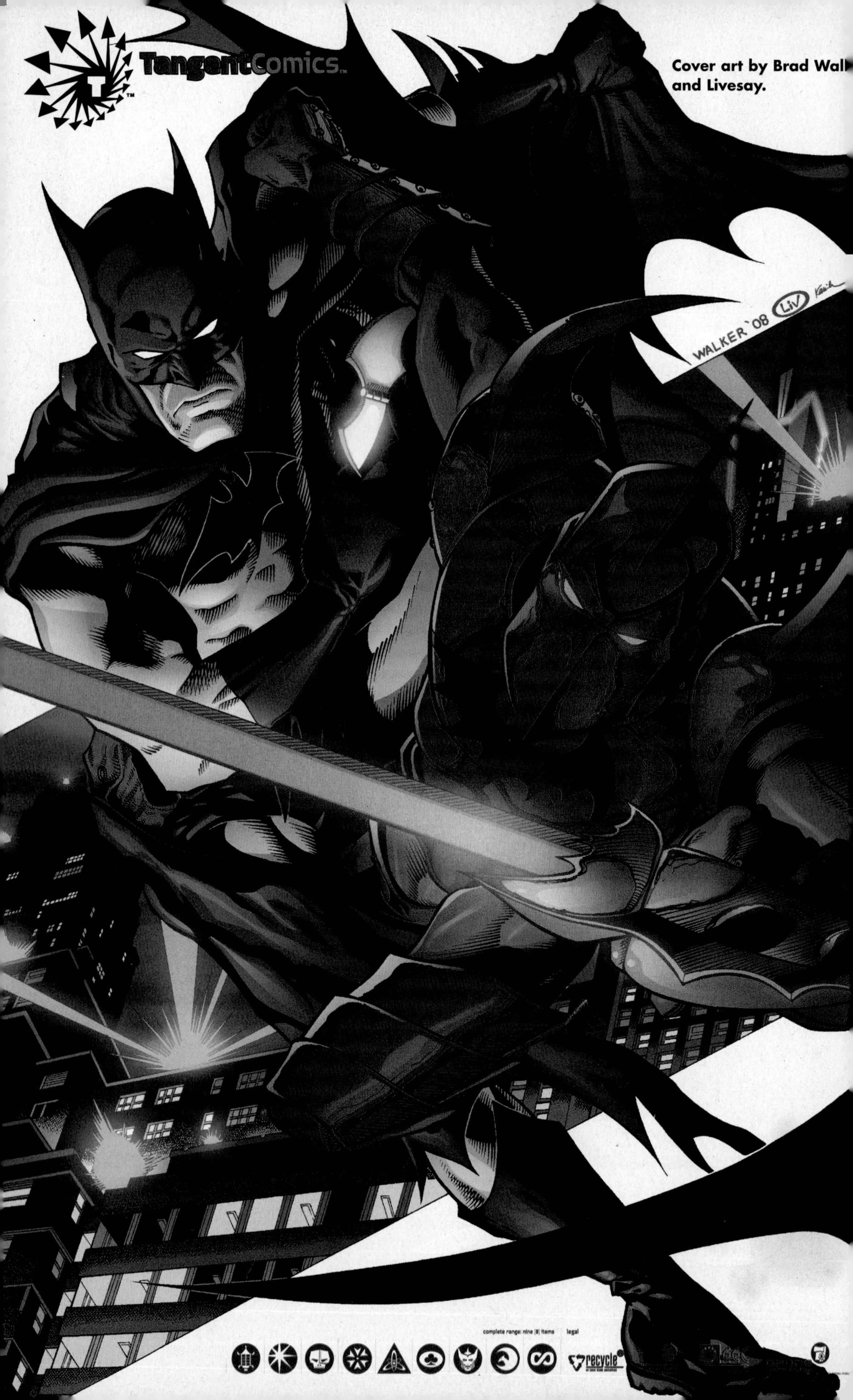
WALKER `08

Cover art by Brad Wal
and Livesay.

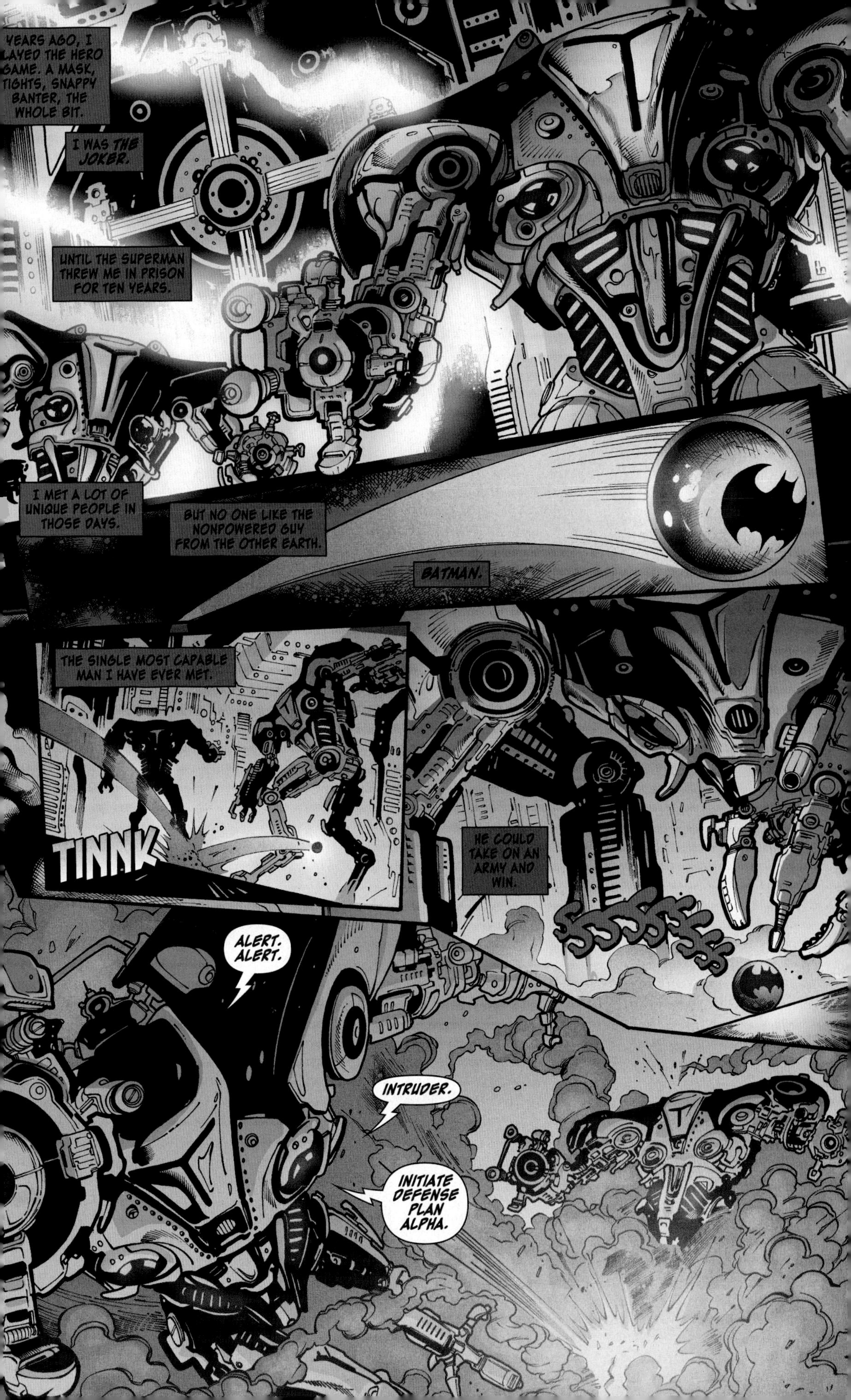
YEARS AGO, I PLAYED THE HERO GAME. A MASK, TIGHTS, SNAPPY BANTER, THE WHOLE BIT.
I WAS THE JOKER.
UNTIL THE SUPERMAN THREW ME IN PRISON FOR TEN YEARS.
I MET A LOT OF UNIQUE PEOPLE IN THOSE DAYS.
BUT NO ONE LIKE THE NONPOWERED GUY FROM THE OTHER EARTH.
BATMAN.
THE SINGLE MOST CAPABLE MAN I HAVE EVER MET.
TINNK
HE COULD TAKE ON AN ARMY AND WIN.
SSSSSHHH
ALERT. ALERT.
INTRUDER.
INITIATE DEFENSE PLAN ALPHA.

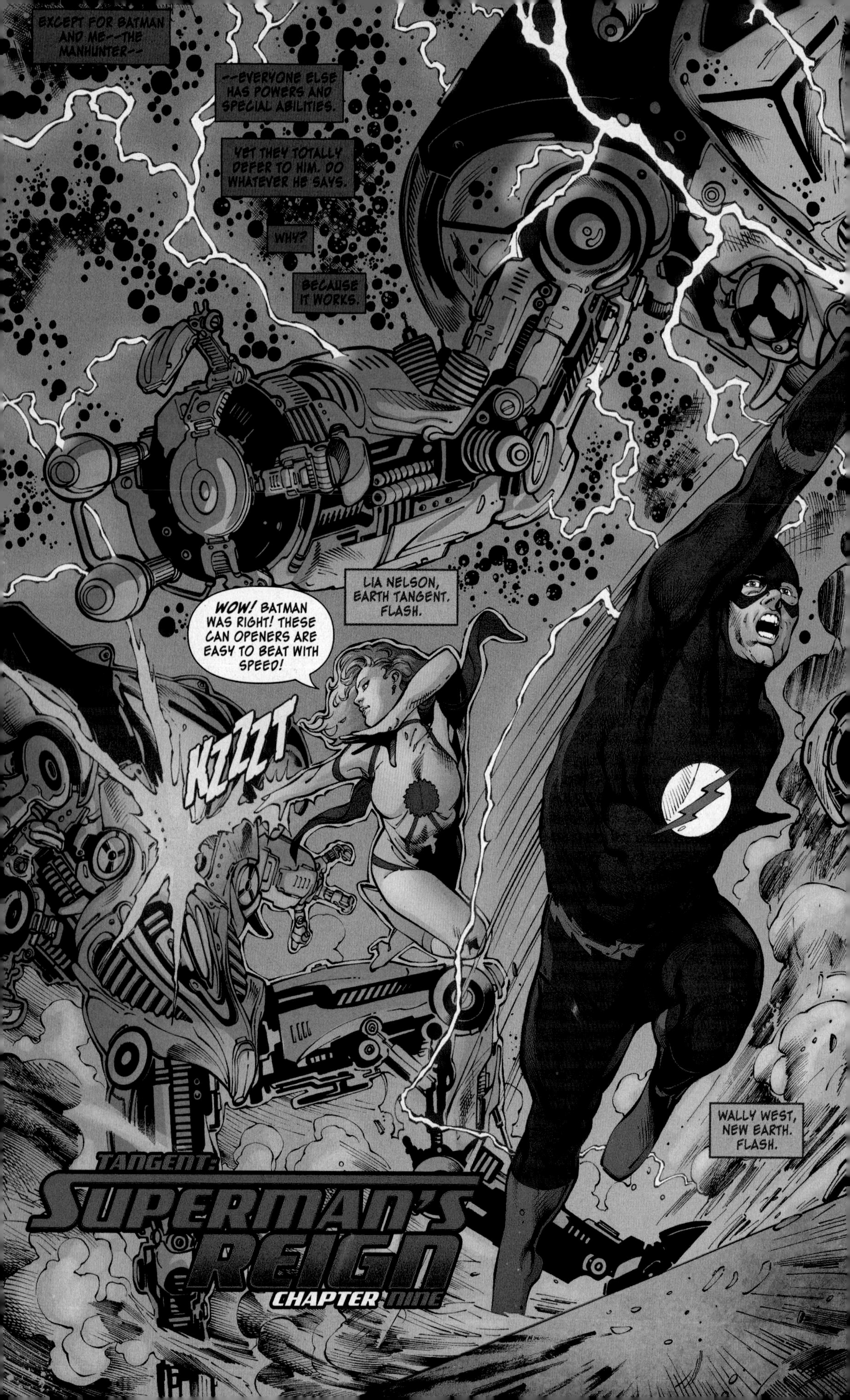
EXCEPT FOR BATMAN AND ME--THE MANHUNTER--
--EVERYONE ELSE HAS POWERS AND SPECIAL ABILITIES.
YET THEY TOTALLY DEFER TO HIM. DO WHATEVER HE SAYS.
WHY?
BECAUSE IT WORKS.
LIA NELSON, EARTH TANGENT. FLASH.
WOW! BATMAN WAS RIGHT! THESE CAN OPENERS ARE EASY TO BEAT WITH SPEED!
KZZZT
WALLY WEST, NEW EARTH. FLASH.
TANGENT: SUPERMAN'S REIGN
CHAPTER NINE

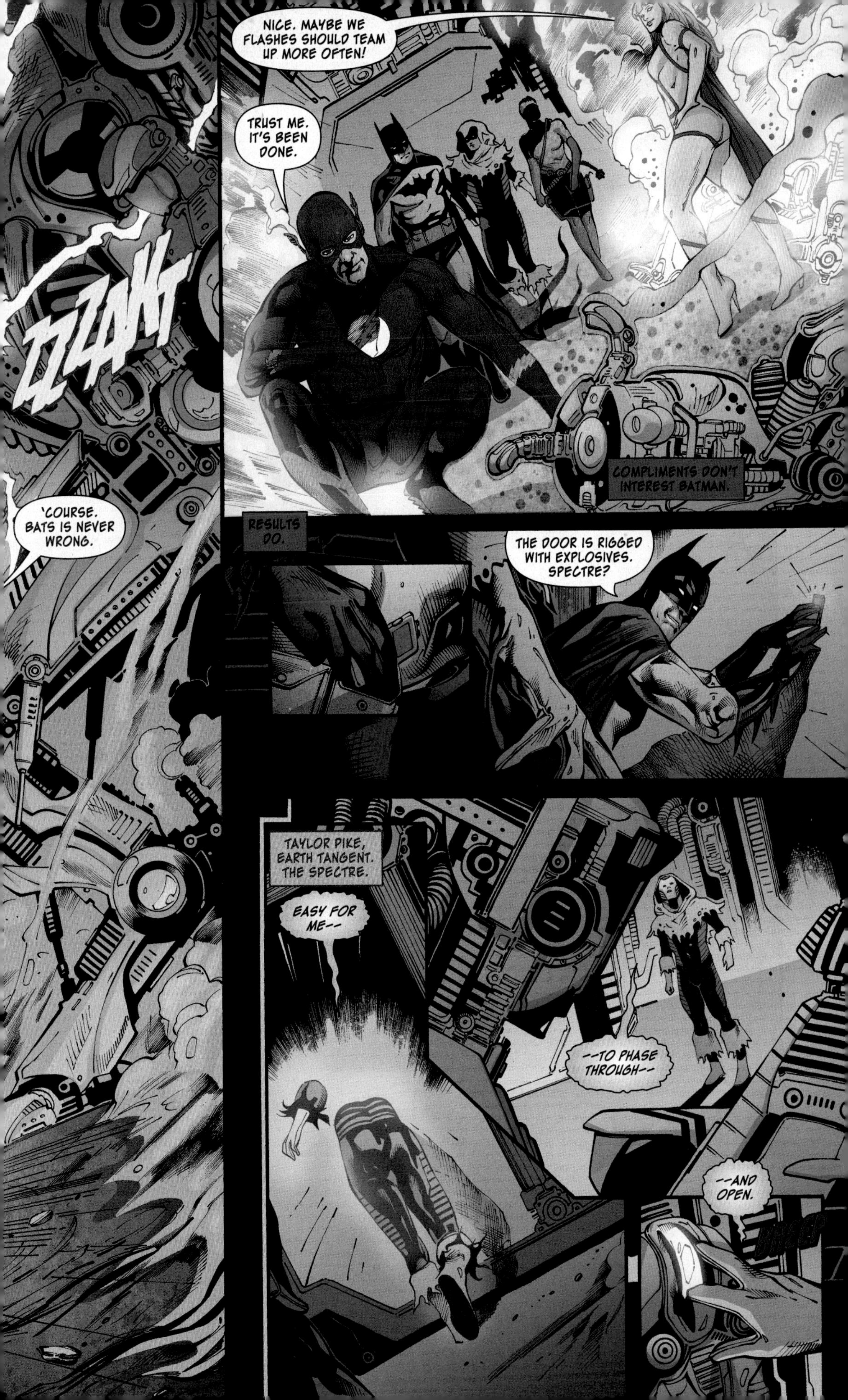
NICE. MAYBE WE FLASHES SHOULD TEAM UP MORE OFTEN!
TRUST ME. IT'S BEEN DONE.
ZZZAKT
COMPLIMENTS DON'T INTEREST BATMAN.
'COURSE. BATS IS NEVER WRONG.
RESULTS DO.
THE DOOR IS RIGGED WITH EXPLOSIVES. SPECTRE?
TAYLOR PIKE, EARTH TANGENT. THE SPECTRE.
EASY FOR ME--
--TO PHASE THROUGH--
--AND OPEN.

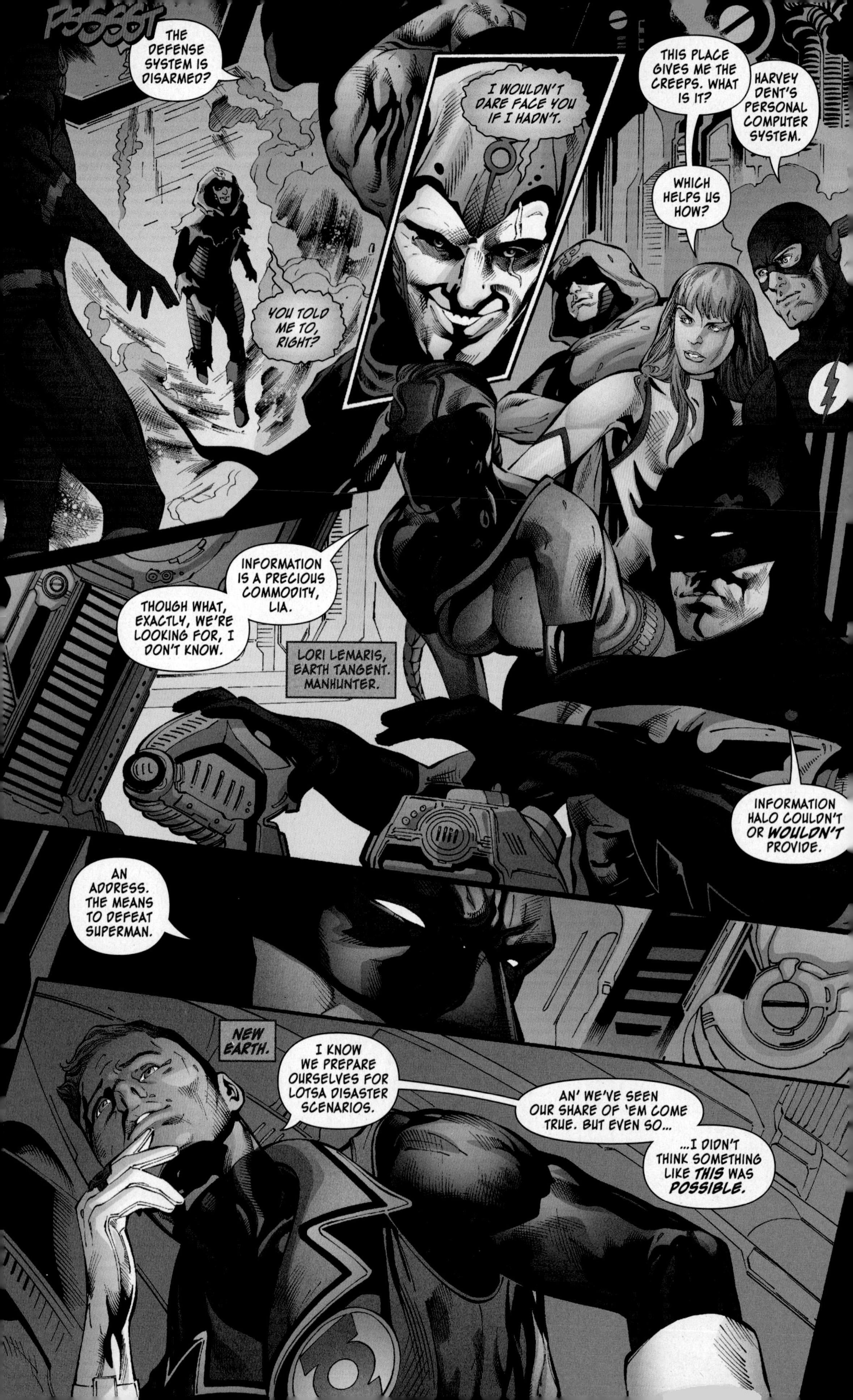
PSSSST
THE DEFENSE SYSTEM IS DISARMED?
I WOULDN'T DARE FACE YOU IF I HADN'T.
YOU TOLD ME TO, RIGHT?
THIS PLACE GIVES ME THE CREEPS. WHAT IS IT?
HARVEY DENT'S PERSONAL COMPUTER SYSTEM.
WHICH HELPS US HOW?
INFORMATION IS A PRECIOUS COMMODITY, LIA.
THOUGH WHAT, EXACTLY, WE'RE LOOKING FOR, I DON'T KNOW.
LORI LEMARIS, EARTH TANGENT. MANHUNTER.
INFORMATION HALO COULDN'T OR WOULDN'T PROVIDE.
AN ADDRESS. THE MEANS TO DEFEAT SUPERMAN.
NEW EARTH.
I KNOW WE PREPARE OURSELVES FOR LOTSA DISASTER SCENARIOS.
AN' WE'VE SEEN OUR SHARE OF 'EM COME TRUE. BUT EVEN SO...
...I DIDN'T THINK SOMETHING LIKE THIS WAS POSSIBLE.

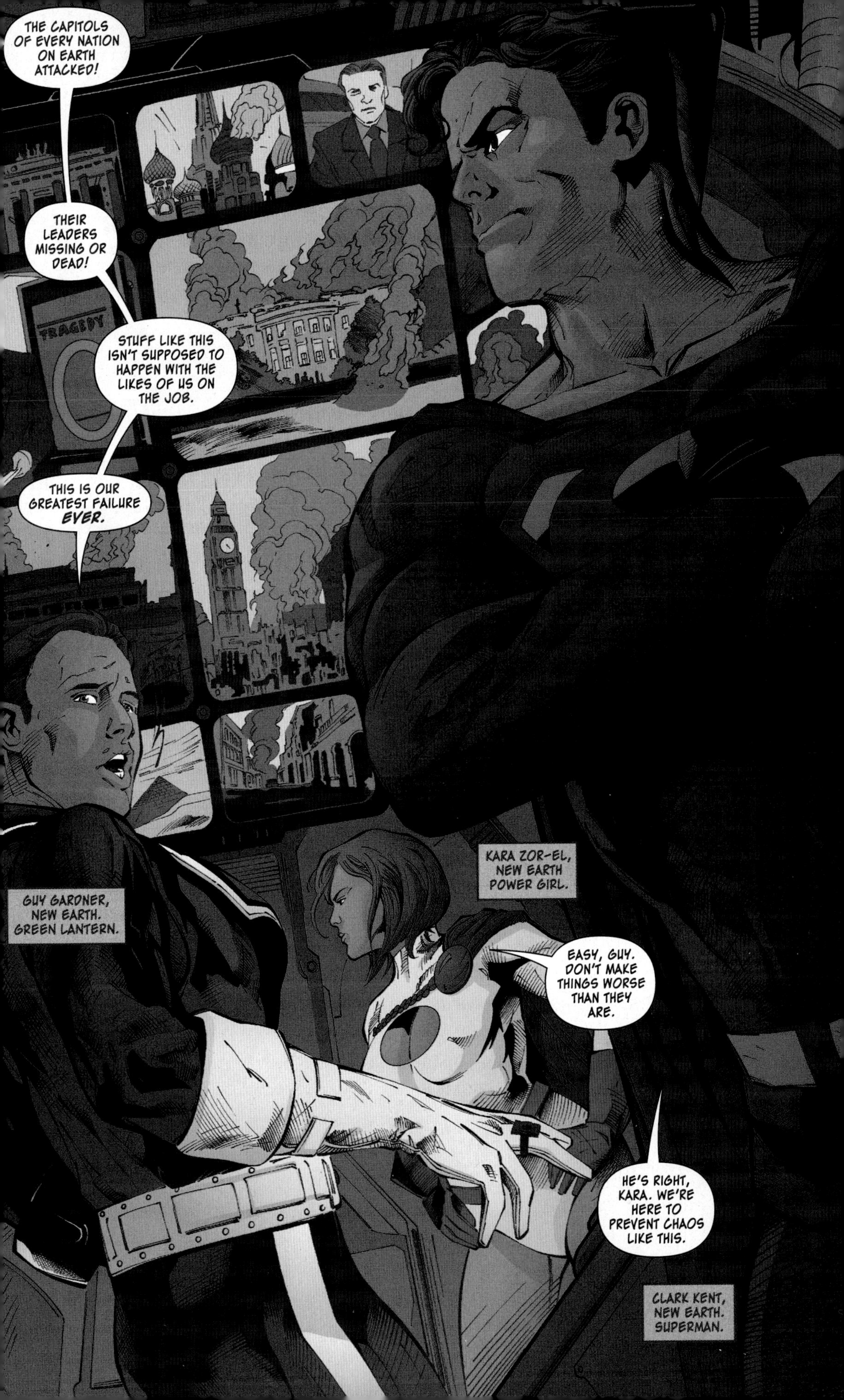
THE CAPITOLS OF EVERY NATION ON EARTH ATTACKED!
THEIR LEADERS MISSING OR DEAD!
TRAGEDY
STUFF LIKE THIS ISN'T SUPPOSED TO HAPPEN WITH THE LIKES OF US ON THE JOB.
THIS IS OUR GREATEST FAILURE *EVER.*
GUY GARDNER, NEW EARTH. GREEN LANTERN.
KARA ZOR-EL, NEW EARTH POWER GIRL.
EASY, GUY. DON'T MAKE THINGS WORSE THAN THEY ARE.
HE'S RIGHT, KARA. WE'RE HERE TO PREVENT CHAOS LIKE THIS.
CLARK KENT, NEW EARTH. SUPERMAN.

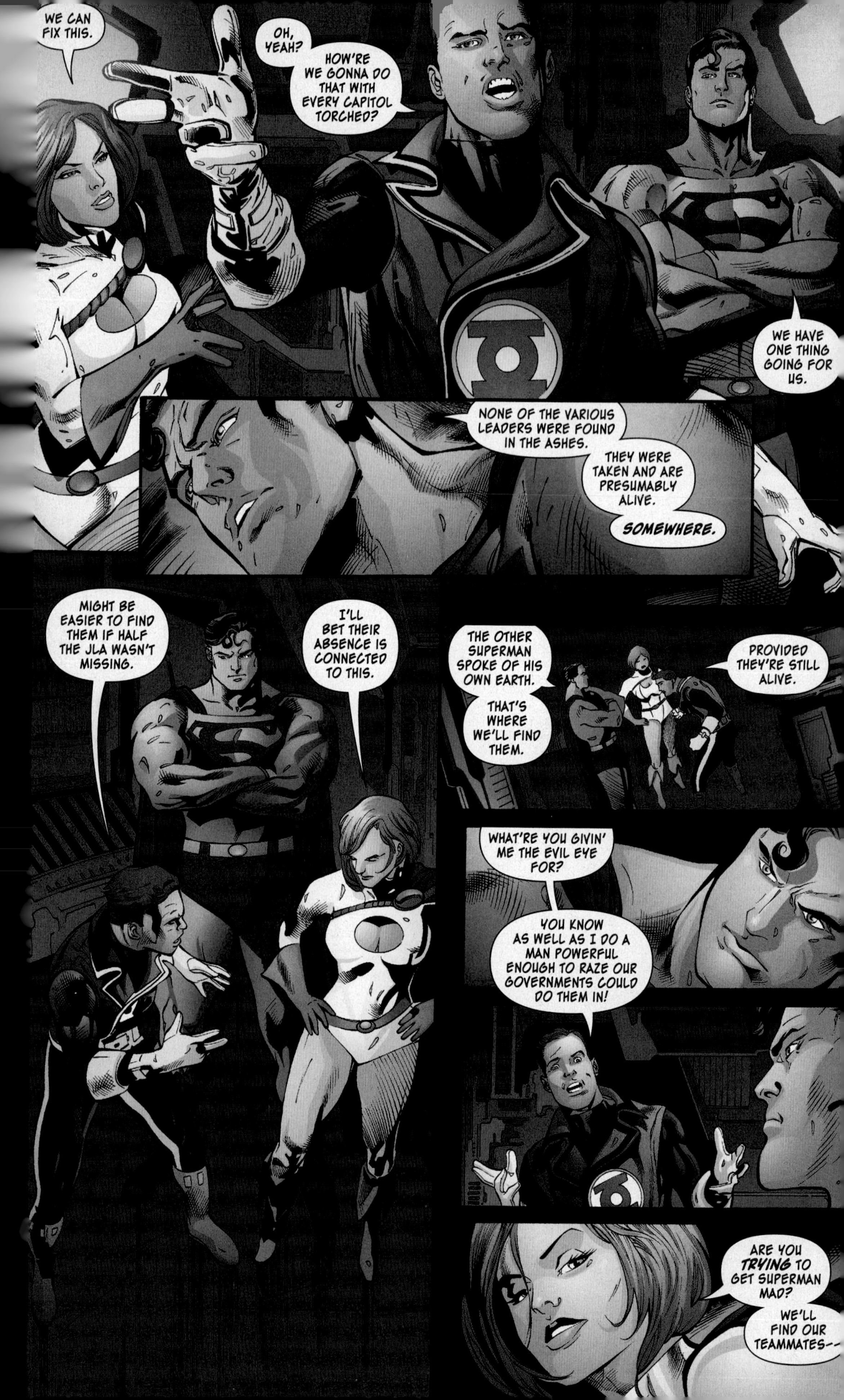
WE CAN FIX THIS.
OH, YEAH?
HOW'RE WE GONNA DO THAT WITH EVERY CAPITOL TORCHED?
WE HAVE ONE THING GOING FOR US.
NONE OF THE VARIOUS LEADERS WERE FOUND IN THE ASHES.
THEY WERE TAKEN AND ARE PRESUMABLY ALIVE.
SOMEWHERE.
MIGHT BE EASIER TO FIND THEM IF HALF THE JLA WASN'T MISSING.
I'LL BET THEIR ABSENCE IS CONNECTED TO THIS.
THE OTHER SUPERMAN SPOKE OF HIS OWN EARTH.
THAT'S WHERE WE'LL FIND THEM.
PROVIDED THEY'RE STILL ALIVE.
WHAT'RE YOU GIVIN' ME THE EVIL EYE FOR?
YOU KNOW AS WELL AS I DO A MAN POWERFUL ENOUGH TO RAZE OUR GOVERNMENTS COULD DO THEM IN!
ARE YOU TRYING TO GET SUPERMAN MAD?
WE'LL FIND OUR TEAMMATES--

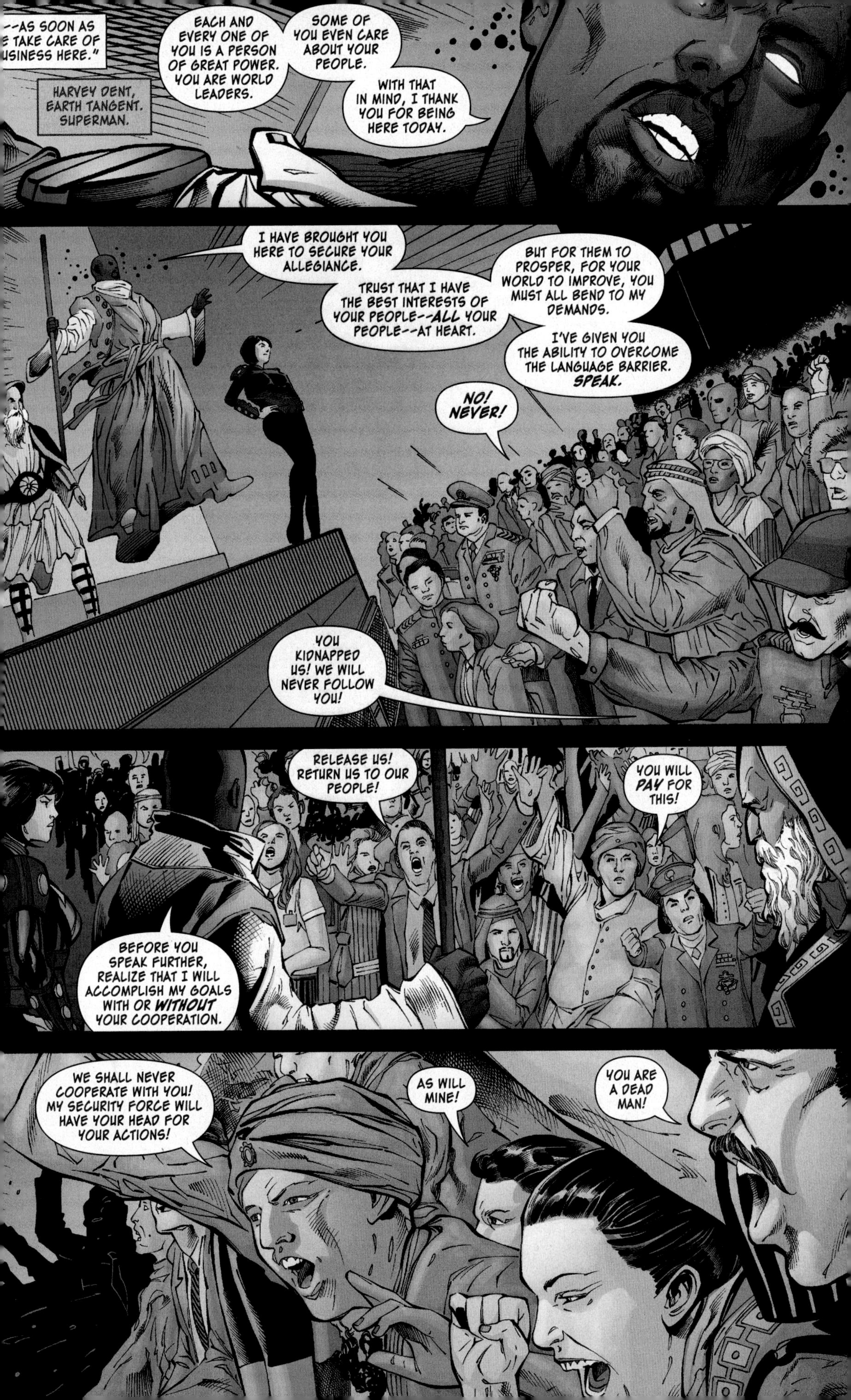
--AS SOON AS
E TAKE CARE OF
USINESS HERE."
HARVEY DENT,
EARTH TANGENT.
SUPERMAN.
EACH AND
EVERY ONE OF
YOU IS A PERSON
OF GREAT POWER.
YOU ARE WORLD
LEADERS.
SOME OF
YOU EVEN CARE
ABOUT YOUR
PEOPLE.
WITH THAT
IN MIND, I THANK
YOU FOR BEING
HERE TODAY.
I HAVE BROUGHT YOU
HERE TO SECURE YOUR
ALLEGIANCE.
TRUST THAT I HAVE
THE BEST INTERESTS OF
YOUR PEOPLE--ALL YOUR
PEOPLE--AT HEART.
BUT FOR THEM TO
PROSPER, FOR YOUR
WORLD TO IMPROVE, YOU
MUST ALL BEND TO MY
DEMANDS.
I'VE GIVEN YOU
THE ABILITY TO OVERCOME
THE LANGUAGE BARRIER.
SPEAK.
NO!
NEVER!
YOU
KIDNAPPED
US! WE WILL
NEVER FOLLOW
YOU!
RELEASE US!
RETURN US TO OUR
PEOPLE!
YOU WILL
PAY FOR
THIS!
BEFORE YOU
SPEAK FURTHER,
REALIZE THAT I WILL
ACCOMPLISH MY GOALS
WITH OR WITHOUT
YOUR COOPERATION.
WE SHALL NEVER
COOPERATE WITH YOU!
MY SECURITY FORCE WILL
HAVE YOUR HEAD FOR
YOUR ACTIONS!
AS WILL
MINE!
YOU ARE
A DEAD
MAN!

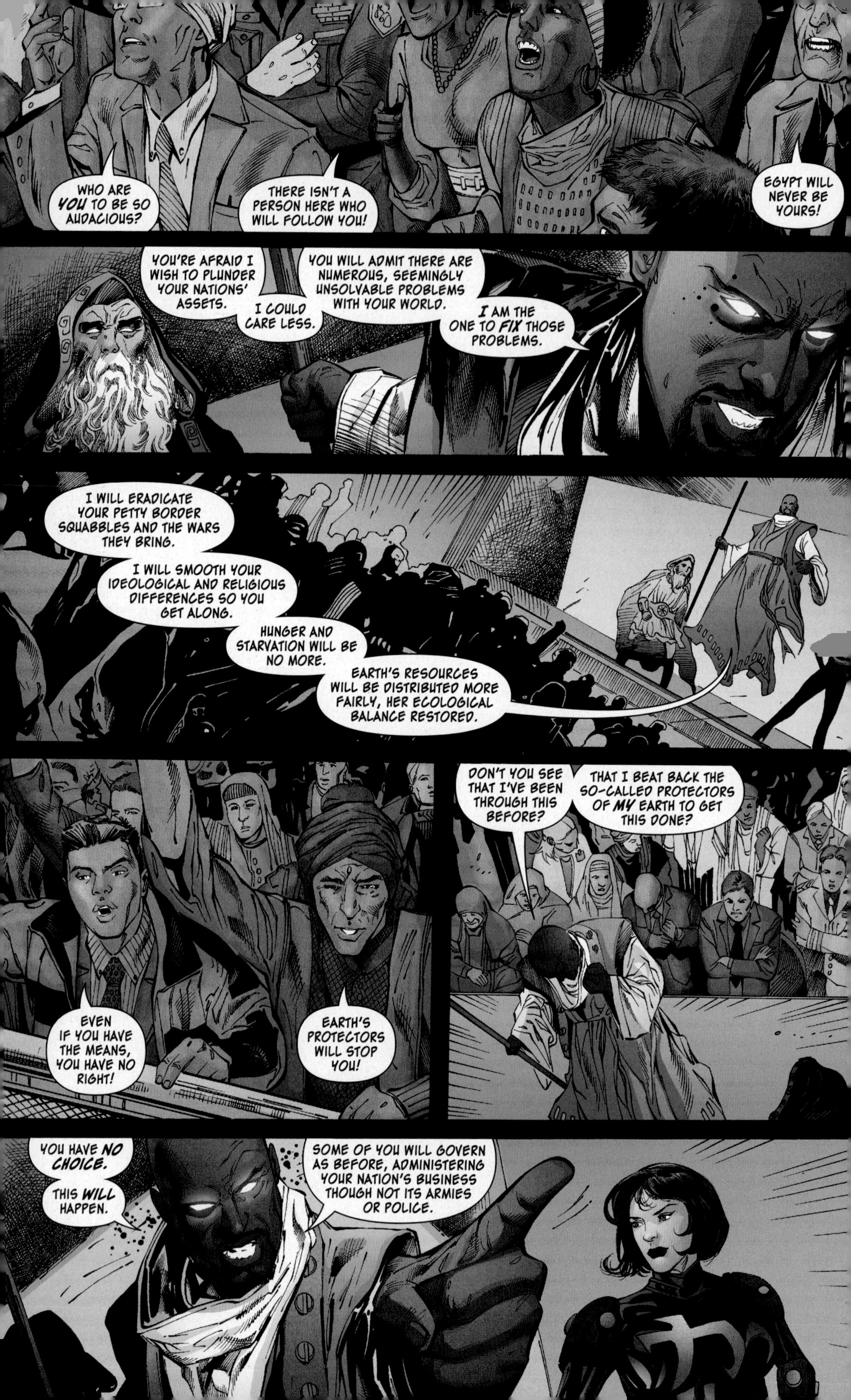
WHO ARE YOU TO BE SO AUDACIOUS?
THERE ISN'T A PERSON HERE WHO WILL FOLLOW YOU!
EGYPT WILL NEVER BE YOURS!
YOU'RE AFRAID I WISH TO PLUNDER YOUR NATIONS' ASSETS.
I COULD CARE LESS.
YOU WILL ADMIT THERE ARE NUMEROUS, SEEMINGLY UNSOLVABLE PROBLEMS WITH YOUR WORLD.
I AM THE ONE TO FIX THOSE PROBLEMS.
I WILL ERADICATE YOUR PETTY BORDER SQUABBLES AND THE WARS THEY BRING.
I WILL SMOOTH YOUR IDEOLOGICAL AND RELIGIOUS DIFFERENCES SO YOU GET ALONG.
HUNGER AND STARVATION WILL BE NO MORE.
EARTH'S RESOURCES WILL BE DISTRIBUTED MORE FAIRLY, HER ECOLOGICAL BALANCE RESTORED.
EVEN IF YOU HAVE THE MEANS, YOU HAVE NO RIGHT!
EARTH'S PROTECTORS WILL STOP YOU!
DON'T YOU SEE THAT I'VE BEEN THROUGH THIS BEFORE?
THAT I BEAT BACK THE SO-CALLED PROTECTORS OF MY EARTH TO GET THIS DONE?
YOU HAVE NO CHOICE.
THIS WILL HAPPEN.
SOME OF YOU WILL GOVERN AS BEFORE, ADMINISTERING YOUR NATION'S BUSINESS THOUGH NOT ITS ARMIES OR POLICE.

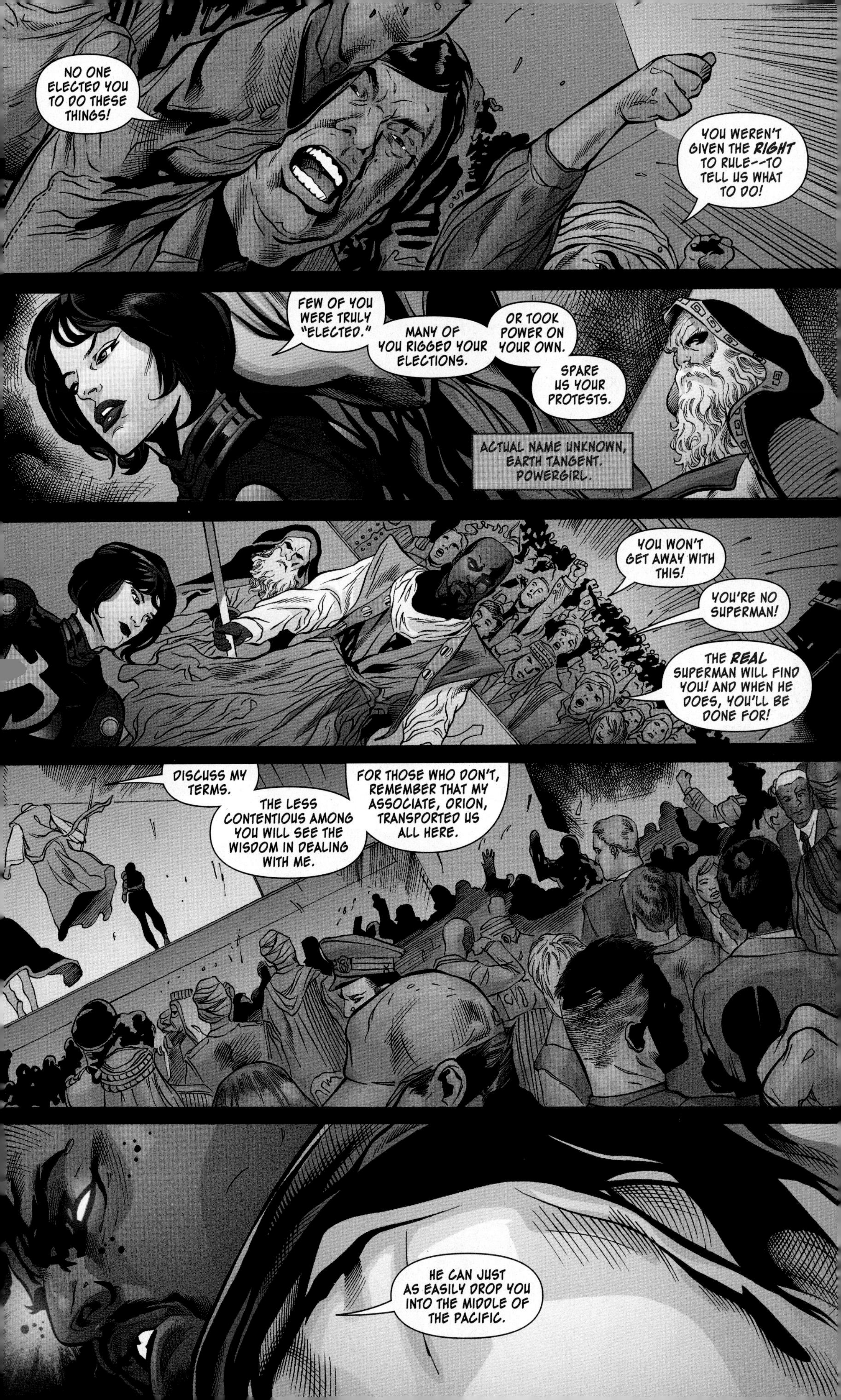

NO ONE ELECTED YOU TO DO THESE THINGS!
YOU WEREN'T GIVEN THE RIGHT TO RULE--TO TELL US WHAT TO DO!
FEW OF YOU WERE TRULY "ELECTED."
MANY OF YOU RIGGED YOUR ELECTIONS.
OR TOOK POWER ON YOUR OWN.
SPARE US YOUR PROTESTS.
ACTUAL NAME UNKNOWN, EARTH TANGENT. POWERGIRL.
YOU WON'T GET AWAY WITH THIS!
YOU'RE NO SUPERMAN!
THE REAL SUPERMAN WILL FIND YOU! AND WHEN HE DOES, YOU'LL BE DONE FOR!
DISCUSS MY TERMS.
THE LESS CONTENTIOUS AMONG YOU WILL SEE THE WISDOM IN DEALING WITH ME.
FOR THOSE WHO DON'T, REMEMBER THAT MY ASSOCIATE, ORION, TRANSPORTED US ALL HERE.
HE CAN JUST AS EASILY DROP YOU INTO THE MIDDLE OF THE PACIFIC.

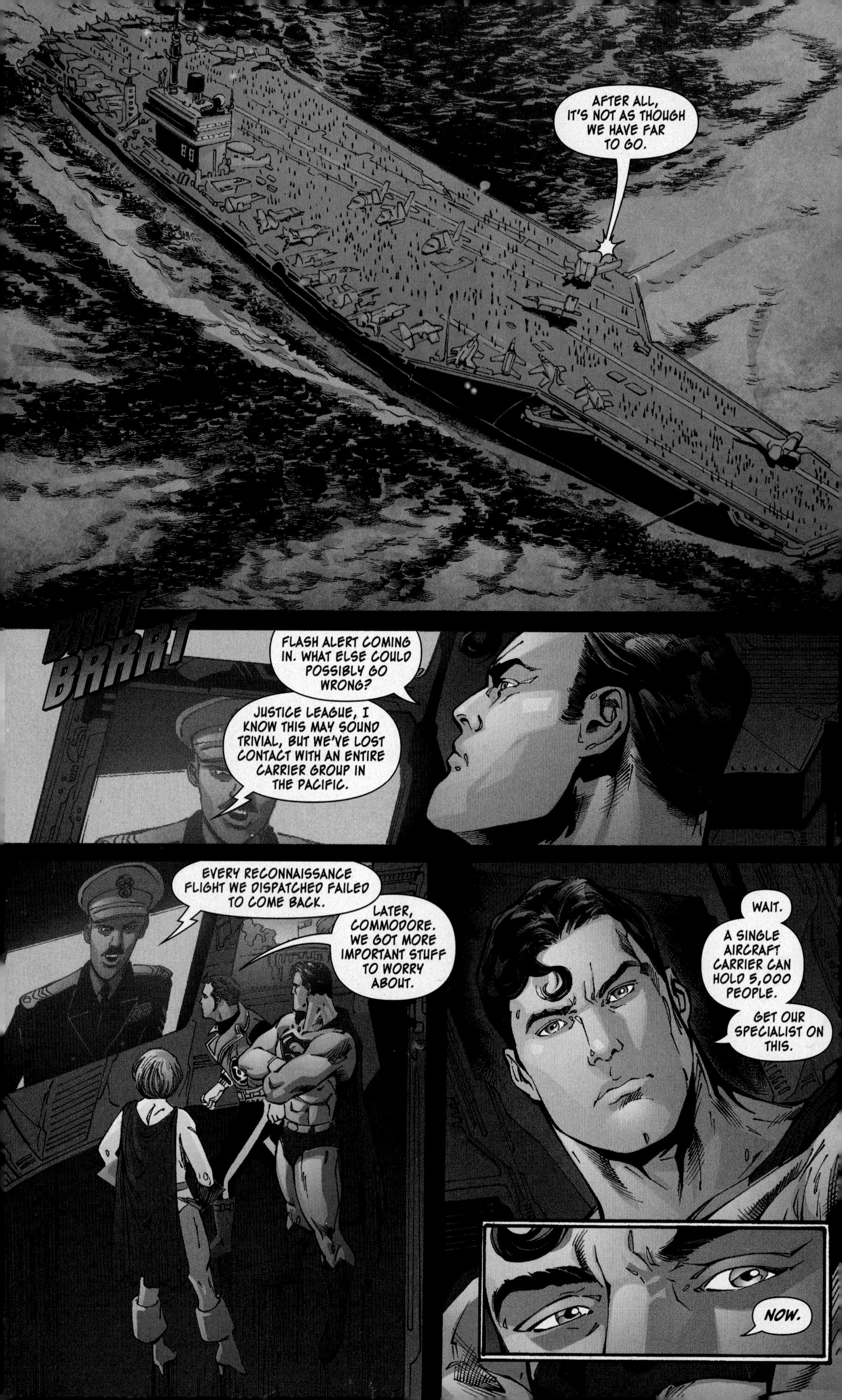
AFTER ALL, IT'S NOT AS THOUGH WE HAVE FAR TO GO.
BRRRT BRRRT
FLASH ALERT COMING IN. WHAT ELSE COULD POSSIBLY GO WRONG?
JUSTICE LEAGUE, I KNOW THIS MAY SOUND TRIVIAL, BUT WE'VE LOST CONTACT WITH AN ENTIRE CARRIER GROUP IN THE PACIFIC.
EVERY RECONNAISSANCE FLIGHT WE DISPATCHED FAILED TO COME BACK.
LATER, COMMODORE. WE GOT MORE IMPORTANT STUFF TO WORRY ABOUT.
WAIT.
A SINGLE AIRCRAFT CARRIER CAN HOLD 5,000 PEOPLE.
GET OUR SPECIALIST ON THIS.
NOW.

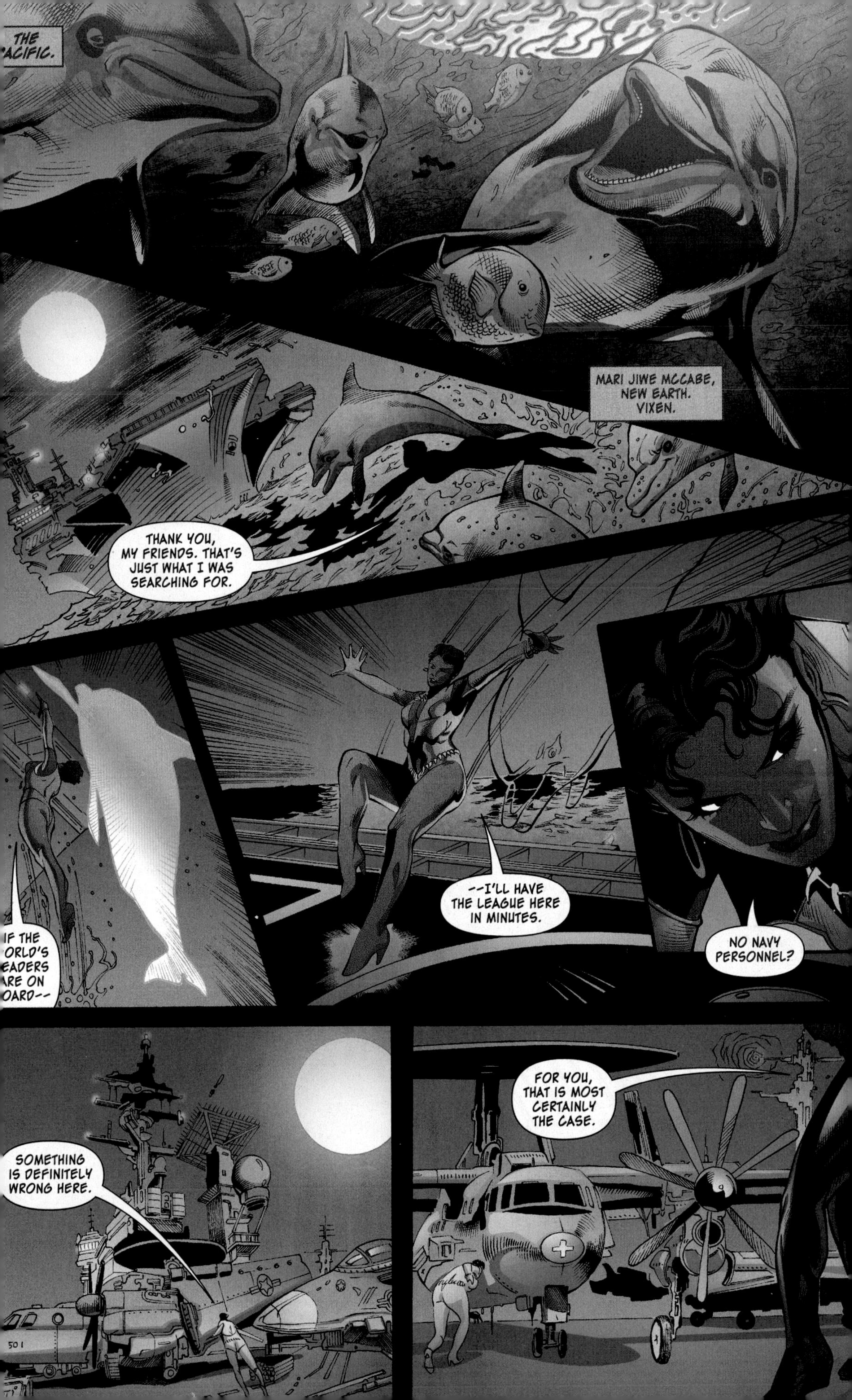
THE ACIFIC.
MARI JIWE MCCABE, NEW EARTH. VIXEN.
THANK YOU, MY FRIENDS. THAT'S JUST WHAT I WAS SEARCHING FOR.
IF THE ORLD'S EADERS ARE ON OARD--
--I'LL HAVE THE LEAGUE HERE IN MINUTES.
NO NAVY PERSONNEL?
SOMETHING IS DEFINITELY WRONG HERE.
FOR YOU, THAT IS MOST CERTAINLY THE CASE.

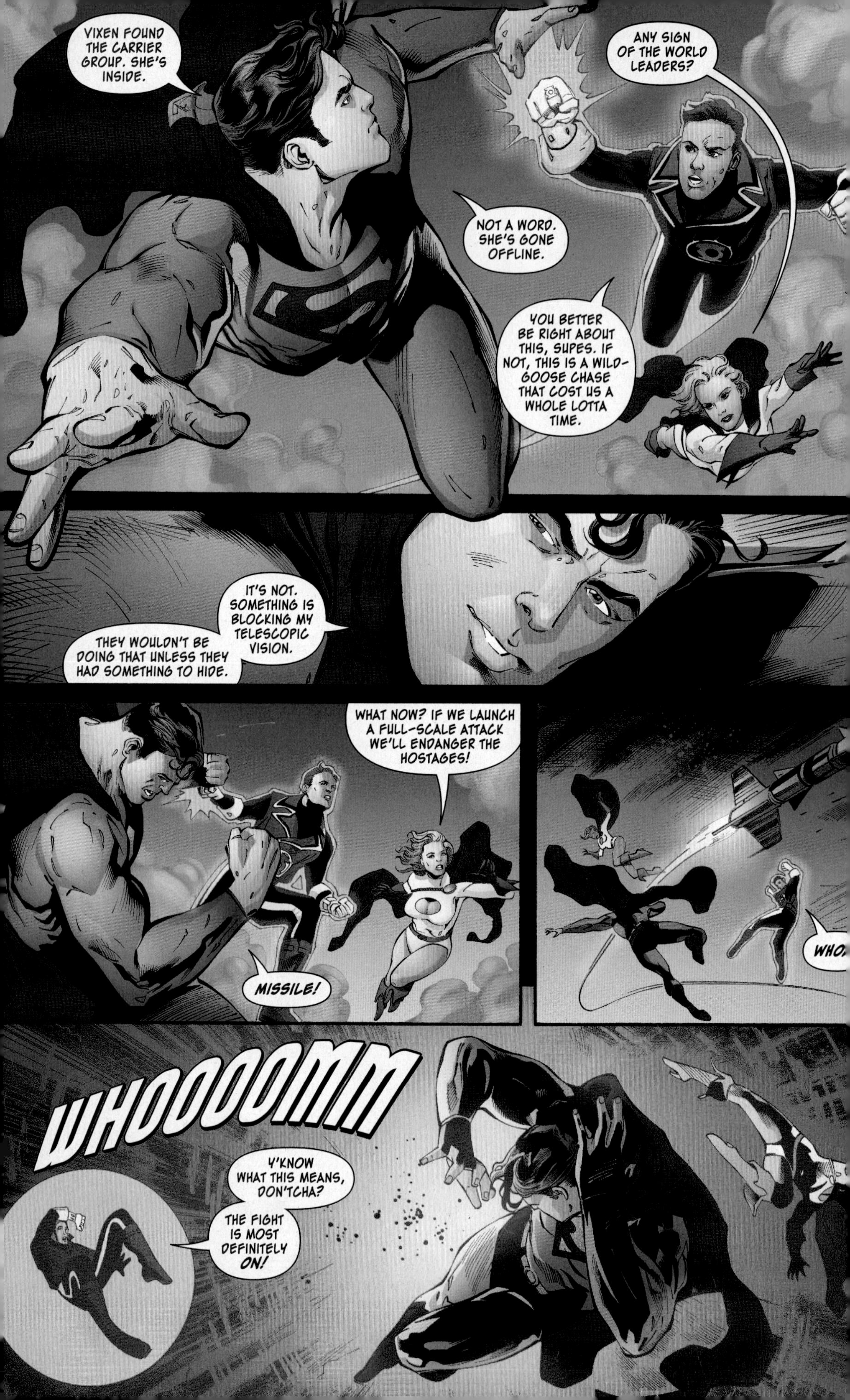
VIXEN FOUND THE CARRIER GROUP. SHE'S INSIDE.
ANY SIGN OF THE WORLD LEADERS?
NOT A WORD. SHE'S GONE OFFLINE.
YOU BETTER BE RIGHT ABOUT THIS, SUPES. IF NOT, THIS IS A WILD-GOOSE CHASE THAT COST US A WHOLE LOTTA TIME.
IT'S NOT. SOMETHING IS BLOCKING MY TELESCOPIC VISION.
THEY WOULDN'T BE DOING THAT UNLESS THEY HAD SOMETHING TO HIDE.
WHAT NOW? IF WE LAUNCH A FULL-SCALE ATTACK WE'LL ENDANGER THE HOSTAGES!
MISSILE!
WHOOOOOMM
Y'KNOW WHAT THIS MEANS, DON'TCHA?
THE FIGHT IS MOST DEFINITELY ON!

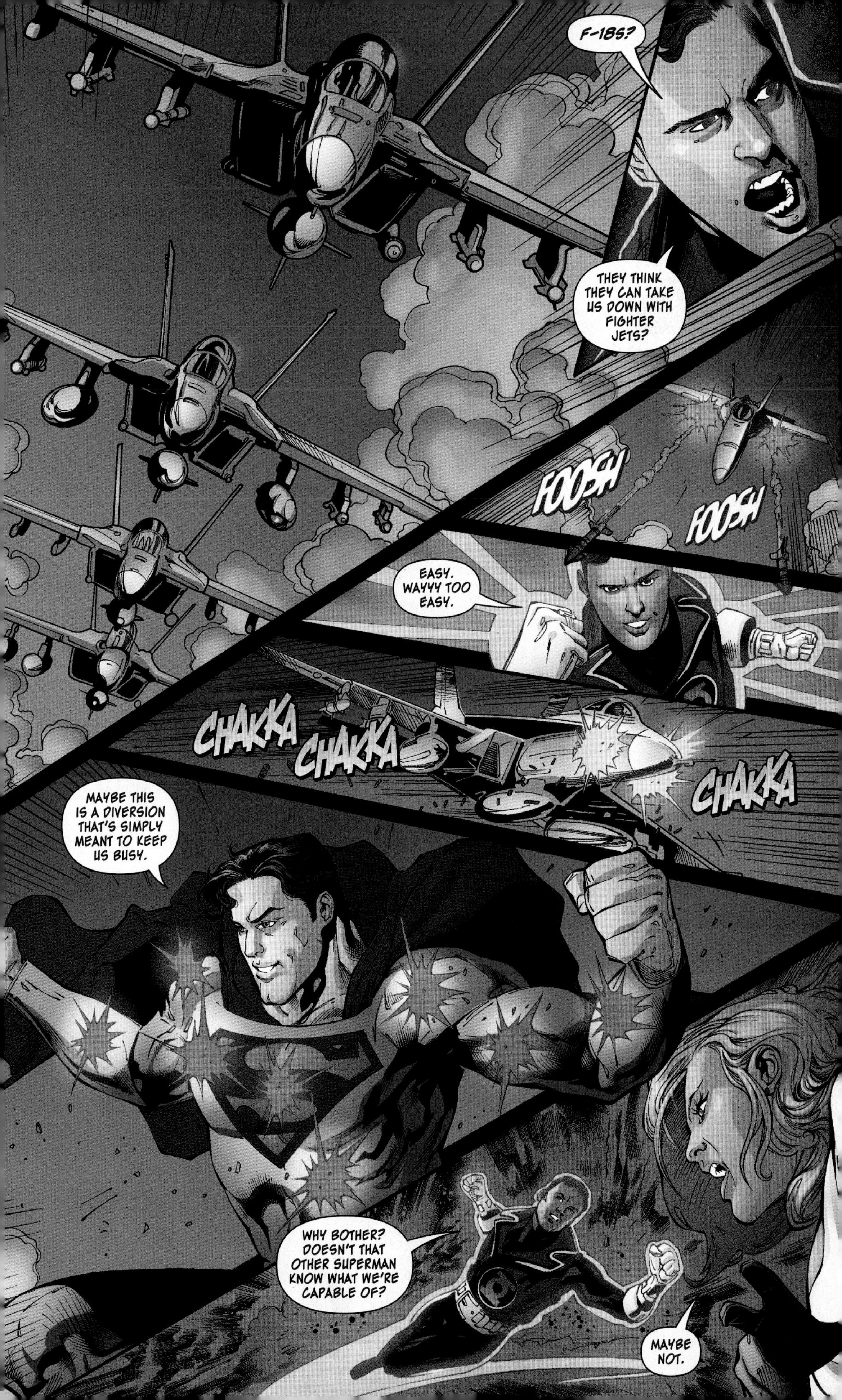
F-18S?
THEY THINK THEY CAN TAKE US DOWN WITH FIGHTER JETS?
FOOSH
FOOSH
EASY. WAYYY TOO EASY.
CHAKKA
CHAKKA
CHAKKA
MAYBE THIS IS A DIVERSION THAT'S SIMPLY MEANT TO KEEP US BUSY.
WHY BOTHER? DOESN'T THAT OTHER SUPERMAN KNOW WHAT WE'RE CAPABLE OF?
MAYBE NOT.

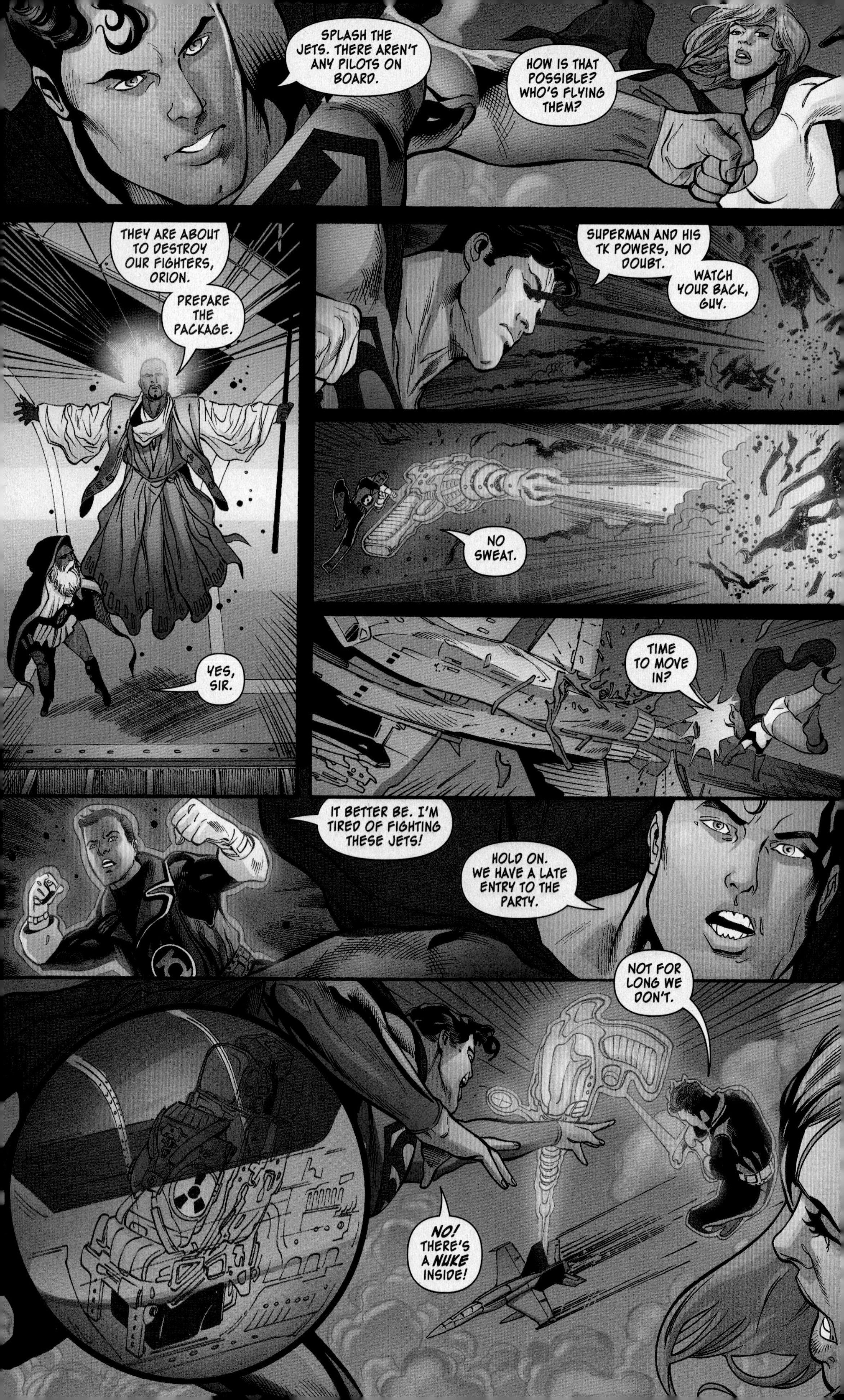
SPLASH THE JETS. THERE AREN'T ANY PILOTS ON BOARD.
HOW IS THAT POSSIBLE? WHO'S FLYING THEM?
THEY ARE ABOUT TO DESTROY OUR FIGHTERS, ORION.
PREPARE THE PACKAGE.
YES, SIR.
SUPERMAN AND HIS TK POWERS, NO DOUBT.
WATCH YOUR BACK, GUY.
NO SWEAT.
TIME TO MOVE IN?
IT BETTER BE. I'M TIRED OF FIGHTING THESE JETS!
HOLD ON. WE HAVE A LATE ENTRY TO THE PARTY.
NOT FOR LONG WE DON'T.
NO! THERE'S A NUKE INSIDE!

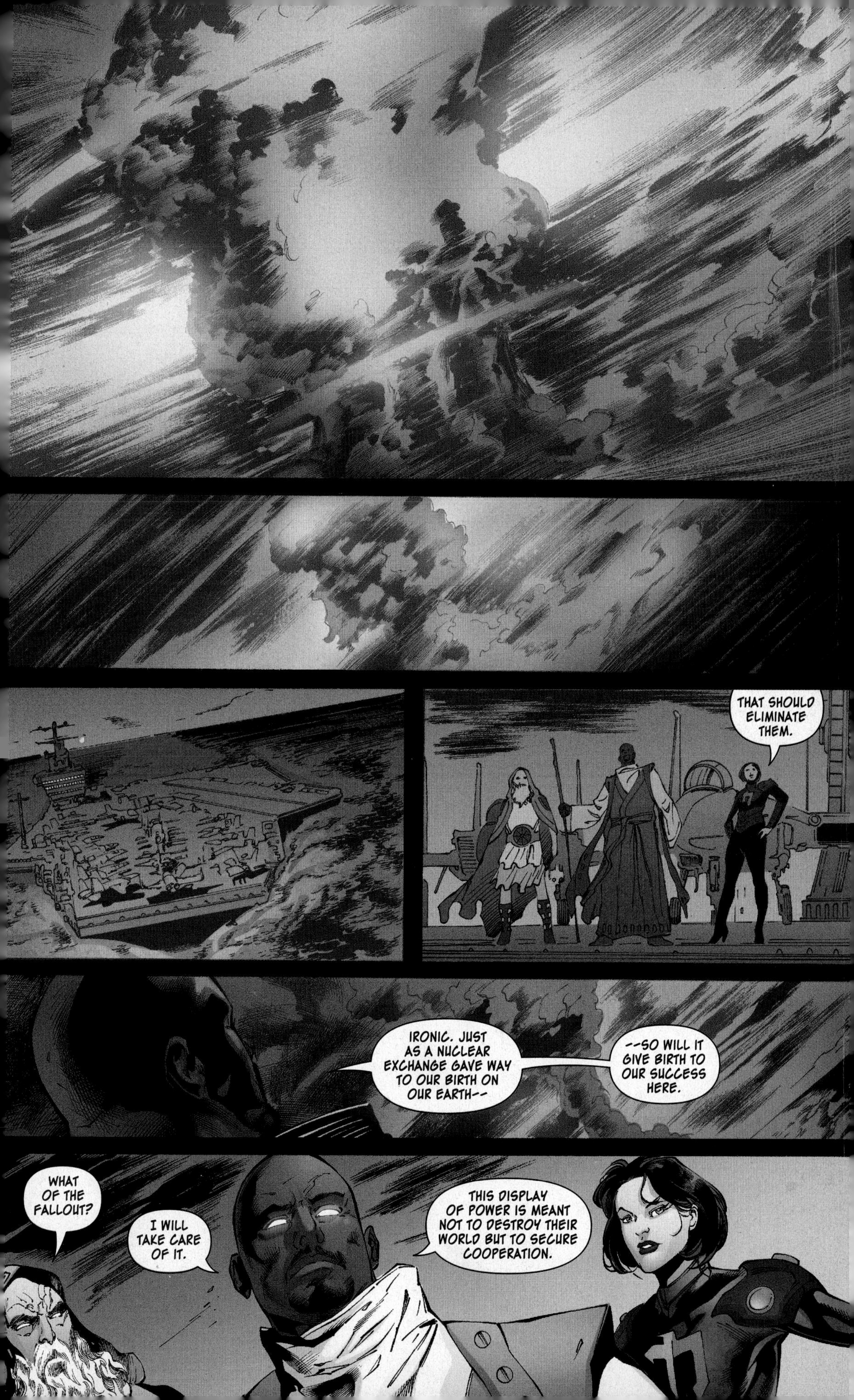
THAT SHOULD ELIMINATE THEM.
IRONIC. JUST AS A NUCLEAR EXCHANGE GAVE WAY TO OUR BIRTH ON OUR EARTH--
--SO WILL IT GIVE BIRTH TO OUR SUCCESS HERE.
WHAT OF THE FALLOUT?
I WILL TAKE CARE OF IT.
THIS DISPLAY OF POWER IS MEANT NOT TO DESTROY THEIR WORLD BUT TO SECURE COOPERATION.

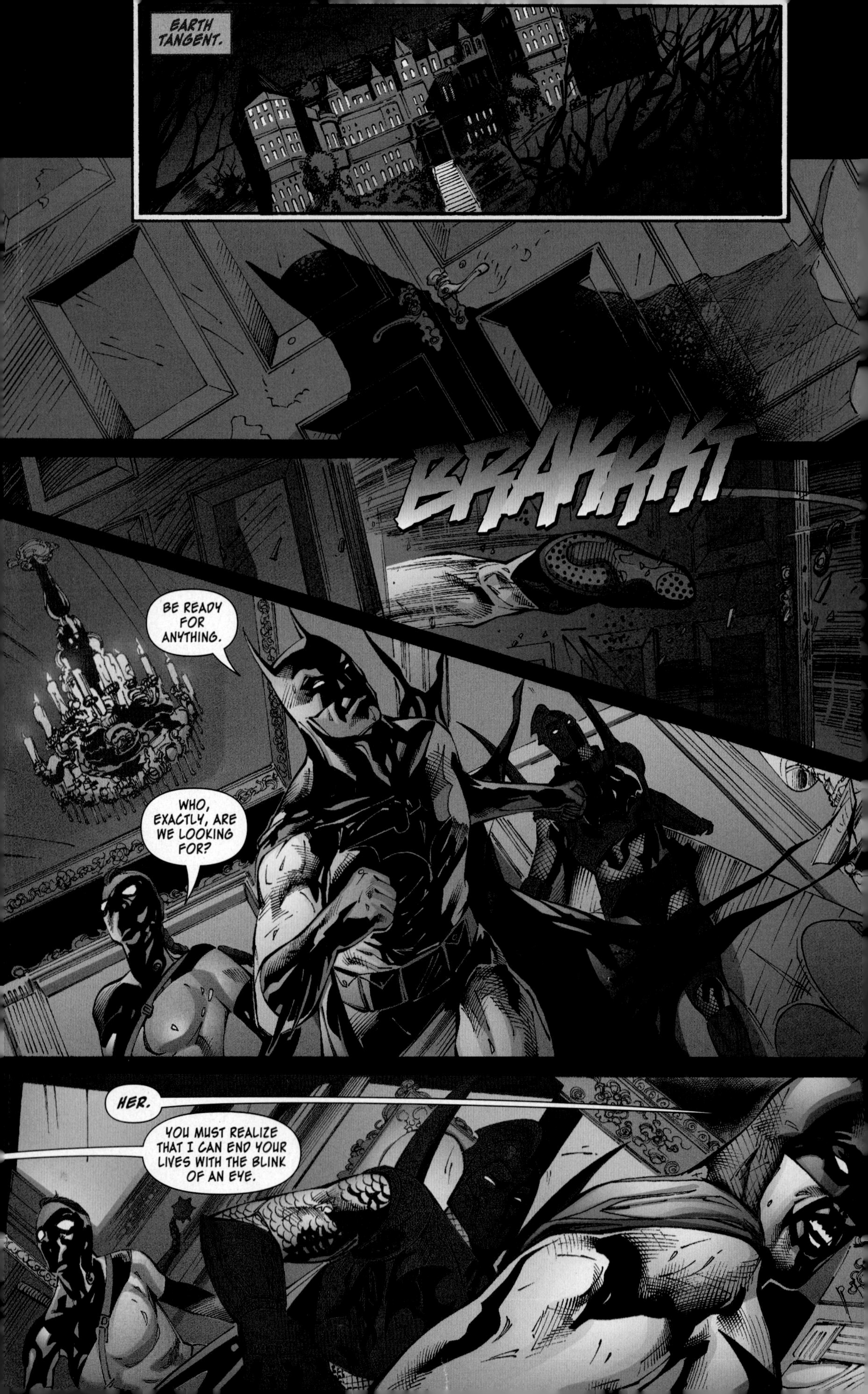
EARTH TANGENT.
BRAKKKT
BE READY FOR ANYTHING.
WHO, EXACTLY, ARE WE LOOKING FOR?
HER.
YOU MUST REALIZE THAT I CAN END YOUR LIVES WITH THE BLINK OF AN EYE.

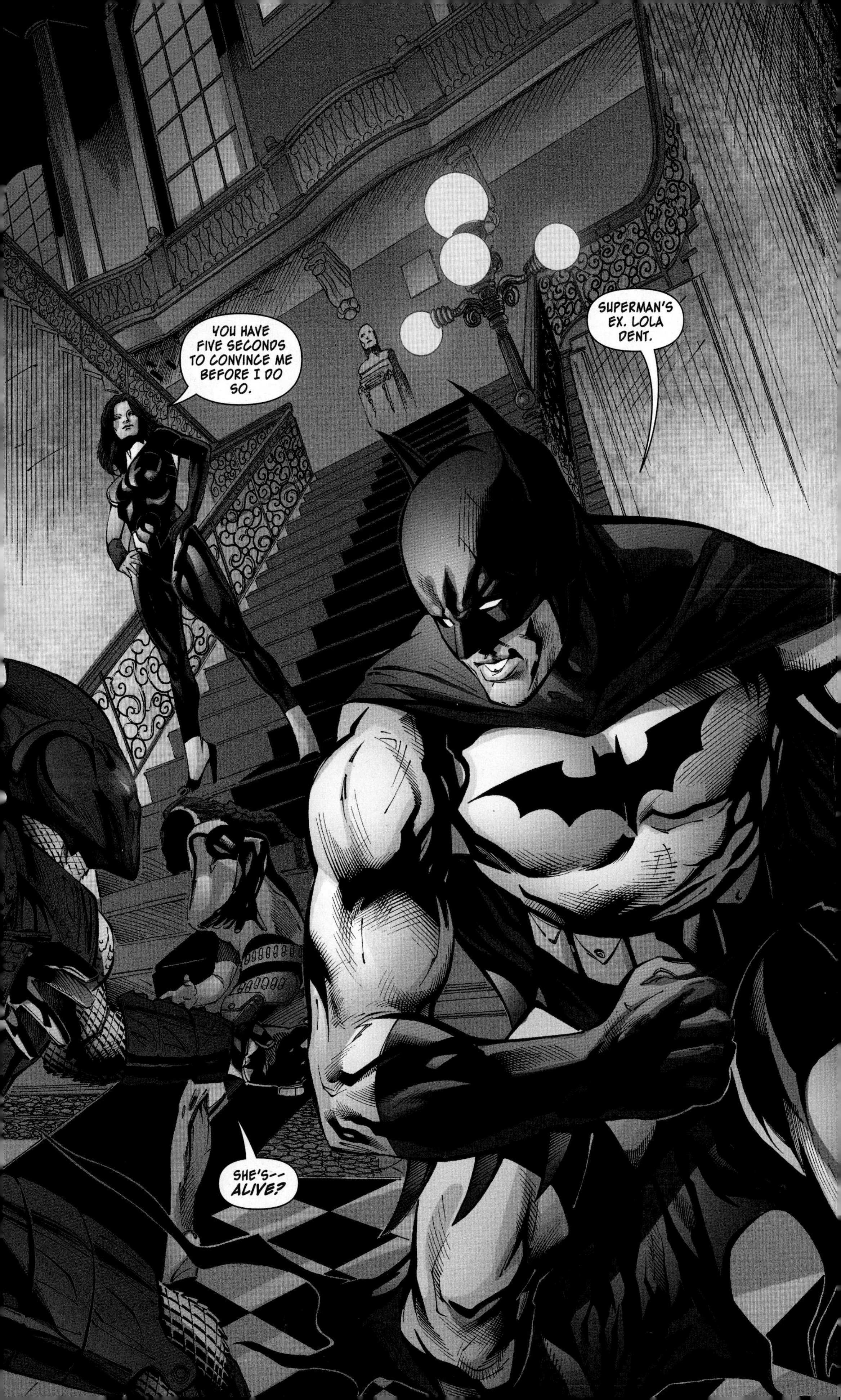
YOU HAVE FIVE SECONDS TO CONVINCE ME BEFORE I DO SO.
SUPERMAN'S EX. LOLA DENT.
SHE'S-- ALIVE?

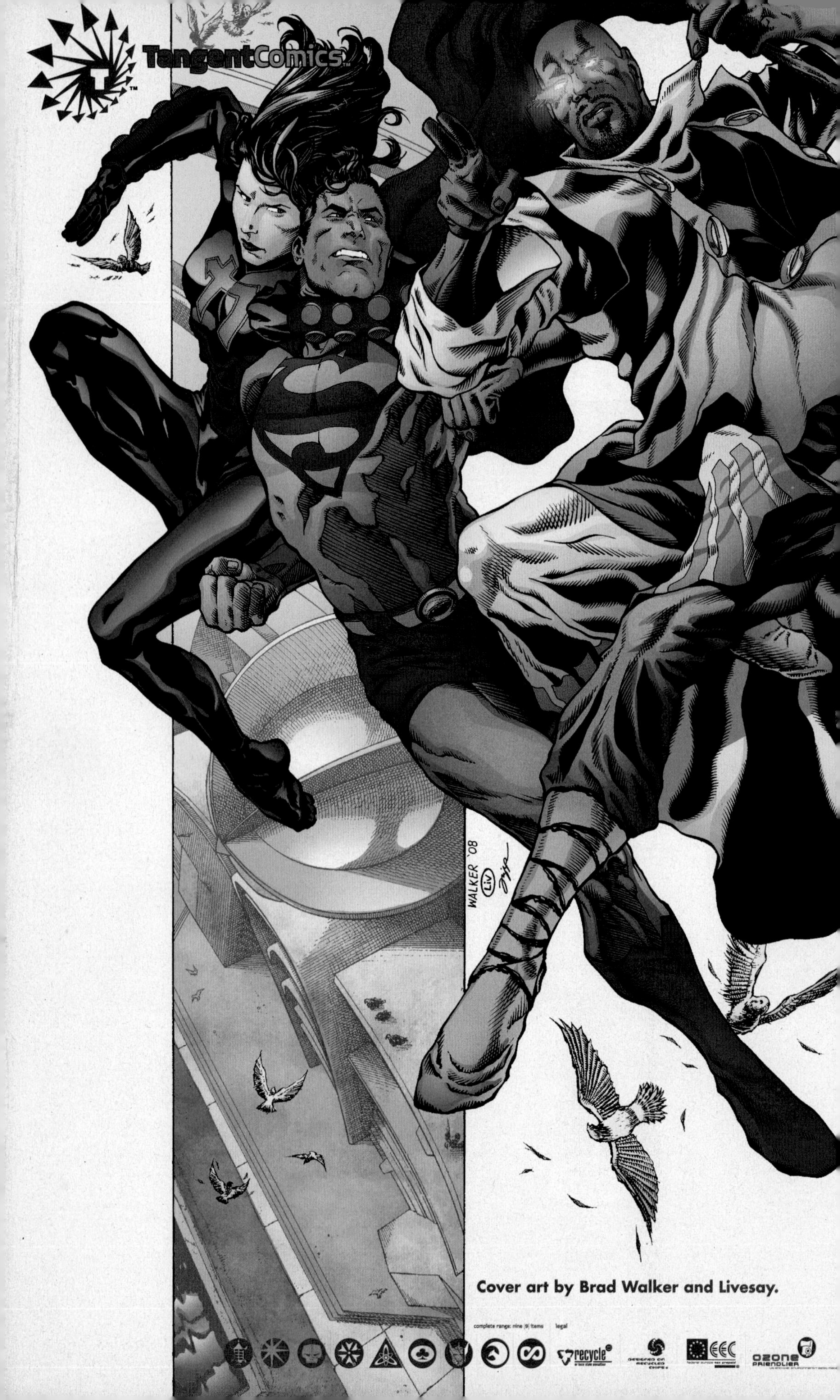
TangentComics
WALKER '08
Liv
complete range: nine [9] items
legal
recycle
ozone friendlier

Cover art by Brad Walker and Livesay.

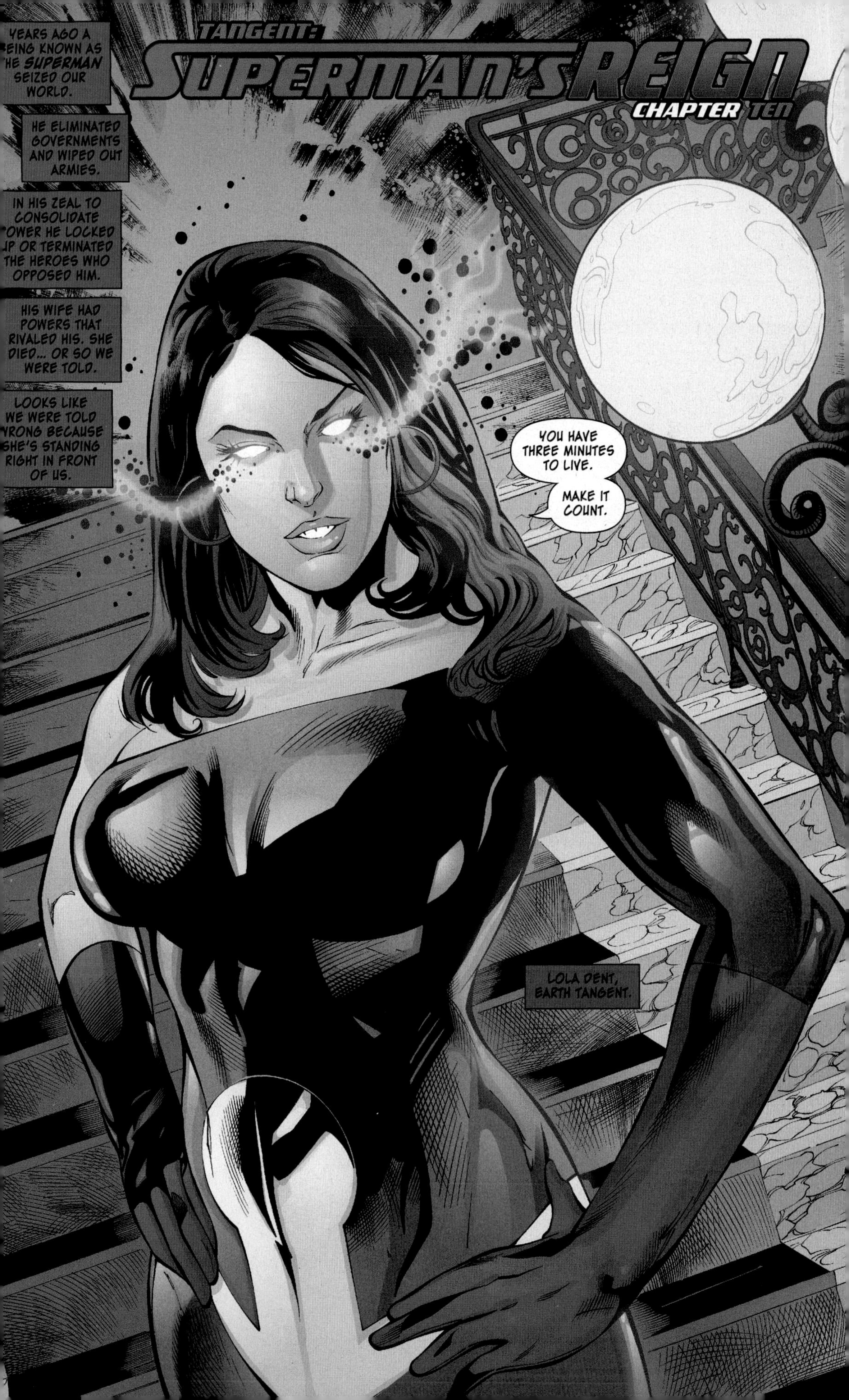
TANGENT:
SUPERMAN'S REIGN
CHAPTER TEN
YEARS AGO A EING KNOWN AS HE SUPERMAN SEIZED OUR WORLD.
HE ELIMINATED GOVERNMENTS AND WIPED OUT ARMIES.
IN HIS ZEAL TO CONSOLIDATE OWER HE LOCKED IP OR TERMINATED THE HEROES WHO OPPOSED HIM.
HIS WIFE HAD POWERS THAT RIVALED HIS. SHE DIED... OR SO WE WERE TOLD.
LOOKS LIKE WE WERE TOLD VRONG BECAUSE SHE'S STANDING RIGHT IN FRONT OF US.
YOU HAVE THREE MINUTES TO LIVE.
MAKE IT COUNT.
LOLA DENT, EARTH TANGENT.

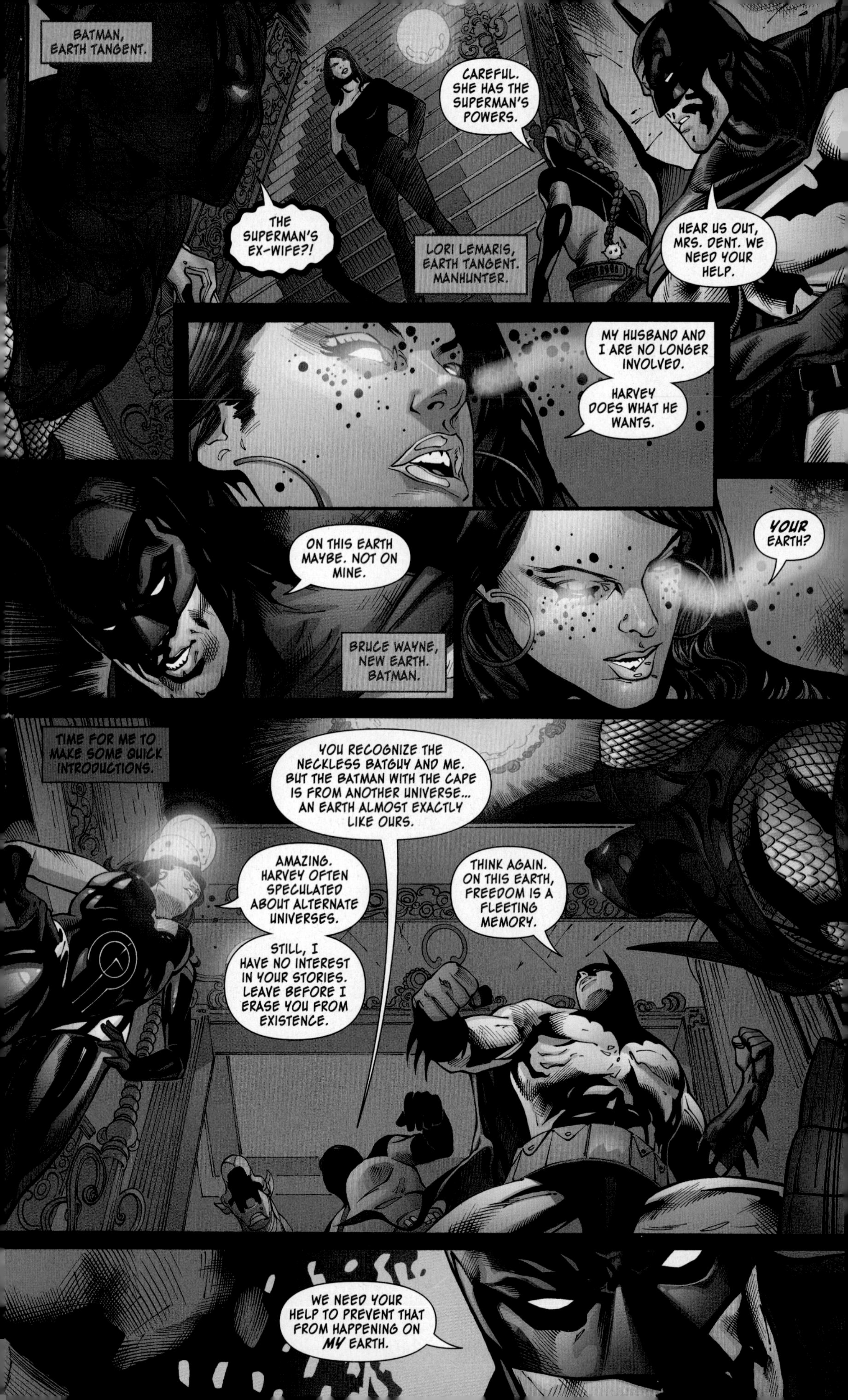
BATMAN, EARTH TANGENT.
CAREFUL. SHE HAS THE SUPERMAN'S POWERS.
THE SUPERMAN'S EX-WIFE?!
LORI LEMARIS, EARTH TANGENT. MANHUNTER.
HEAR US OUT, MRS. DENT. WE NEED YOUR HELP.
MY HUSBAND AND I ARE NO LONGER INVOLVED.
HARVEY DOES WHAT HE WANTS.
ON THIS EARTH MAYBE. NOT ON MINE.
BRUCE WAYNE, NEW EARTH. BATMAN.
YOUR EARTH?
TIME FOR ME TO MAKE SOME QUICK INTRODUCTIONS.
YOU RECOGNIZE THE NECKLESS BATGUY AND ME. BUT THE BATMAN WITH THE CAPE IS FROM ANOTHER UNIVERSE... AN EARTH ALMOST EXACTLY LIKE OURS.
AMAZING. HARVEY OFTEN SPECULATED ABOUT ALTERNATE UNIVERSES.
STILL, I HAVE NO INTEREST IN YOUR STORIES. LEAVE BEFORE I ERASE YOU FROM EXISTENCE.
THINK AGAIN. ON THIS EARTH, FREEDOM IS A FLEETING MEMORY.
WE NEED YOUR HELP TO PREVENT THAT FROM HAPPENING ON MY EARTH.

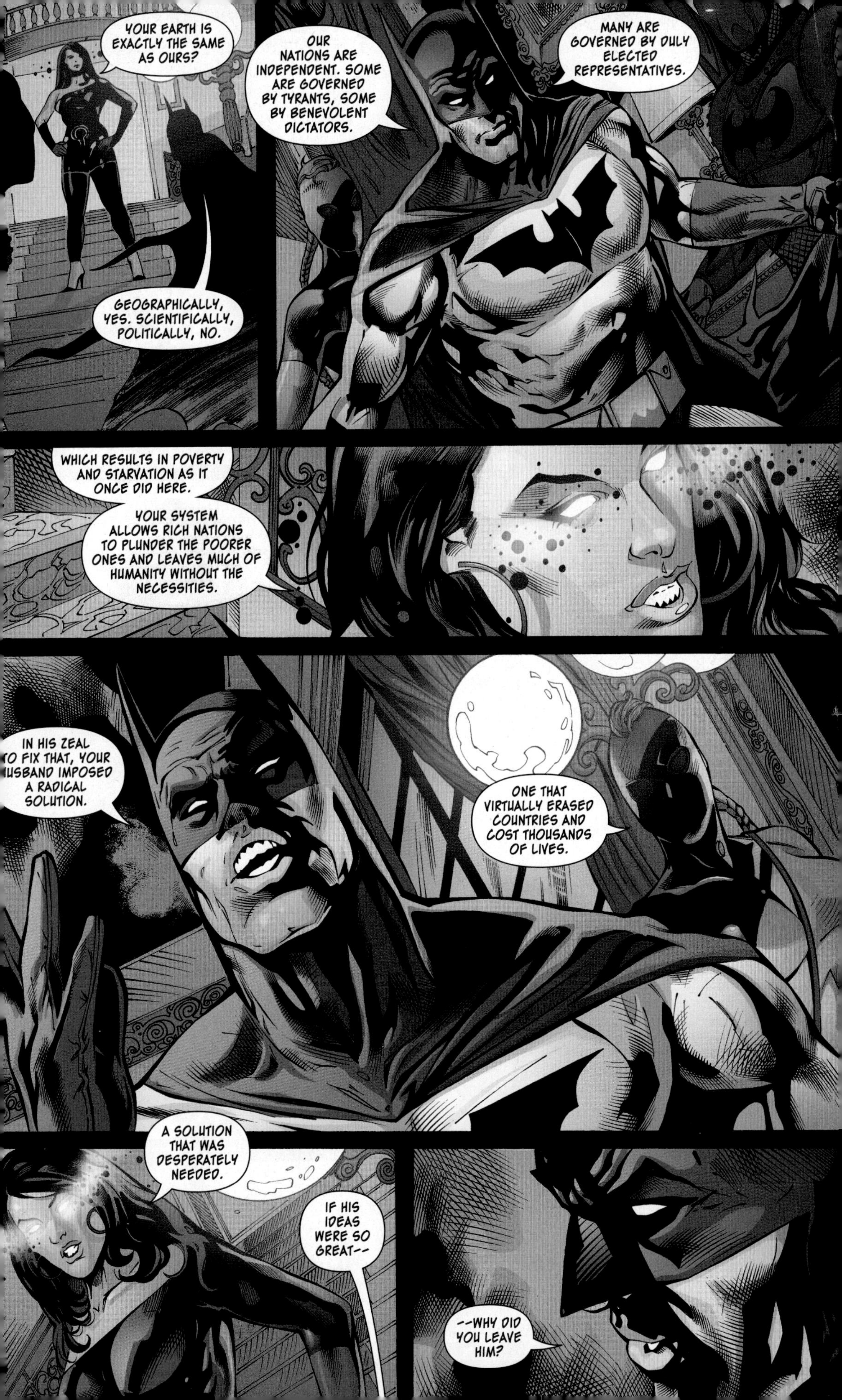
YOUR EARTH IS EXACTLY THE SAME AS OURS?
GEOGRAPHICALLY, YES. SCIENTIFICALLY, POLITICALLY, NO.
OUR NATIONS ARE INDEPENDENT. SOME ARE GOVERNED BY TYRANTS, SOME BY BENEVOLENT DICTATORS.
MANY ARE GOVERNED BY DULY ELECTED REPRESENTATIVES.
WHICH RESULTS IN POVERTY AND STARVATION AS IT ONCE DID HERE.
YOUR SYSTEM ALLOWS RICH NATIONS TO PLUNDER THE POORER ONES AND LEAVES MUCH OF HUMANITY WITHOUT THE NECESSITIES.
IN HIS ZEAL TO FIX THAT, YOUR HUSBAND IMPOSED A RADICAL SOLUTION.
ONE THAT VIRTUALLY ERASED COUNTRIES AND COST THOUSANDS OF LIVES.
A SOLUTION THAT WAS DESPERATELY NEEDED.
IF HIS IDEAS WERE SO GREAT--
--WHY DID YOU LEAVE HIM?

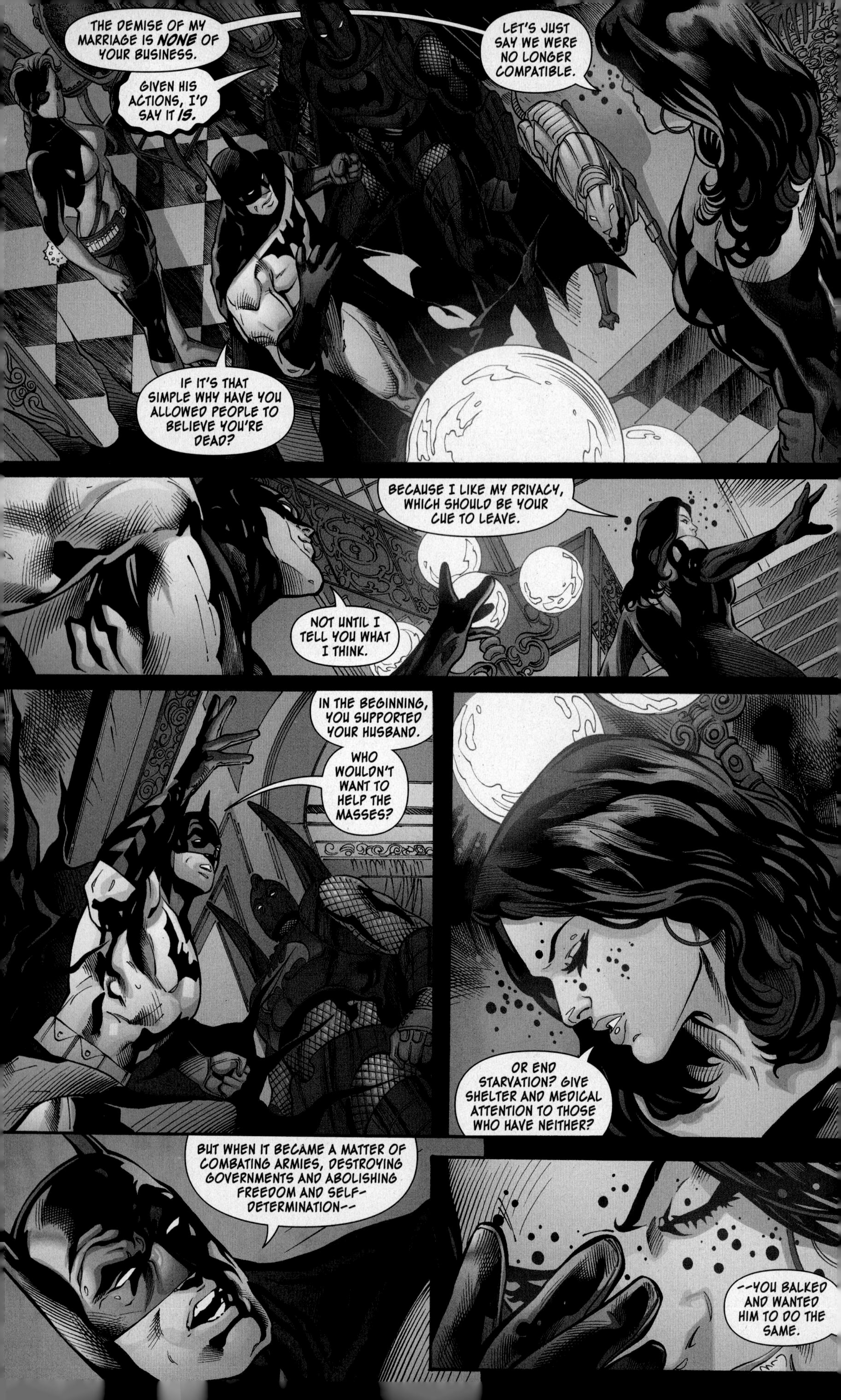

THE DEMISE OF MY MARRIAGE IS NONE OF YOUR BUSINESS.
GIVEN HIS ACTIONS, I'D SAY IT IS.
LET'S JUST SAY WE WERE NO LONGER COMPATIBLE.
IF IT'S THAT SIMPLE WHY HAVE YOU ALLOWED PEOPLE TO BELIEVE YOU'RE DEAD?
BECAUSE I LIKE MY PRIVACY, WHICH SHOULD BE YOUR CUE TO LEAVE.
NOT UNTIL I TELL YOU WHAT I THINK.
IN THE BEGINNING, YOU SUPPORTED YOUR HUSBAND.
WHO WOULDN'T WANT TO HELP THE MASSES?
OR END STARVATION? GIVE SHELTER AND MEDICAL ATTENTION TO THOSE WHO HAVE NEITHER?
BUT WHEN IT BECAME A MATTER OF COMBATING ARMIES, DESTROYING GOVERNMENTS AND ABOLISHING FREEDOM AND SELF-DETERMINATION--
--YOU BALKED AND WANTED HIM TO DO THE SAME.

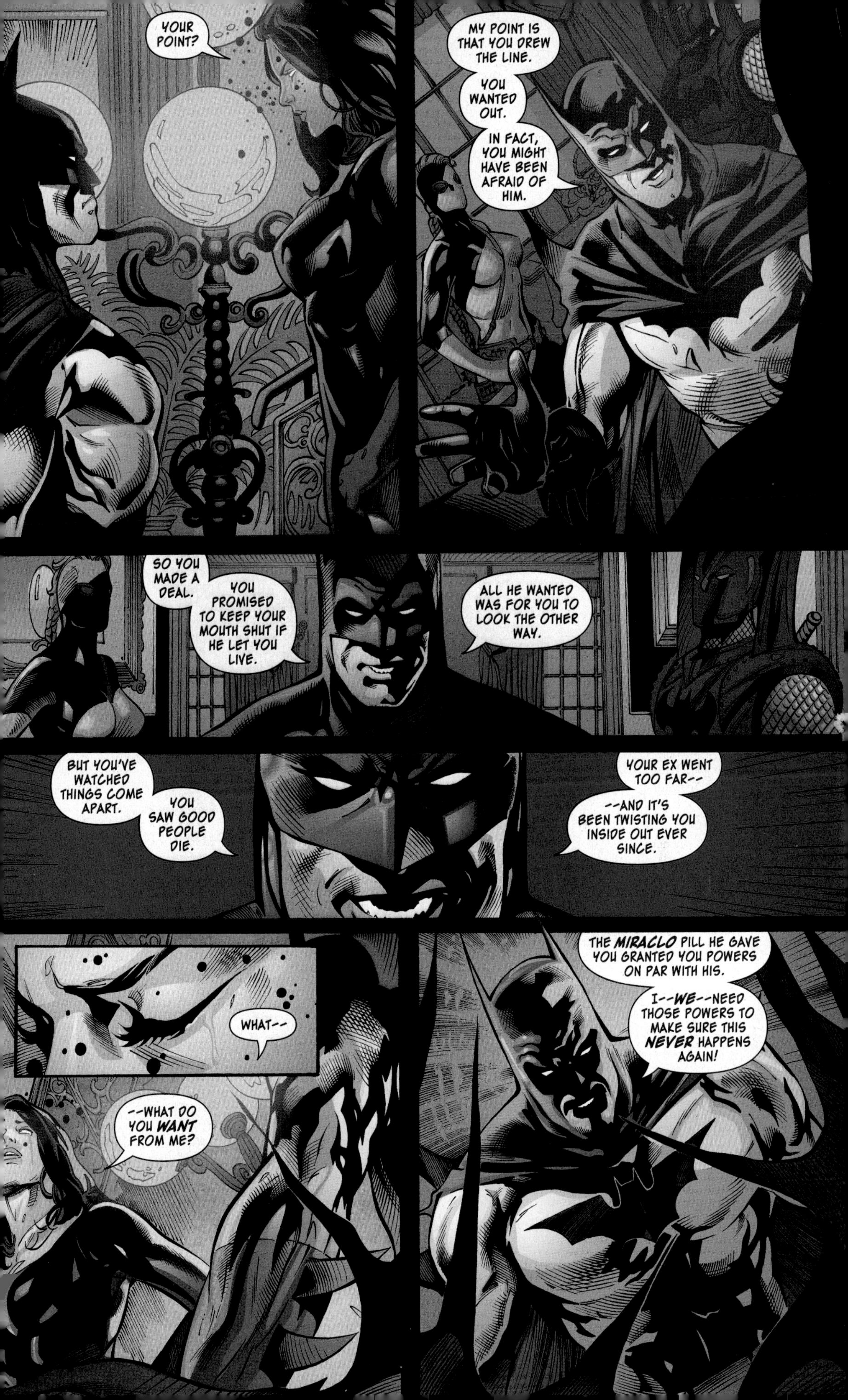
YOUR POINT?
MY POINT IS THAT YOU DREW THE LINE.
YOU WANTED OUT.
IN FACT, YOU MIGHT HAVE BEEN AFRAID OF HIM.
SO YOU MADE A DEAL.
YOU PROMISED TO KEEP YOUR MOUTH SHUT IF HE LET YOU LIVE.
ALL HE WANTED WAS FOR YOU TO LOOK THE OTHER WAY.
BUT YOU'VE WATCHED THINGS COME APART.
YOU SAW GOOD PEOPLE DIE.
YOUR EX WENT TOO FAR--
--AND IT'S BEEN TWISTING YOU INSIDE OUT EVER SINCE.
WHAT--
--WHAT DO YOU WANT FROM ME?
THE MIRACLO PILL HE GAVE YOU GRANTED YOU POWERS ON PAR WITH HIS.
I--WE--NEED THOSE POWERS TO MAKE SURE THIS NEVER HAPPENS AGAIN!

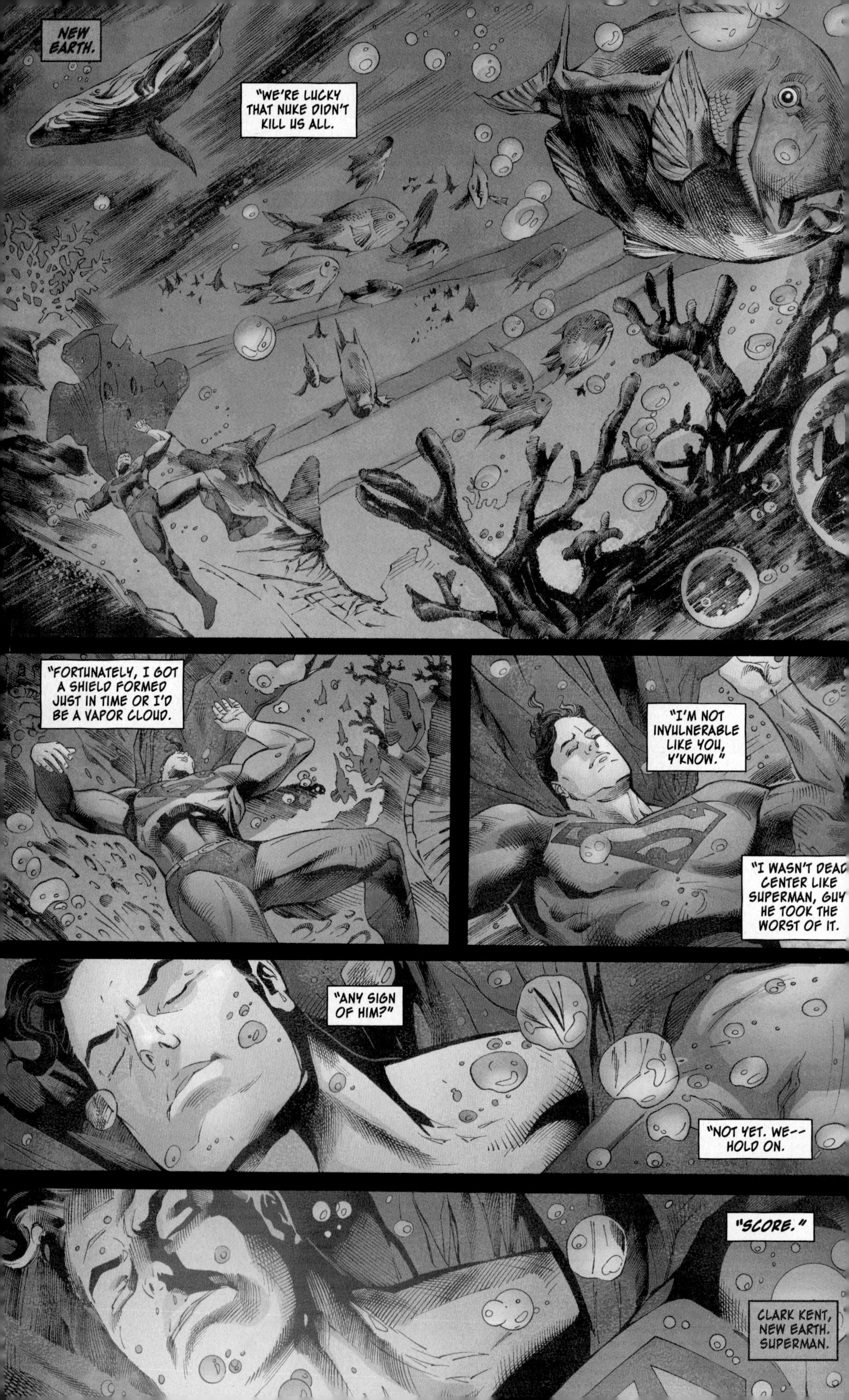
NEW EARTH.
"WE'RE LUCKY THAT NUKE DIDN'T KILL US ALL.
"FORTUNATELY, I GOT A SHIELD FORMED JUST IN TIME OR I'D BE A VAPOR CLOUD.
"I'M NOT INVULNERABLE LIKE YOU, Y'KNOW."
"I WASN'T DEAD CENTER LIKE SUPERMAN, GUY HE TOOK THE WORST OF IT.
"ANY SIGN OF HIM?"
"NOT YET. WE-- HOLD ON.
"SCORE."
CLARK KENT, NEW EARTH. SUPERMAN.

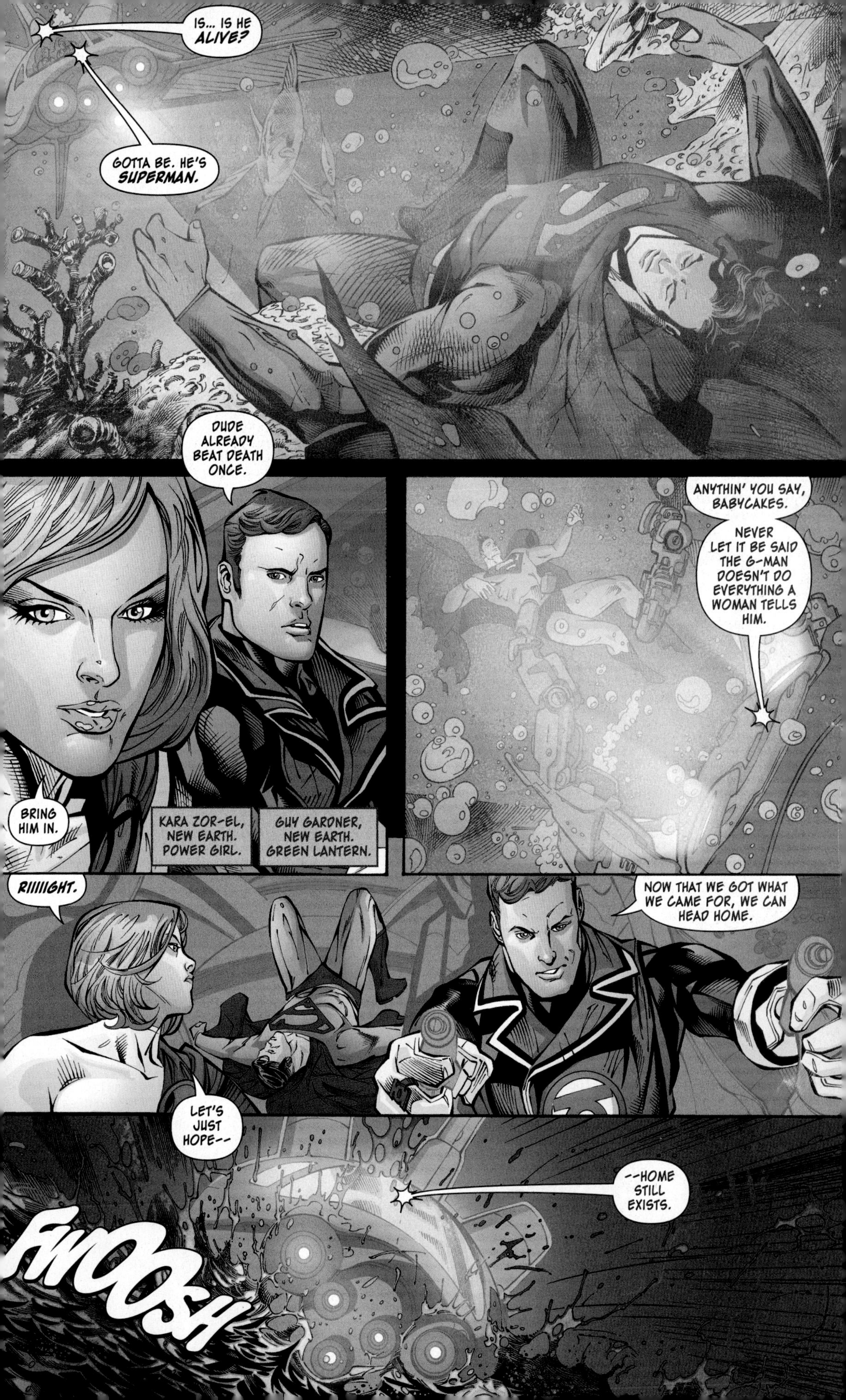

IS... IS HE ALIVE?
GOTTA BE. HE'S SUPERMAN.
DUDE ALREADY BEAT DEATH ONCE.
BRING HIM IN.
KARA ZOR-EL, NEW EARTH. POWER GIRL.
GUY GARDNER, NEW EARTH. GREEN LANTERN.
ANYTHIN' YOU SAY, BABYCAKES.
NEVER LET IT BE SAID THE G-MAN DOESN'T DO EVERYTHING A WOMAN TELLS HIM.
RIIIIIGHT.
NOW THAT WE GOT WHAT WE CAME FOR, WE CAN HEAD HOME.
LET'S JUST HOPE--
--HOME STILL EXISTS.
FWOOSH

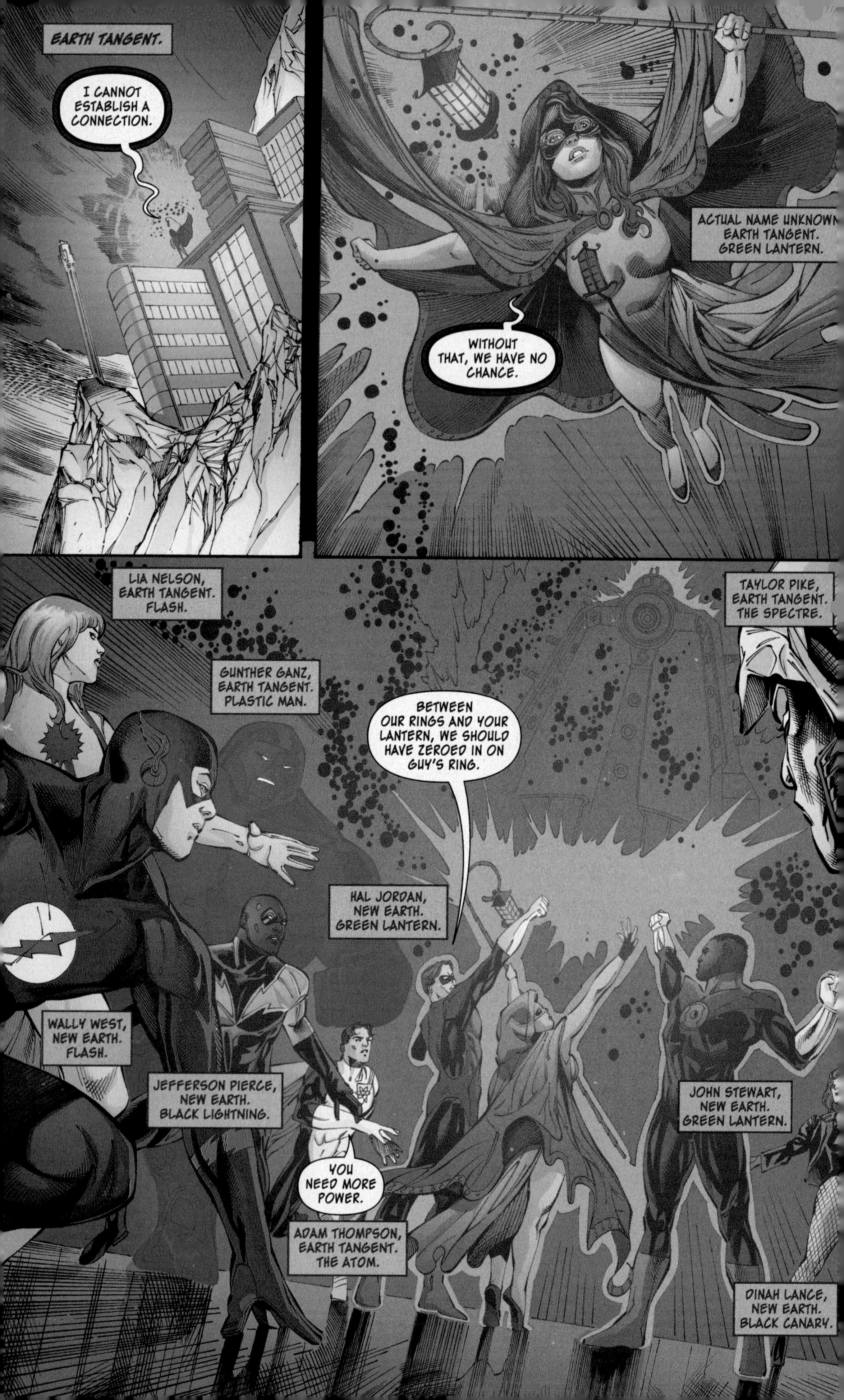
EARTH TANGENT.
I CANNOT ESTABLISH A CONNECTION.
ACTUAL NAME UNKNOWN EARTH TANGENT. GREEN LANTERN.
WITHOUT THAT, WE HAVE NO CHANCE.
LIA NELSON, EARTH TANGENT. FLASH.
GUNTHER GANZ, EARTH TANGENT. PLASTIC MAN.
TAYLOR PIKE, EARTH TANGENT. THE SPECTRE.
BETWEEN OUR RINGS AND YOUR LANTERN, WE SHOULD HAVE ZEROED IN ON GUY'S RING.
HAL JORDAN, NEW EARTH. GREEN LANTERN.
WALLY WEST, NEW EARTH. FLASH.
JEFFERSON PIERCE, NEW EARTH. BLACK LIGHTNING.
YOU NEED MORE POWER.
ADAM THOMPSON, EARTH TANGENT. THE ATOM.
JOHN STEWART, NEW EARTH. GREEN LANTERN.
DINAH LANCE, NEW EARTH. BLACK CANARY.

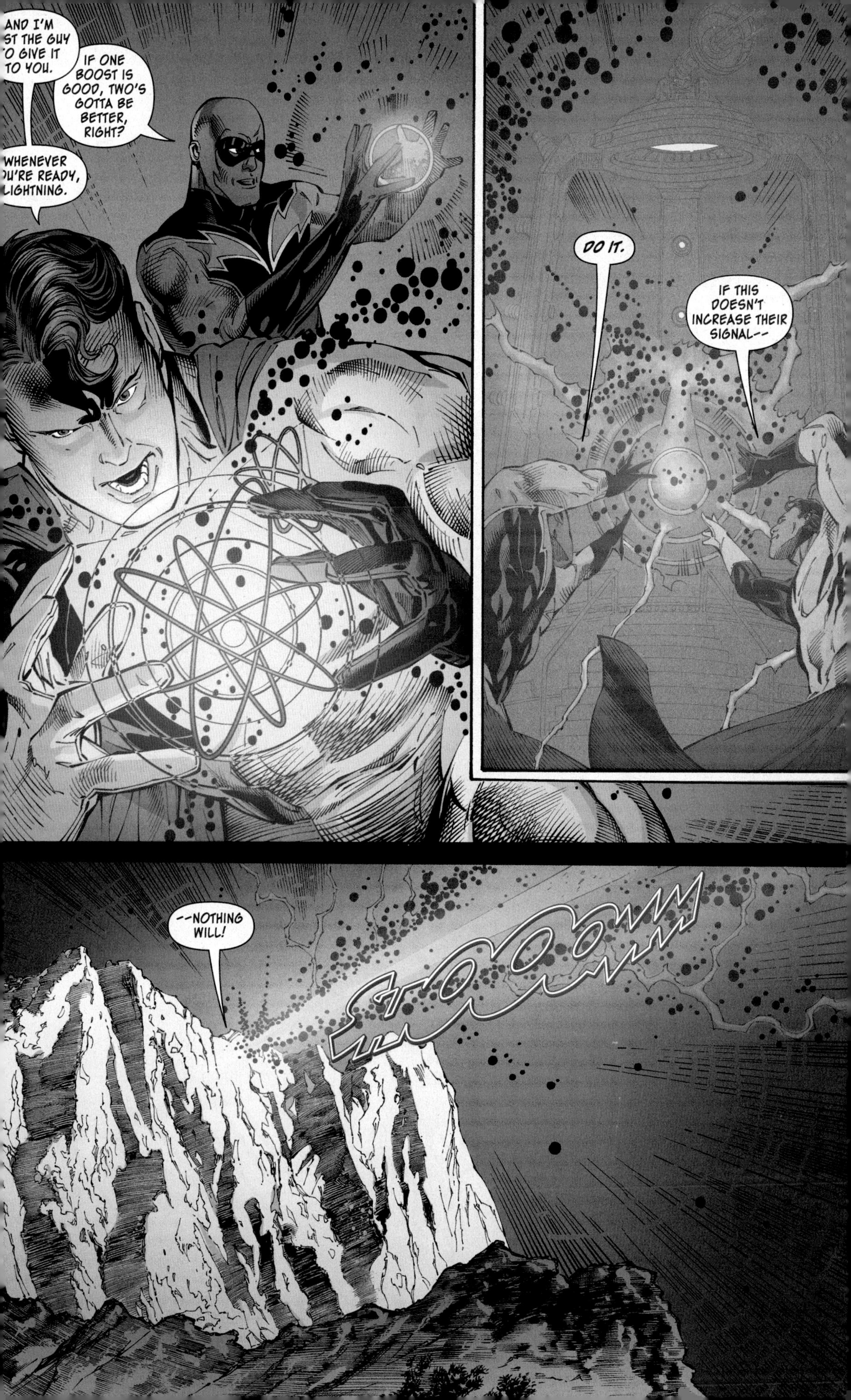
AND I'M ST THE GUY O GIVE IT TO YOU.
IF ONE BOOST IS GOOD, TWO'S GOTTA BE BETTER, RIGHT?
WHENEVER U'RE READY, LIGHTNING.
DO IT.
IF THIS DOESN'T INCREASE THEIR SIGNAL--
--NOTHING WILL!

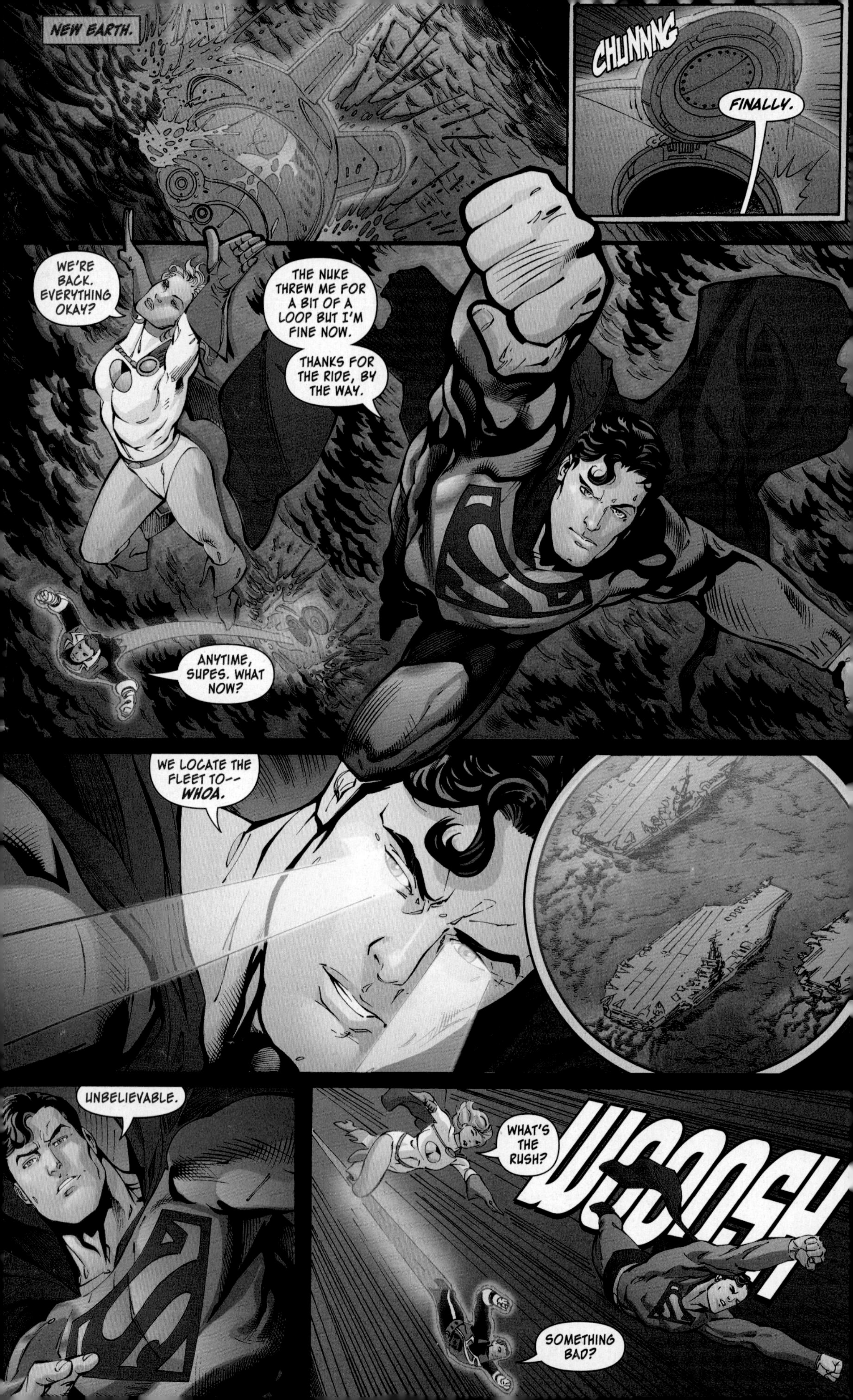
NEW EARTH.
CHUNNNG
FINALLY.
WE'RE BACK. EVERYTHING OKAY?
THE NUKE THREW ME FOR A BIT OF A LOOP BUT I'M FINE NOW.
THANKS FOR THE RIDE, BY THE WAY.
ANYTIME, SUPES. WHAT NOW?
WE LOCATE THE FLEET TO-- WHOA.
UNBELIEVABLE.
WHAT'S THE RUSH?
WOOOSH
SOMETHING BAD?

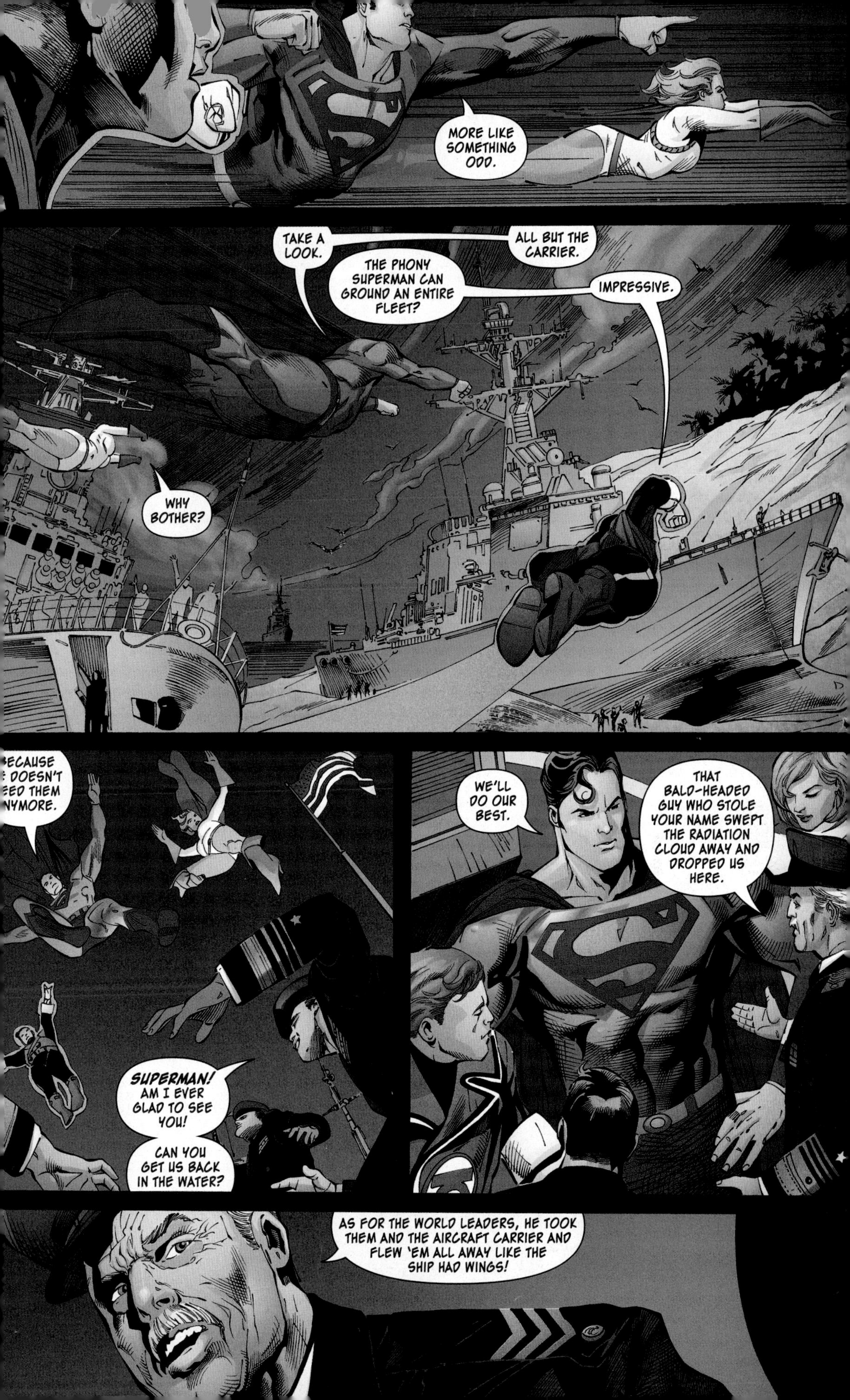
MORE LIKE SOMETHING ODD.
TAKE A LOOK.
ALL BUT THE CARRIER.
THE PHONY SUPERMAN CAN GROUND AN ENTIRE FLEET?
IMPRESSIVE.
WHY BOTHER?
ECAUSE E DOESN'T EED THEM NYMORE.
SUPERMAN! AM I EVER GLAD TO SEE YOU!
CAN YOU GET US BACK IN THE WATER?
WE'LL DO OUR BEST.
THAT BALD-HEADED GUY WHO STOLE YOUR NAME SWEPT THE RADIATION CLOUD AWAY AND DROPPED US HERE.
AS FOR THE WORLD LEADERS, HE TOOK THEM AND THE AIRCRAFT CARRIER AND FLEW 'EM ALL AWAY LIKE THE SHIP HAD WINGS!

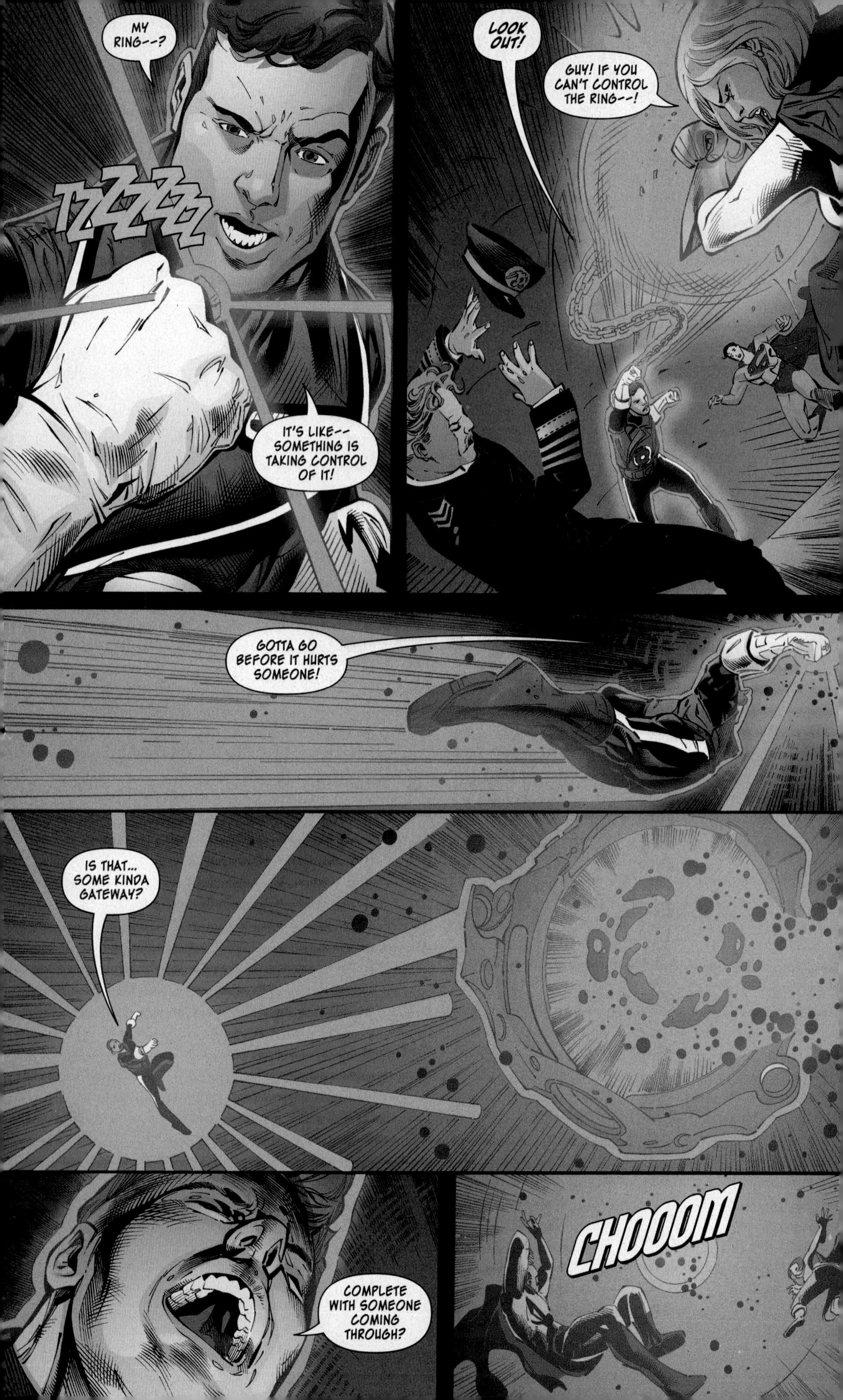
MY RING--?
TZZZZZZ
IT'S LIKE-- SOMETHING IS TAKING CONTROL OF IT!
LOOK OUT!
GUY! IF YOU CAN'T CONTROL THE RING--!
GOTTA GO BEFORE IT HURTS SOMEONE!
IS THAT... SOME KINDA GATEWAY?
COMPLETE WITH SOMEONE COMING THROUGH?
CHOOOM

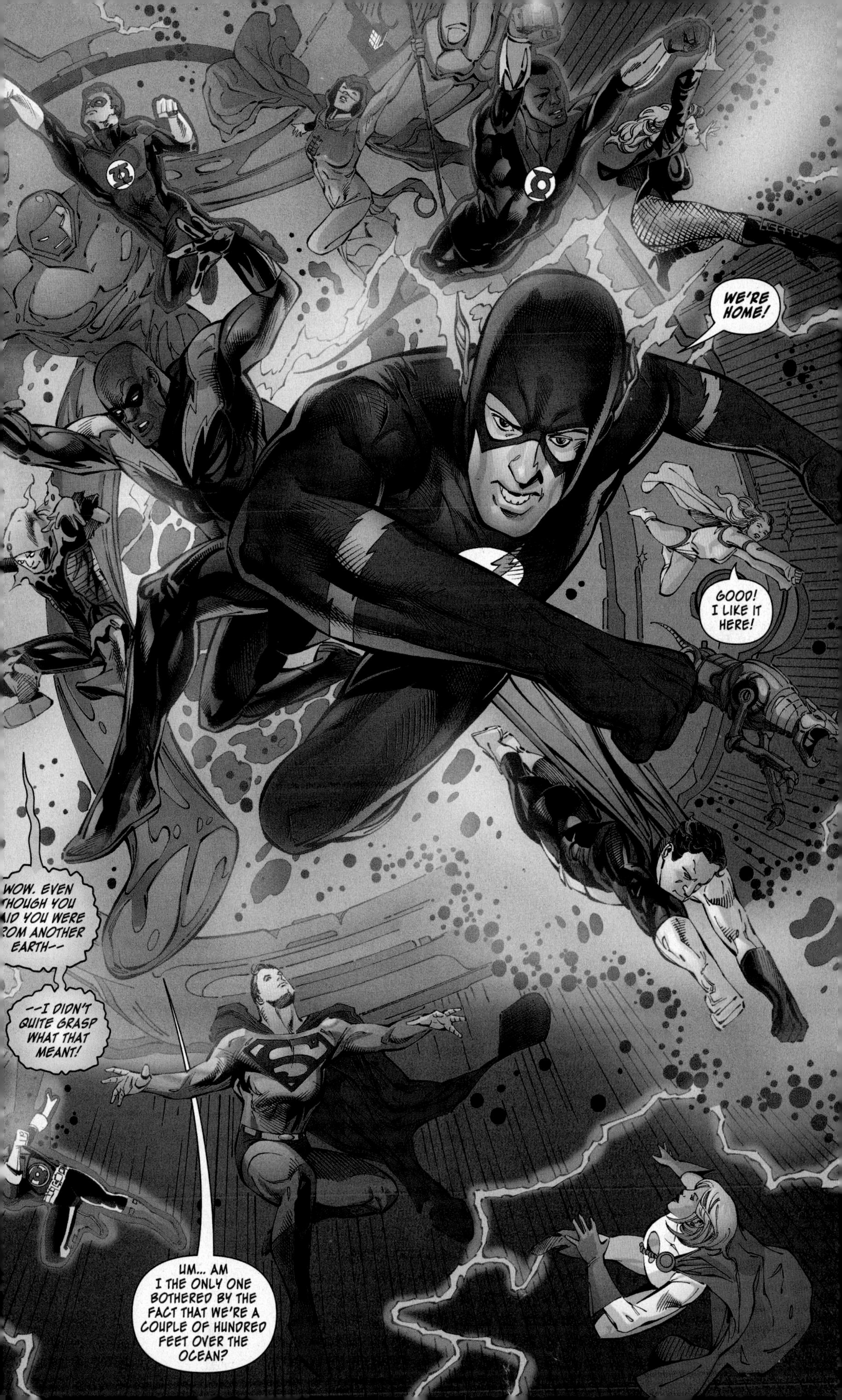
WE'RE HOME!
GOOD! I LIKE IT HERE!
WOW. EVEN THOUGH YOU AID YOU WERE ROM ANOTHER EARTH--
--I DIDN'T QUITE GRASP WHAT THAT MEANT!
UM... AM I THE ONLY ONE BOTHERED BY THE FACT THAT WE'RE A COUPLE OF HUNDRED FEET OVER THE OCEAN?

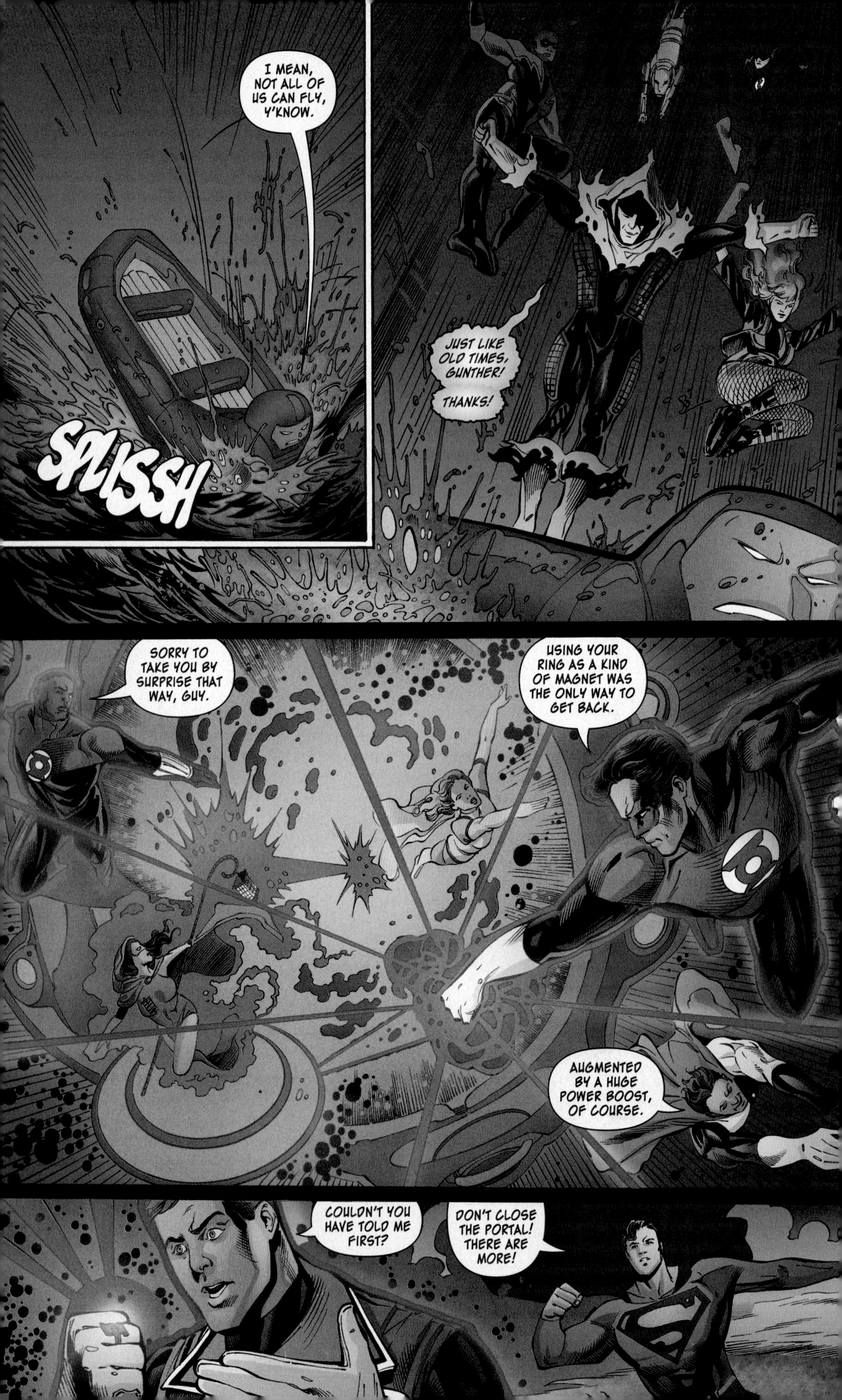
I MEAN, NOT ALL OF US CAN FLY, Y'KNOW.
SPLSSH
JUST LIKE OLD TIMES, GUNTHER!
THANKS!
SORRY TO TAKE YOU BY SURPRISE THAT WAY, GUY.
USING YOUR RING AS A KIND OF MAGNET WAS THE ONLY WAY TO GET BACK.
AUGMENTED BY A HUGE POWER BOOST, OF COURSE.
COULDN'T YOU HAVE TOLD ME FIRST?
DON'T CLOSE THE PORTAL! THERE ARE MORE!

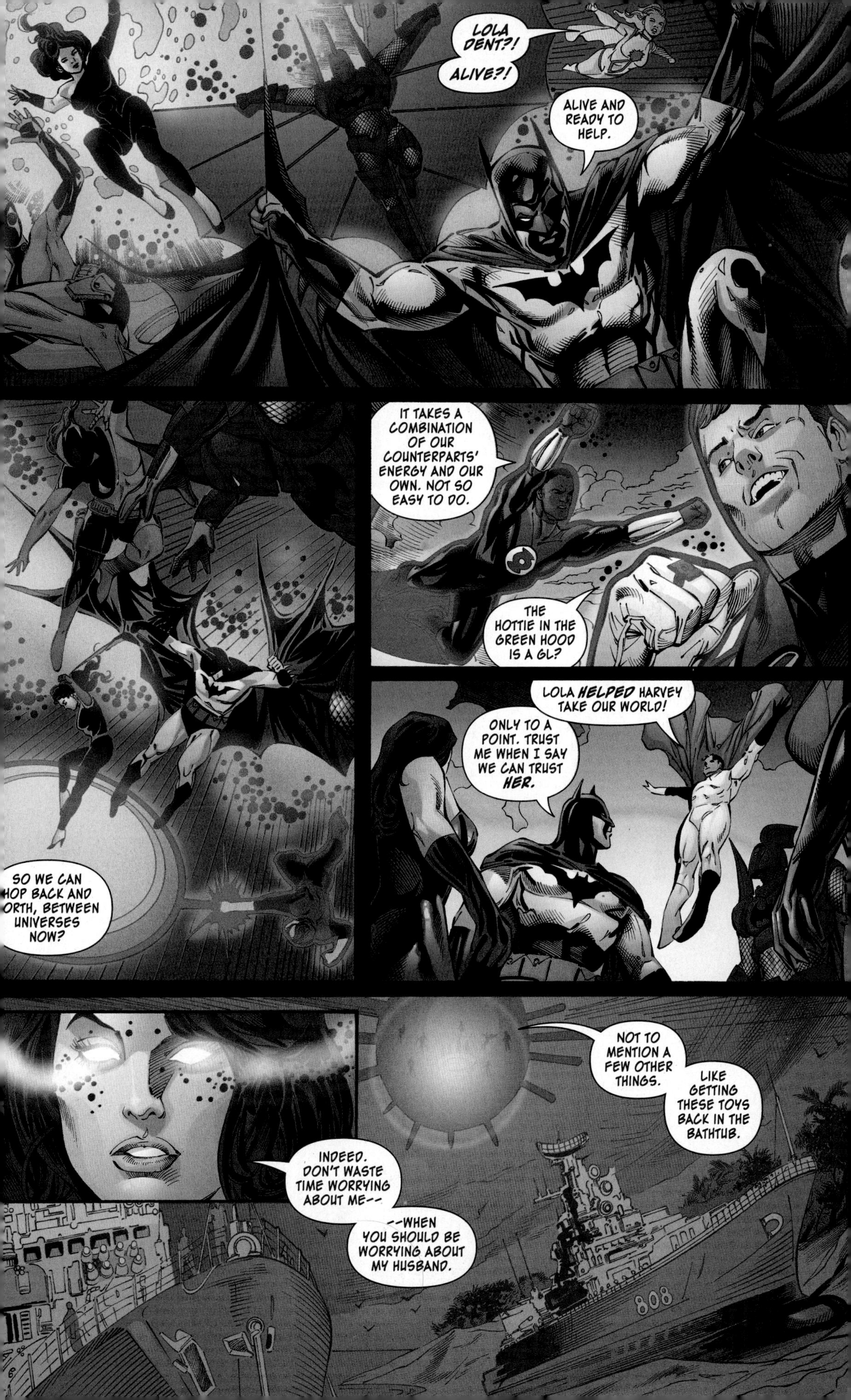
LOLA DENT?!
ALIVE?!
ALIVE AND READY TO HELP.
IT TAKES A COMBINATION OF OUR COUNTERPARTS' ENERGY AND OUR OWN. NOT SO EASY TO DO.
THE HOTTIE IN THE GREEN HOOD IS A GL?
SO WE CAN HOP BACK AND ORTH, BETWEEN UNIVERSES NOW?
LOLA HELPED HARVEY TAKE OUR WORLD!
ONLY TO A POINT. TRUST ME WHEN I SAY WE CAN TRUST HER.
NOT TO MENTION A FEW OTHER THINGS.
LIKE GETTING THESE TOYS BACK IN THE BATHTUB.
INDEED. DON'T WASTE TIME WORRYING ABOUT ME--
--WHEN YOU SHOULD BE WORRYING ABOUT MY HUSBAND.
808

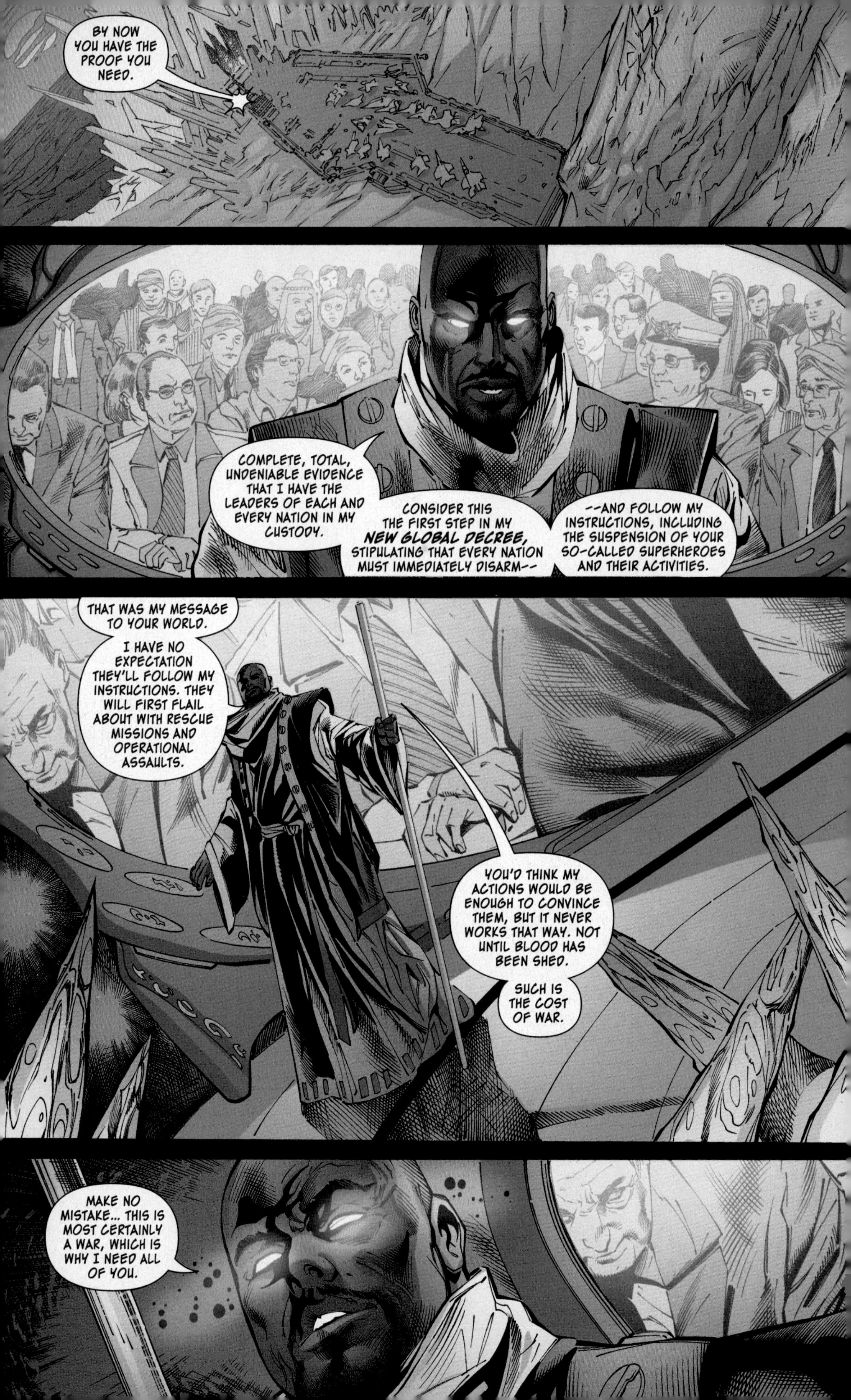
BY NOW YOU HAVE THE PROOF YOU NEED.
COMPLETE, TOTAL, UNDENIABLE EVIDENCE THAT I HAVE THE LEADERS OF EACH AND EVERY NATION IN MY CUSTODY.
CONSIDER THIS THE FIRST STEP IN MY NEW GLOBAL DECREE, STIPULATING THAT EVERY NATION MUST IMMEDIATELY DISARM--
--AND FOLLOW MY INSTRUCTIONS, INCLUDING THE SUSPENSION OF YOUR SO-CALLED SUPERHEROES AND THEIR ACTIVITIES.
THAT WAS MY MESSAGE TO YOUR WORLD.
I HAVE NO EXPECTATION THEY'LL FOLLOW MY INSTRUCTIONS. THEY WILL FIRST FLAIL ABOUT WITH RESCUE MISSIONS AND OPERATIONAL ASSAULTS.
YOU'D THINK MY ACTIONS WOULD BE ENOUGH TO CONVINCE THEM, BUT IT NEVER WORKS THAT WAY. NOT UNTIL BLOOD HAS BEEN SHED.
SUCH IS THE COST OF WAR.
MAKE NO MISTAKE... THIS IS MOST CERTAINLY A WAR, WHICH IS WHY I NEED ALL OF YOU.

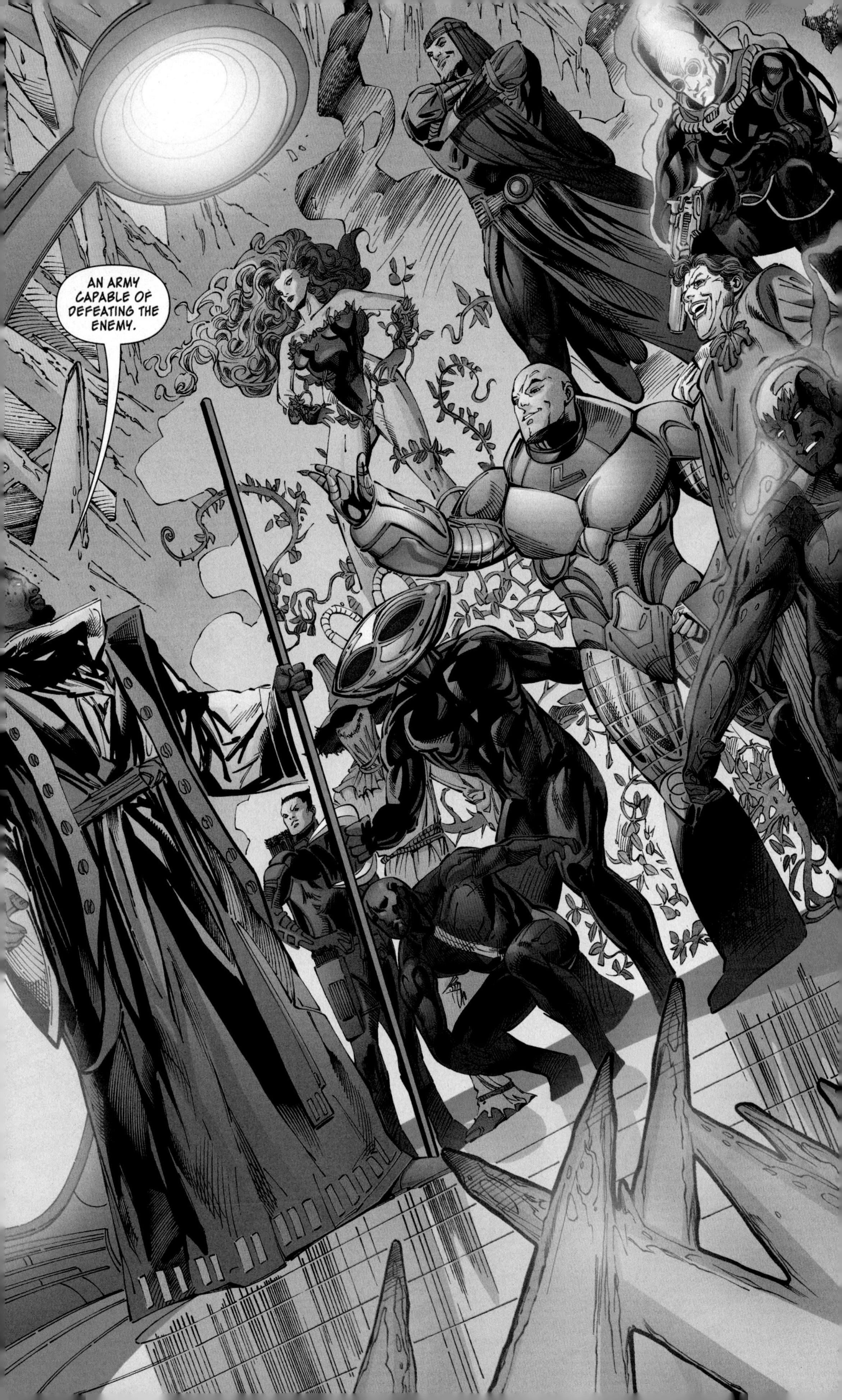
AN ARMY CAPABLE OF DEFEATING THE ENEMY.

Cover art by Ivan Reis and Joe Prado.

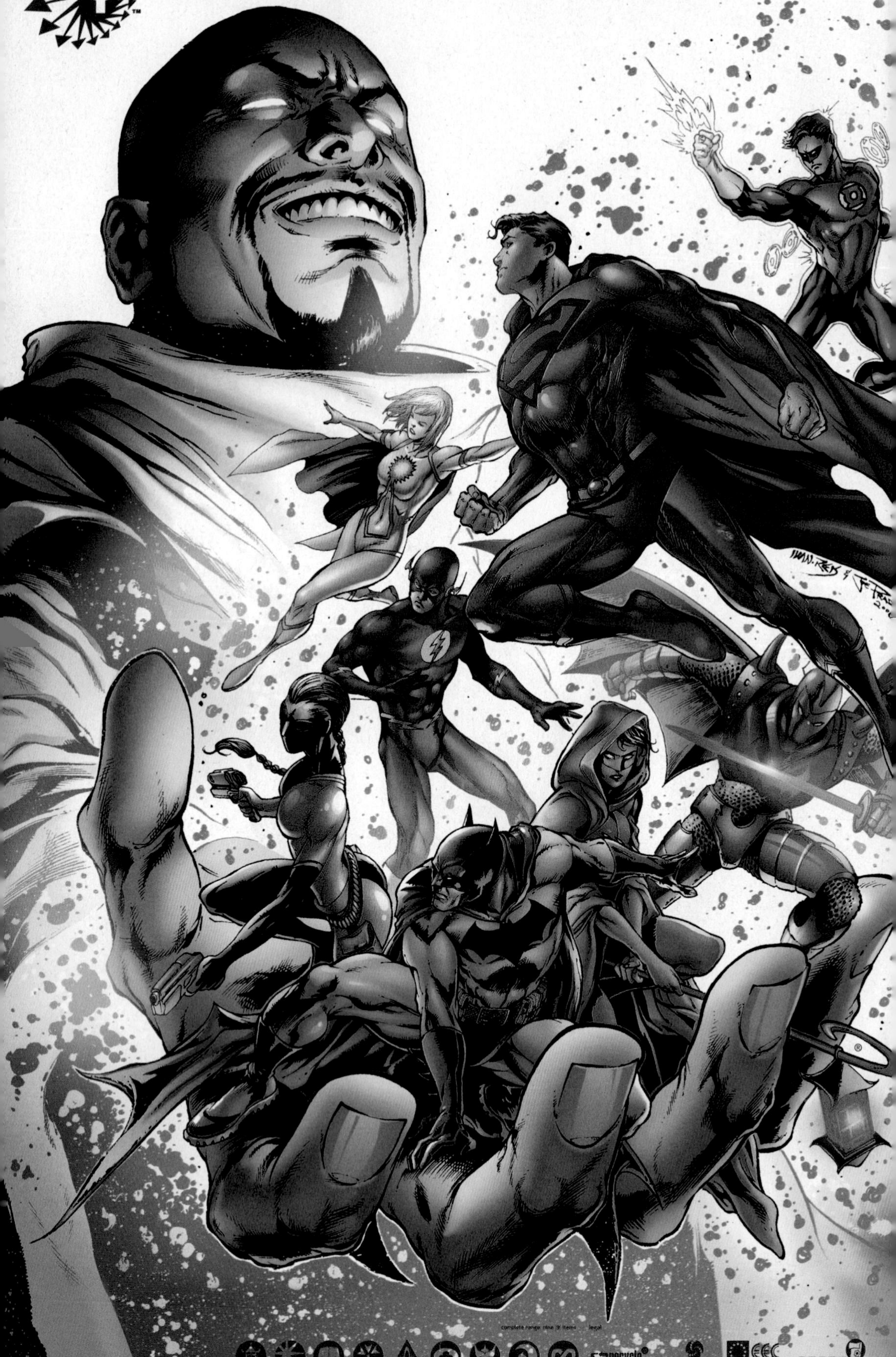

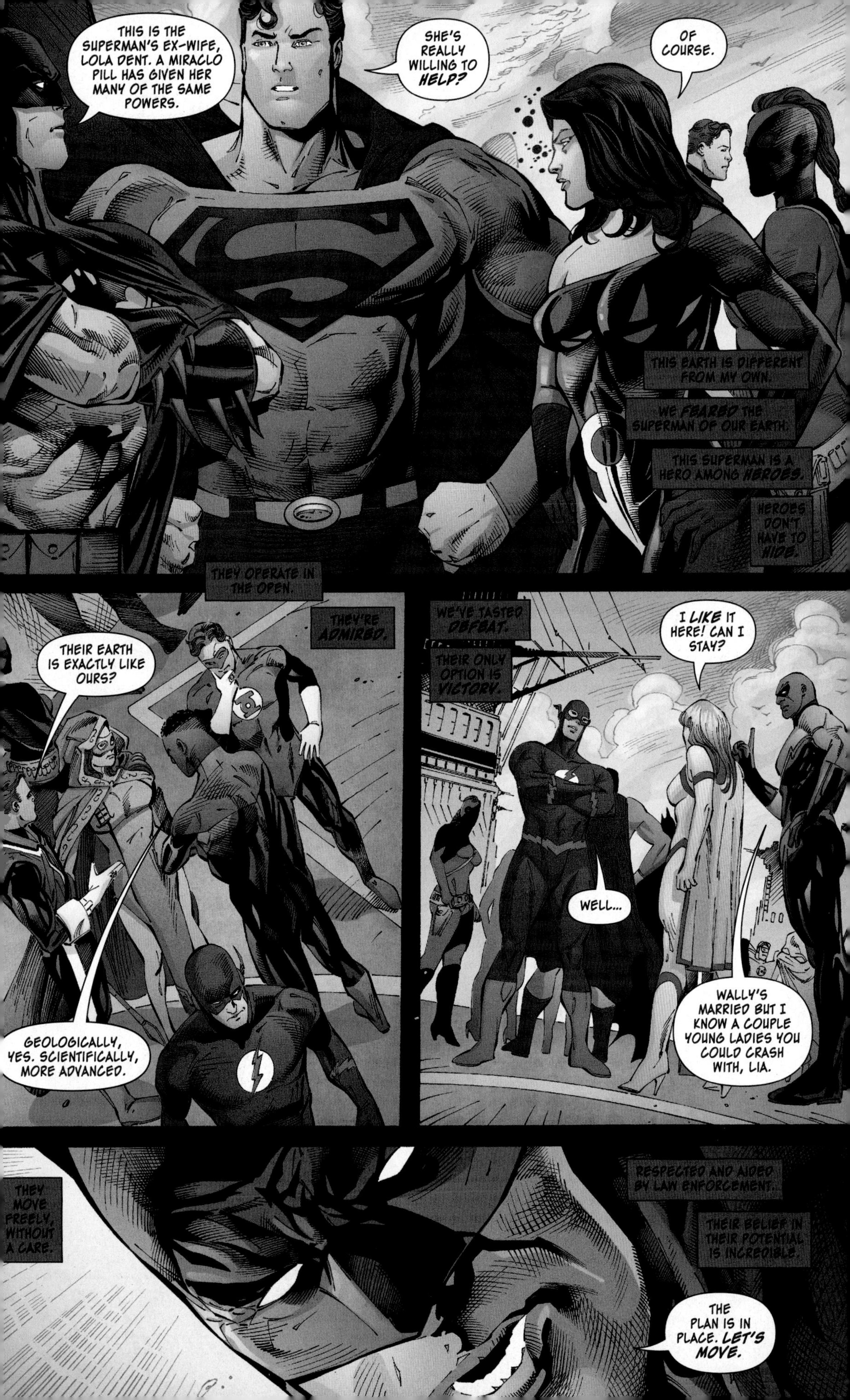
THIS IS THE SUPERMAN'S EX-WIFE, LOLA DENT. A MIRACLO PILL HAS GIVEN HER MANY OF THE SAME POWERS.
SHE'S REALLY WILLING TO *HELP?*
OF COURSE.
THIS EARTH IS DIFFERENT FROM MY OWN.
WE *FEARED* THE SUPERMAN OF OUR EARTH.
THIS SUPERMAN IS A HERO AMONG *HEROES.*
HEROES DON'T HAVE TO *HIDE.*
THEY OPERATE IN THE OPEN.
THEY'RE *ADMIRED.*
THEIR EARTH IS EXACTLY LIKE OURS?
GEOLOGICALLY, YES. SCIENTIFICALLY, MORE ADVANCED.
WE'VE TASTED *DEFEAT.*
THEIR ONLY OPTION IS *VICTORY.*
I *LIKE* IT HERE! CAN I STAY?
WELL...
WALLY'S MARRIED BUT I KNOW A COUPLE YOUNG LADIES YOU COULD CRASH WITH, LIA.
THEY MOVE FREELY, WITHOUT A CARE.
RESPECTED AND AIDED BY LAW ENFORCEMENT.
THEIR BELIEF IN THEIR POTENTIAL IS INCREDIBLE.
THE PLAN IS IN PLACE. *LET'S MOVE.*

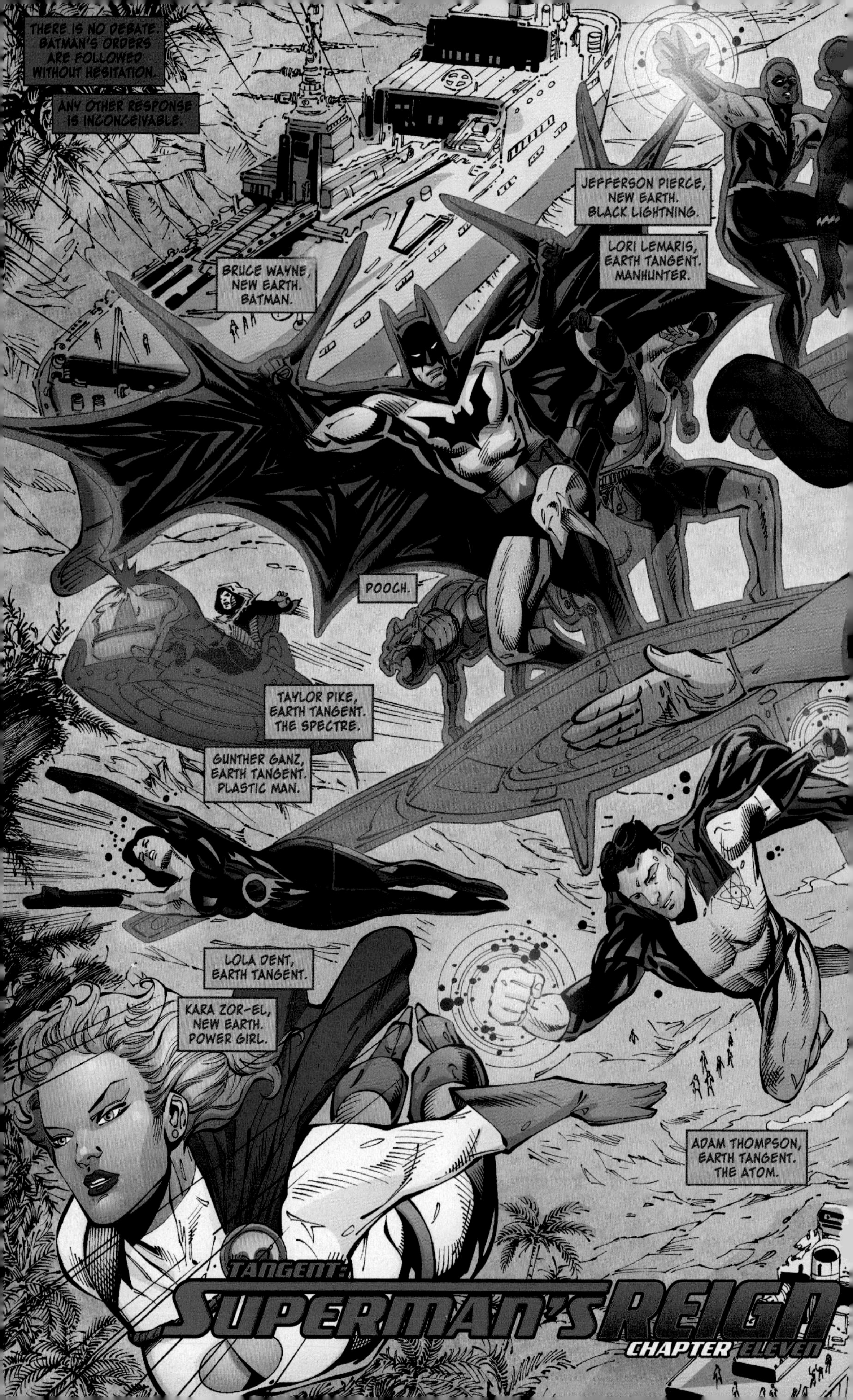
THERE IS NO DEBATE. BATMAN'S ORDERS ARE FOLLOWED WITHOUT HESITATION.
ANY OTHER RESPONSE IS INCONCEIVABLE.
JEFFERSON PIERCE, NEW EARTH. BLACK LIGHTNING.
LORI LEMARIS, EARTH TANGENT. MANHUNTER.
BRUCE WAYNE, NEW EARTH. BATMAN.
POOCH.
TAYLOR PIKE, EARTH TANGENT. THE SPECTRE.
GUNTHER GANZ, EARTH TANGENT. PLASTIC MAN.
LOLA DENT, EARTH TANGENT.
KARA ZOR-EL, NEW EARTH. POWER GIRL.
ADAM THOMPSON, EARTH TANGENT. THE ATOM.
TANGENT:
SUPERMAN'S REIGN
CHAPTER ELEVEN

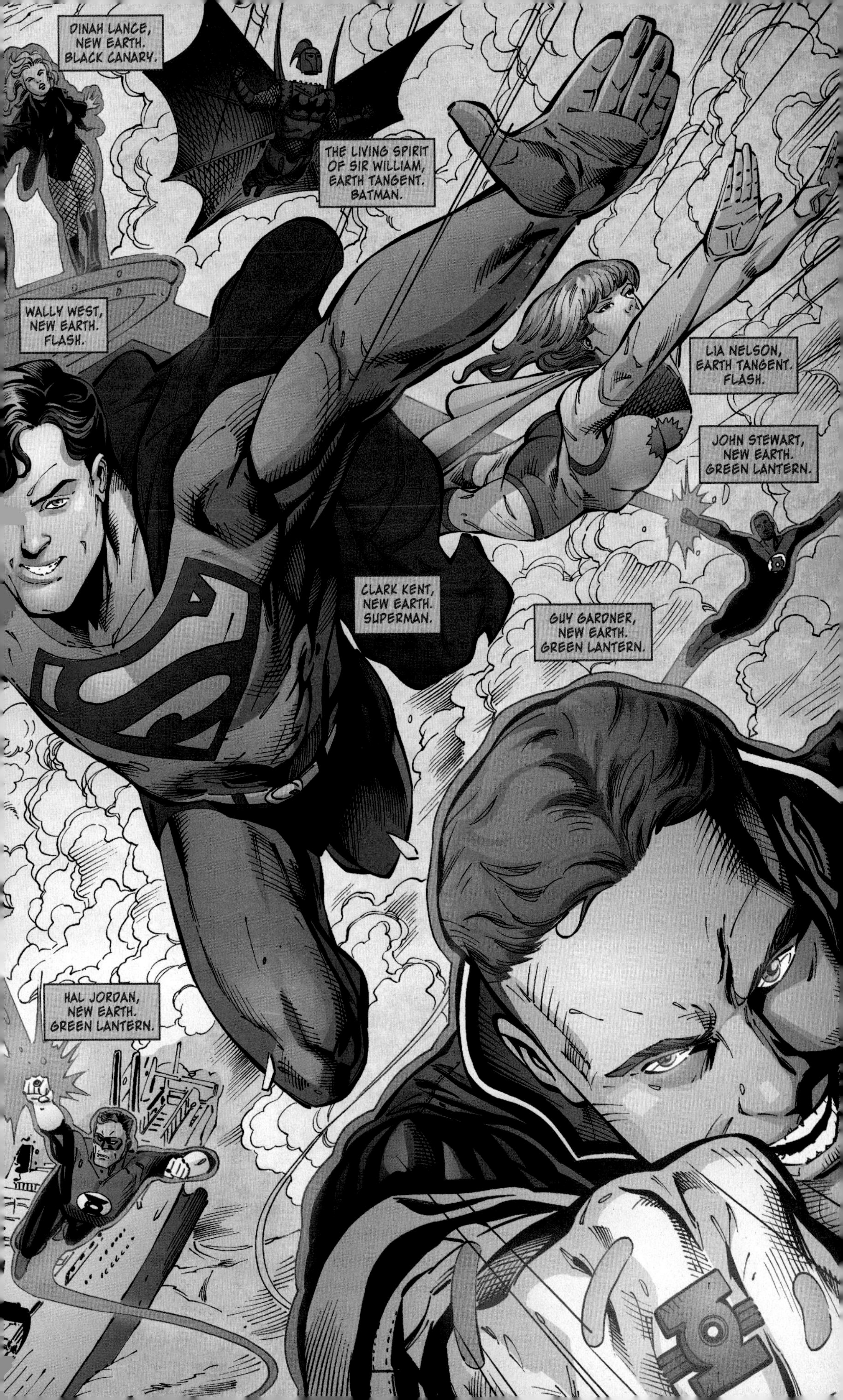
DINAH LANCE, NEW EARTH. BLACK CANARY.
THE LIVING SPIRIT OF SIR WILLIAM, EARTH TANGENT. BATMAN.
WALLY WEST, NEW EARTH. FLASH.
LIA NELSON, EARTH TANGENT. FLASH.
JOHN STEWART, NEW EARTH. GREEN LANTERN.
CLARK KENT, NEW EARTH. SUPERMAN.
GUY GARDNER, NEW EARTH. GREEN LANTERN.
HAL JORDAN, NEW EARTH. GREEN LANTERN.

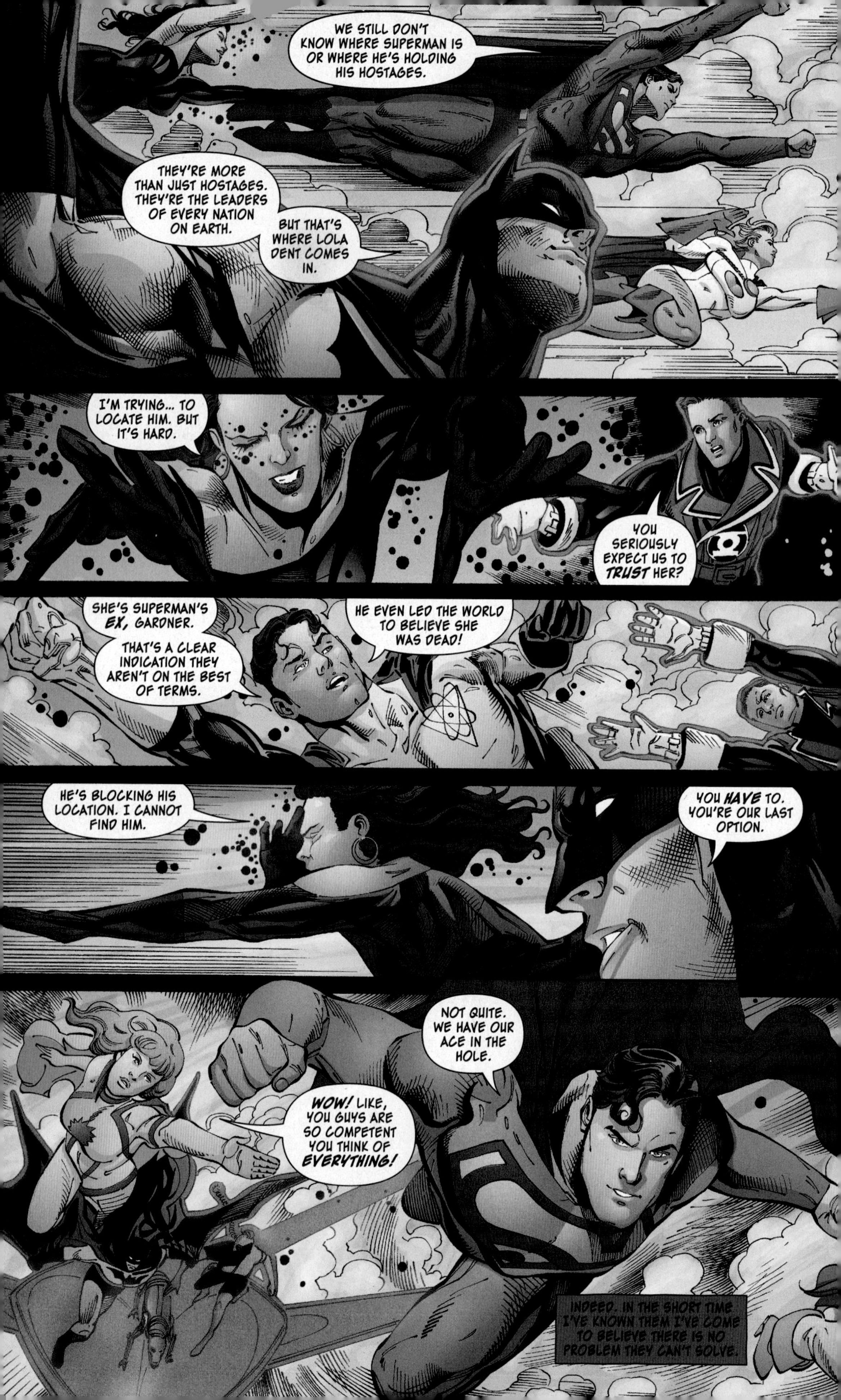
WE STILL DON'T KNOW WHERE SUPERMAN IS OR WHERE HE'S HOLDING HIS HOSTAGES.
THEY'RE MORE THAN JUST HOSTAGES. THEY'RE THE LEADERS OF EVERY NATION ON EARTH.
BUT THAT'S WHERE LOLA DENT COMES IN.
I'M TRYING... TO LOCATE HIM. BUT IT'S HARD.
YOU SERIOUSLY EXPECT US TO TRUST HER?
SHE'S SUPERMAN'S EX, GARDNER.
THAT'S A CLEAR INDICATION THEY AREN'T ON THE BEST OF TERMS.
HE EVEN LED THE WORLD TO BELIEVE SHE WAS DEAD!
HE'S BLOCKING HIS LOCATION. I CANNOT FIND HIM.
YOU HAVE TO. YOU'RE OUR LAST OPTION.
NOT QUITE. WE HAVE OUR ACE IN THE HOLE.
WOW! LIKE, YOU GUYS ARE SO COMPETENT YOU THINK OF EVERYTHING!
INDEED. IN THE SHORT TIME I'VE KNOWN THEM I'VE COME TO BELIEVE THERE IS NO PROBLEM THEY CAN'T SOLVE.

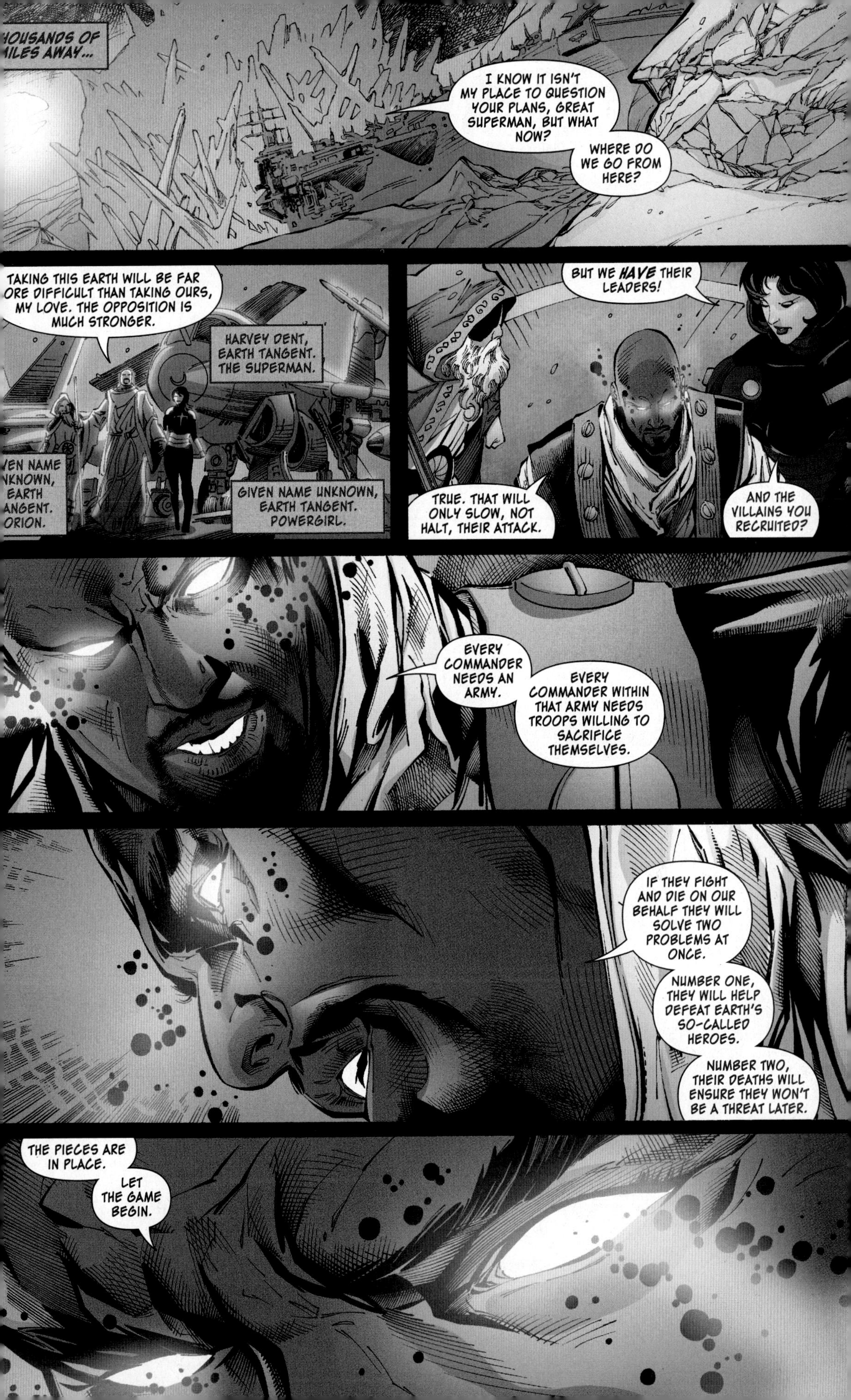
HOUSANDS OF
ILES AWAY...
I KNOW IT ISN'T MY PLACE TO QUESTION YOUR PLANS, GREAT SUPERMAN, BUT WHAT NOW?
WHERE DO WE GO FROM HERE?
TAKING THIS EARTH WILL BE FAR ORE DIFFICULT THAN TAKING OURS, MY LOVE. THE OPPOSITION IS MUCH STRONGER.
HARVEY DENT, EARTH TANGENT. THE SUPERMAN.
VEN NAME NKNOWN, EARTH ANGENT. ORION.
GIVEN NAME UNKNOWN, EARTH TANGENT. POWERGIRL.
BUT WE HAVE THEIR LEADERS!
TRUE. THAT WILL ONLY SLOW, NOT HALT, THEIR ATTACK.
AND THE VILLAINS YOU RECRUITED?
EVERY COMMANDER NEEDS AN ARMY.
EVERY COMMANDER WITHIN THAT ARMY NEEDS TROOPS WILLING TO SACRIFICE THEMSELVES.
IF THEY FIGHT AND DIE ON OUR BEHALF THEY WILL SOLVE TWO PROBLEMS AT ONCE.
NUMBER ONE, THEY WILL HELP DEFEAT EARTH'S SO-CALLED HEROES.
NUMBER TWO, THEIR DEATHS WILL ENSURE THEY WON'T BE A THREAT LATER.
THE PIECES ARE IN PLACE.
LET THE GAME BEGIN.

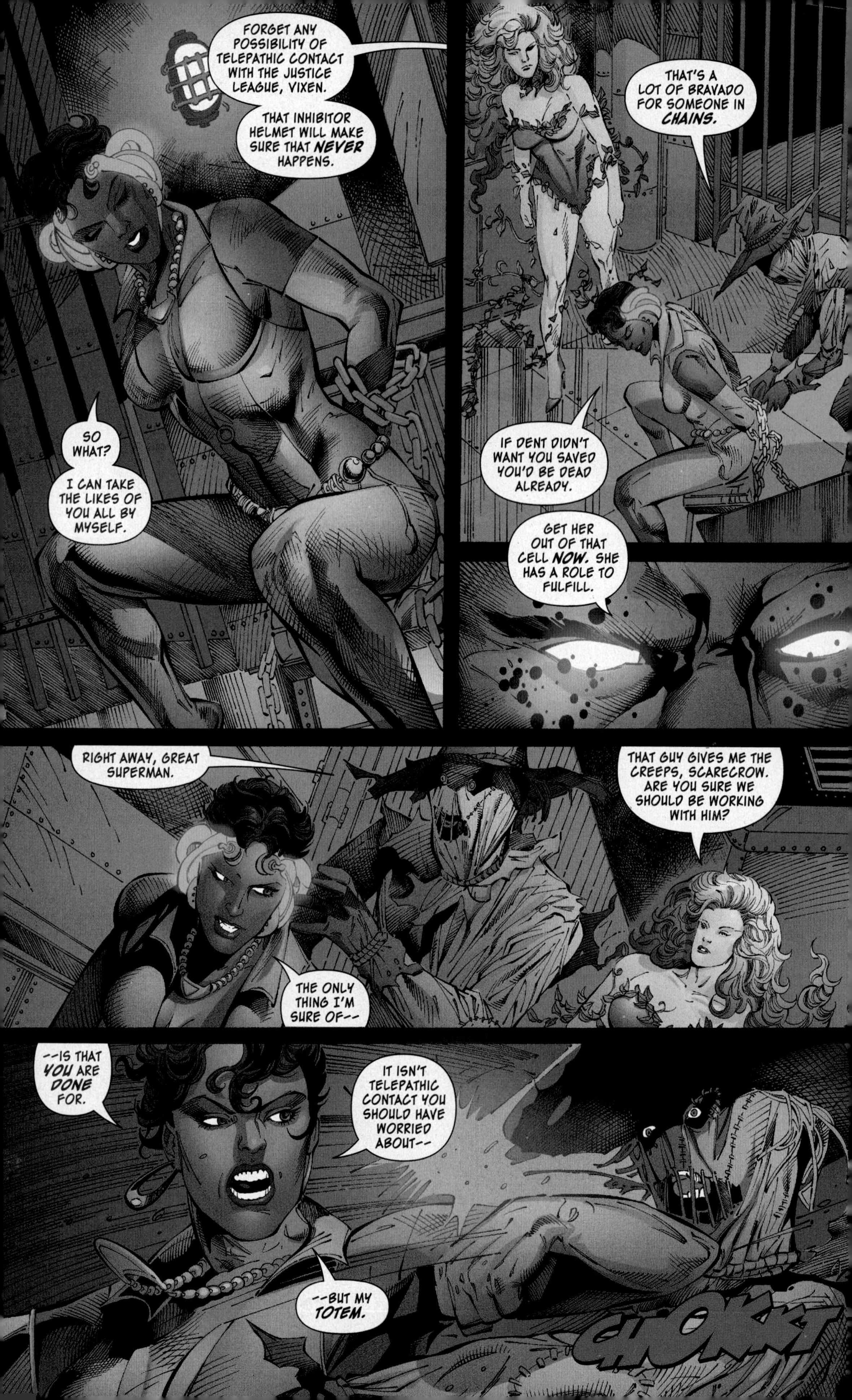
FORGET ANY POSSIBILITY OF TELEPATHIC CONTACT WITH THE JUSTICE LEAGUE, VIXEN.
THAT INHIBITOR HELMET WILL MAKE SURE THAT **NEVER** HAPPENS.
SO WHAT?
I CAN TAKE THE LIKES OF YOU ALL BY MYSELF.
THAT'S A LOT OF BRAVADO FOR SOMEONE IN **CHAINS.**
IF DENT DIDN'T WANT YOU SAVED YOU'D BE DEAD ALREADY.
GET HER OUT OF THAT CELL **NOW.** SHE HAS A ROLE TO FULFILL.
RIGHT AWAY, GREAT SUPERMAN.
THAT GUY GIVES ME THE CREEPS, SCARECROW. ARE YOU SURE WE SHOULD BE WORKING WITH HIM?
THE ONLY THING I'M SURE OF--
--IS THAT **YOU** ARE **DONE** FOR.
IT ISN'T TELEPATHIC CONTACT YOU SHOULD HAVE WORRIED ABOUT--
--BUT MY **TOTEM.**
CHOKK

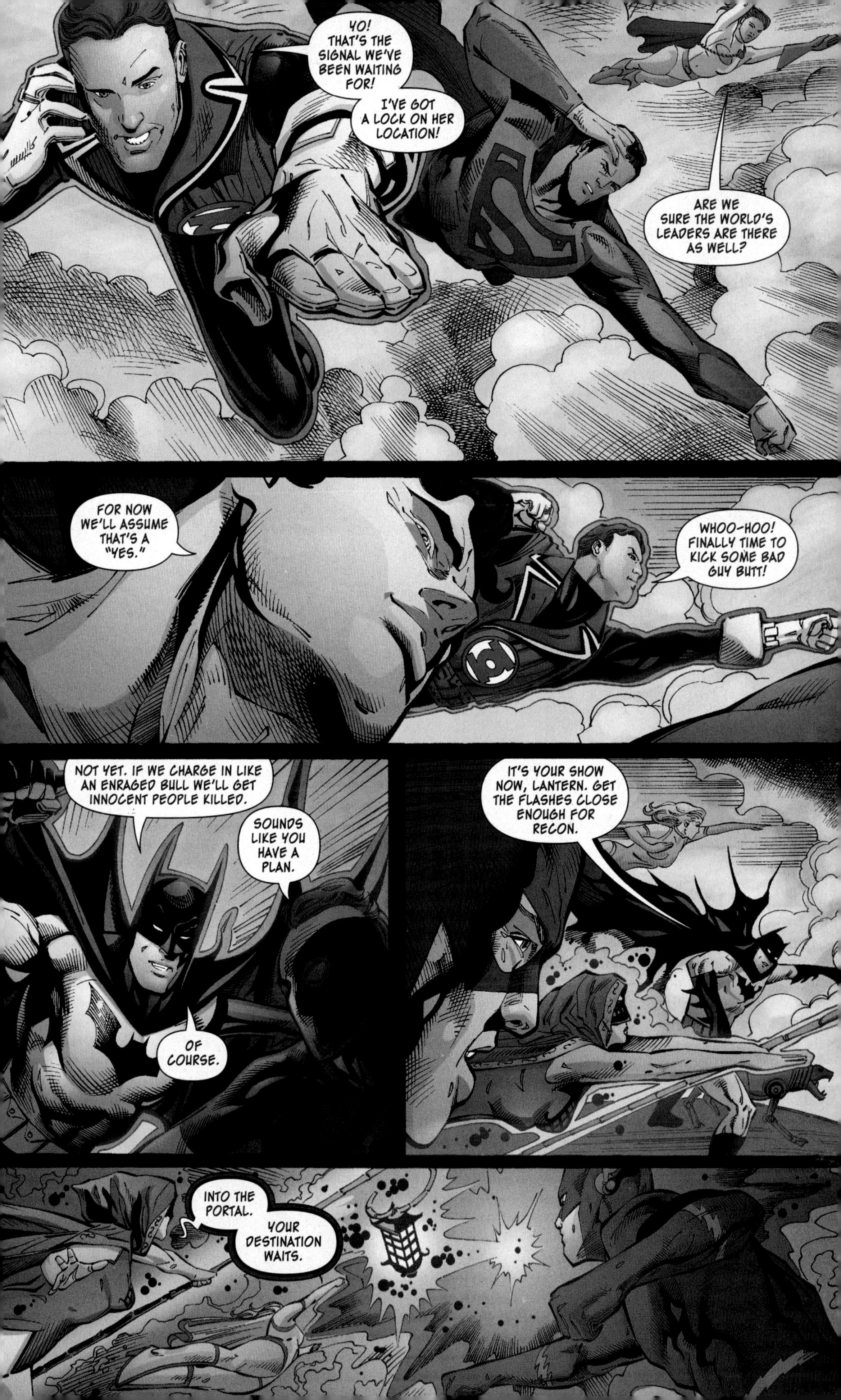

YO! THAT'S THE SIGNAL WE'VE BEEN WAITING FOR!
I'VE GOT A LOCK ON HER LOCATION!
ARE WE SURE THE WORLD'S LEADERS ARE THERE AS WELL?
FOR NOW WE'LL ASSUME THAT'S A "YES."
WHOO-HOO! FINALLY TIME TO KICK SOME BAD GUY BUTT!
NOT YET. IF WE CHARGE IN LIKE AN ENRAGED BULL WE'LL GET INNOCENT PEOPLE KILLED.
SOUNDS LIKE YOU HAVE A PLAN.
OF COURSE.
IT'S YOUR SHOW NOW, LANTERN. GET THE FLASHES CLOSE ENOUGH FOR RECON.
INTO THE PORTAL.
YOUR DESTINATION WAITS.

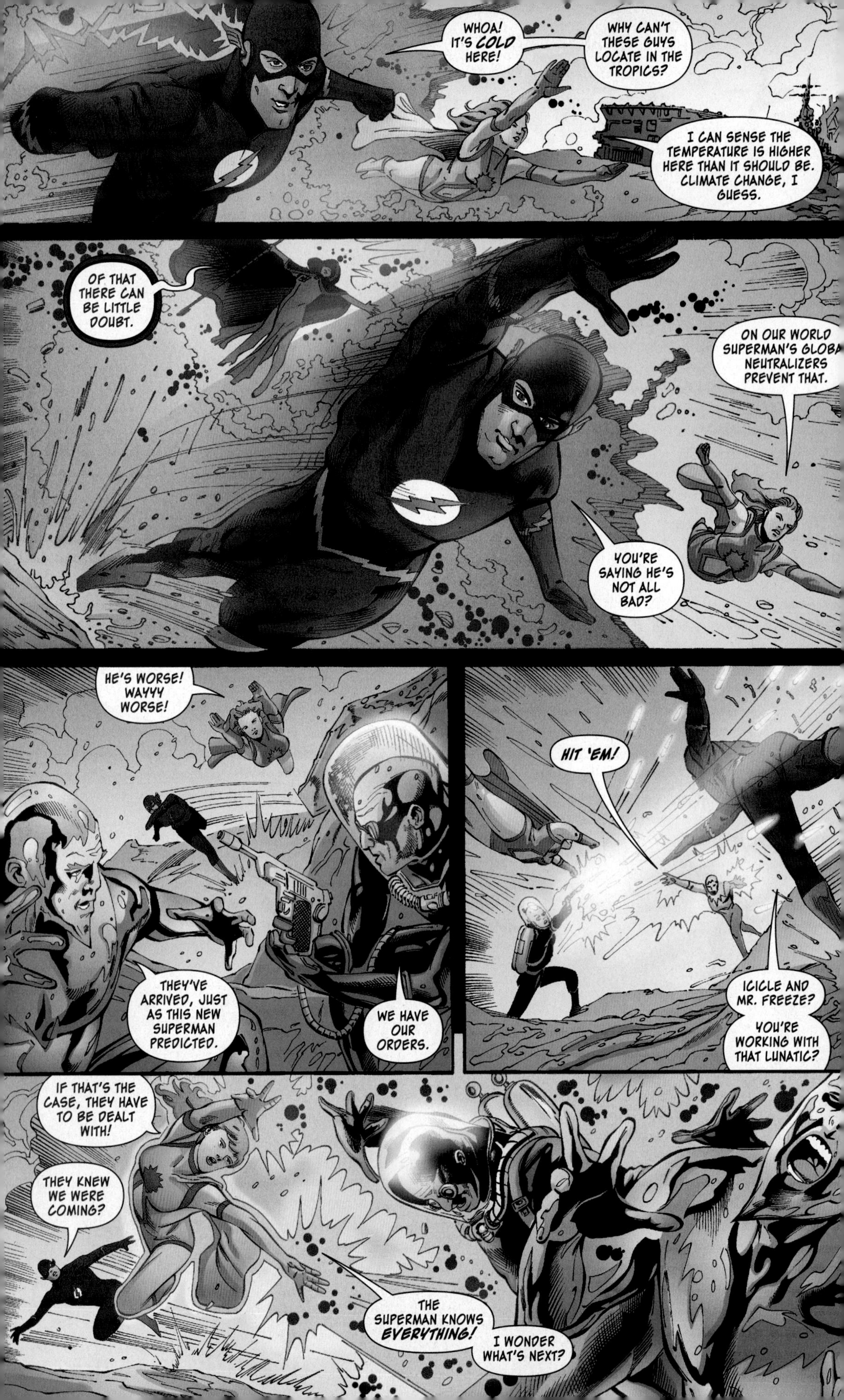
WHOA! IT'S *COLD* HERE!
WHY CAN'T THESE GUYS LOCATE IN THE TROPICS?
I CAN SENSE THE TEMPERATURE IS HIGHER HERE THAN IT SHOULD BE. CLIMATE CHANGE, I GUESS.
OF THAT THERE CAN BE LITTLE DOUBT.
ON OUR WORLD SUPERMAN'S GLOBA NEUTRALIZERS PREVENT THAT.
YOU'RE SAYING HE'S NOT ALL BAD?
HE'S WORSE! WAYYY WORSE!
THEY'VE ARRIVED, JUST AS THIS NEW SUPERMAN PREDICTED.
WE HAVE OUR ORDERS.
HIT 'EM!
ICICLE AND MR. FREEZE?
YOU'RE WORKING WITH THAT LUNATIC?
IF THAT'S THE CASE, THEY HAVE TO BE DEALT WITH!
THEY KNEW WE WERE COMING?
THE SUPERMAN KNOWS *EVERYTHING!*
I WONDER WHAT'S NEXT?

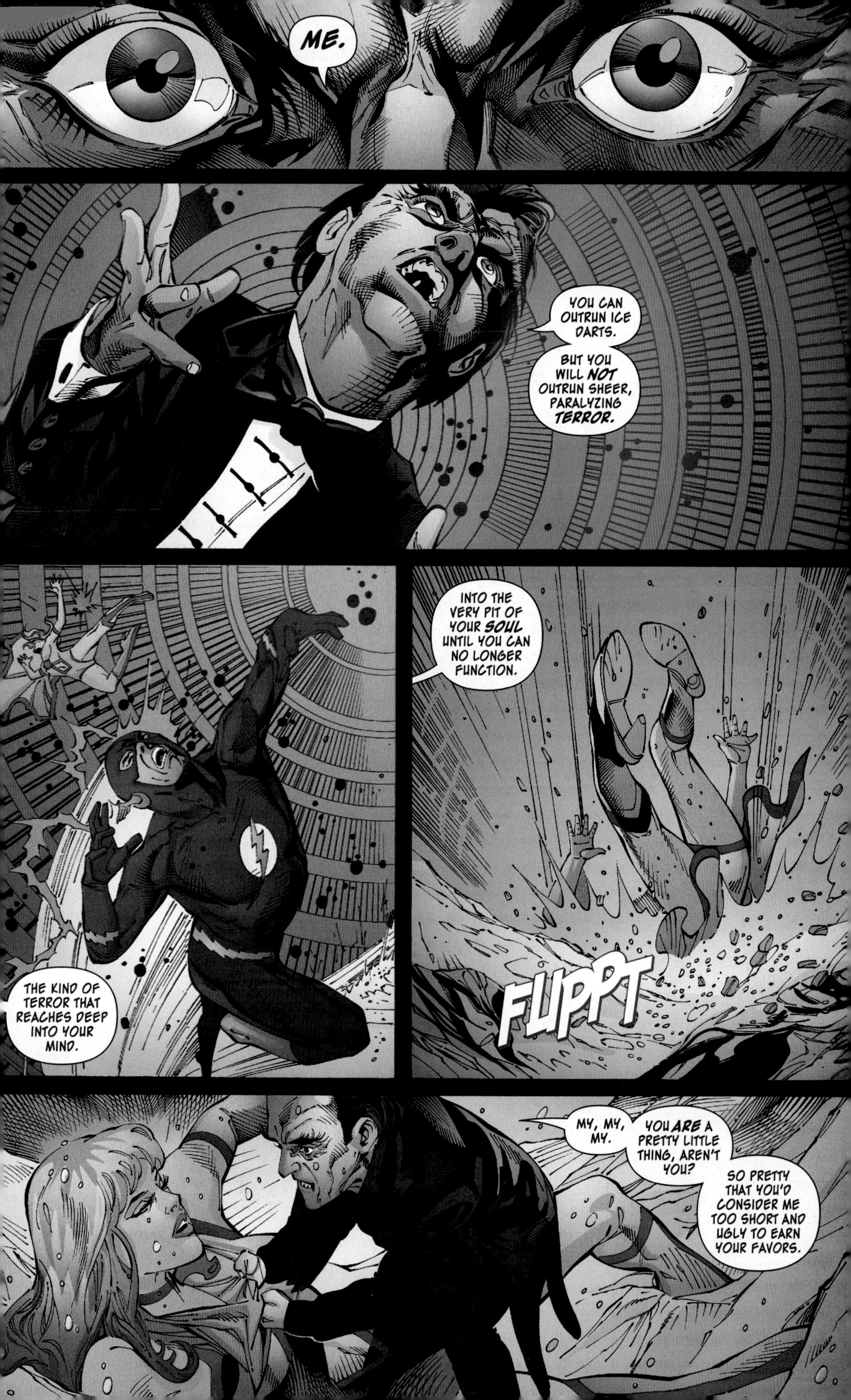
ME.
YOU CAN OUTRUN ICE DARTS.
BUT YOU WILL NOT OUTRUN SHEER, PARALYZING TERROR.
THE KIND OF TERROR THAT REACHES DEEP INTO YOUR MIND.
INTO THE VERY PIT OF YOUR SOUL UNTIL YOU CAN NO LONGER FUNCTION.
FLIPPT
MY, MY, MY.
YOU ARE A PRETTY LITTLE THING, AREN'T YOU?
SO PRETTY THAT YOU'D CONSIDER ME TOO SHORT AND UGLY TO EARN YOUR FAVORS.

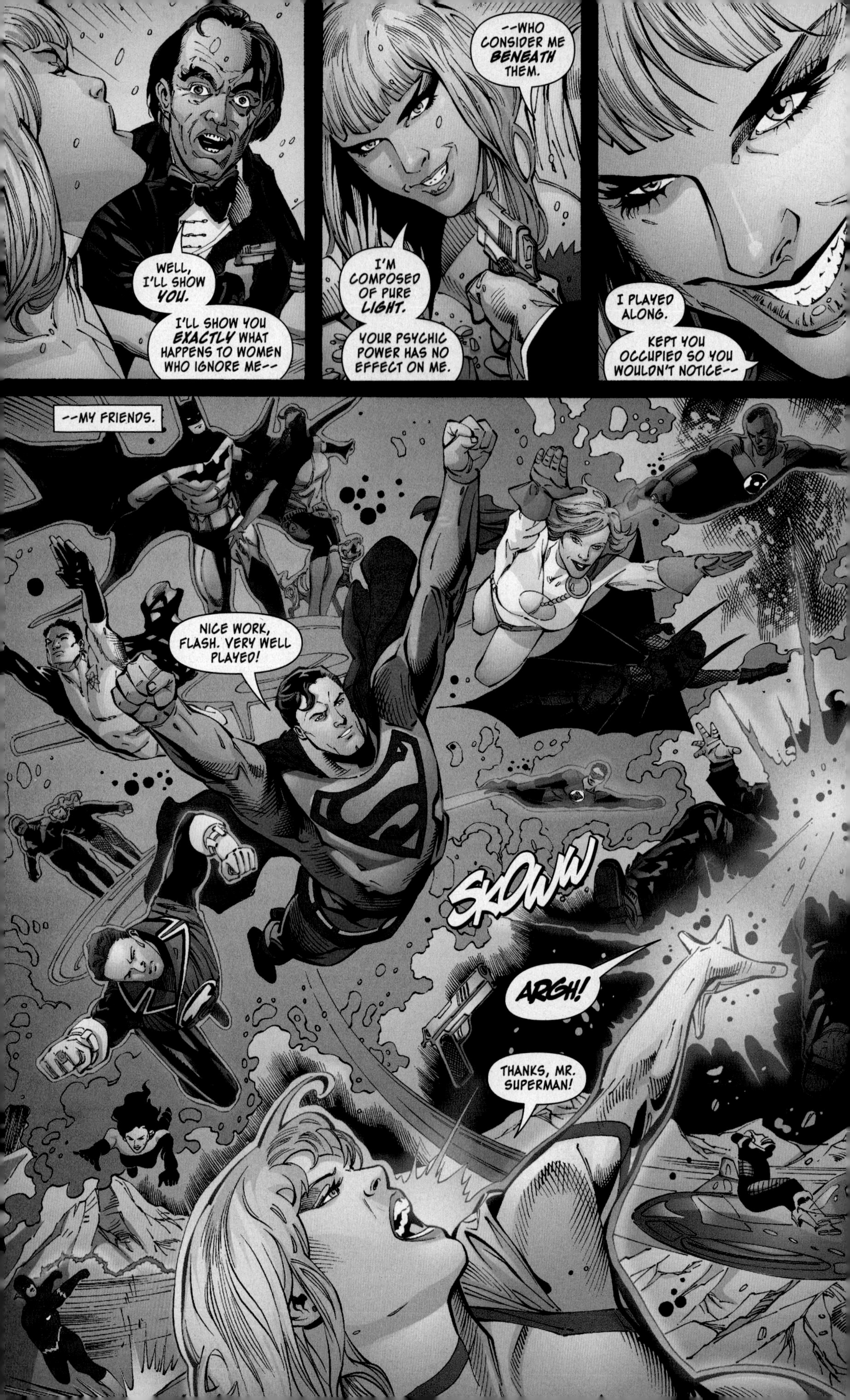
WELL, I'LL SHOW YOU.
I'LL SHOW YOU EXACTLY WHAT HAPPENS TO WOMEN WHO IGNORE ME--
--WHO CONSIDER ME BENEATH THEM.
I'M COMPOSED OF PURE LIGHT.
YOUR PSYCHIC POWER HAS NO EFFECT ON ME.
I PLAYED ALONG.
KEPT YOU OCCUPIED SO YOU WOULDN'T NOTICE--
--MY FRIENDS.
NICE WORK, FLASH. VERY WELL PLAYED!
SKOWW
ARGH!
THANKS, MR. SUPERMAN!

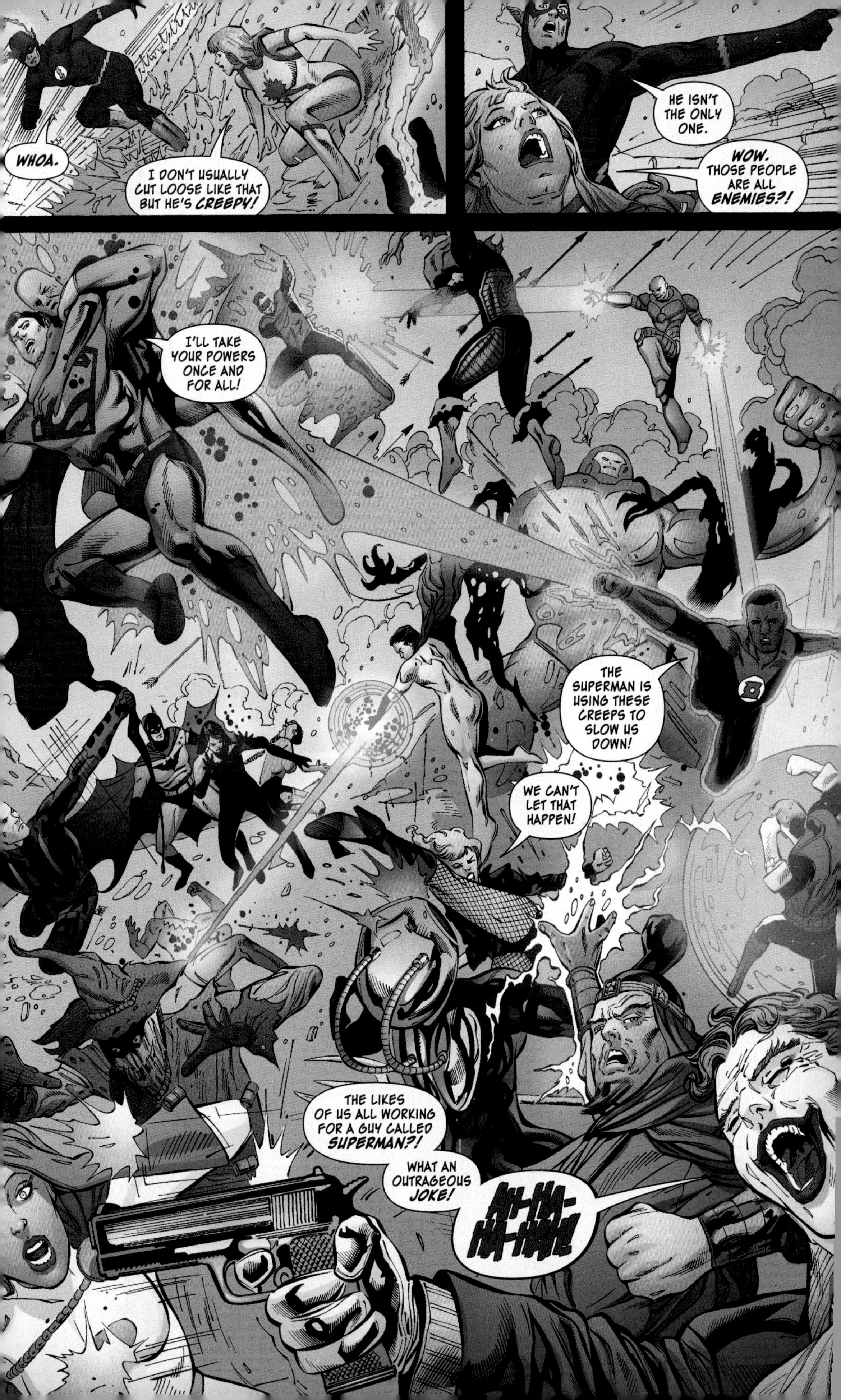
WHOA.
I DON'T USUALLY CUT LOOSE LIKE THAT BUT HE'S CREEPY!
HE ISN'T THE ONLY ONE.
WOW. THOSE PEOPLE ARE ALL ENEMIES?!
I'LL TAKE YOUR POWERS ONCE AND FOR ALL!
THE SUPERMAN IS USING THESE CREEPS TO SLOW US DOWN!
WE CAN'T LET THAT HAPPEN!
THE LIKES OF US ALL WORKING FOR A GUY CALLED SUPERMAN?!
WHAT AN OUTRAGEOUS JOKE!
AH-HA-HA-HA!!

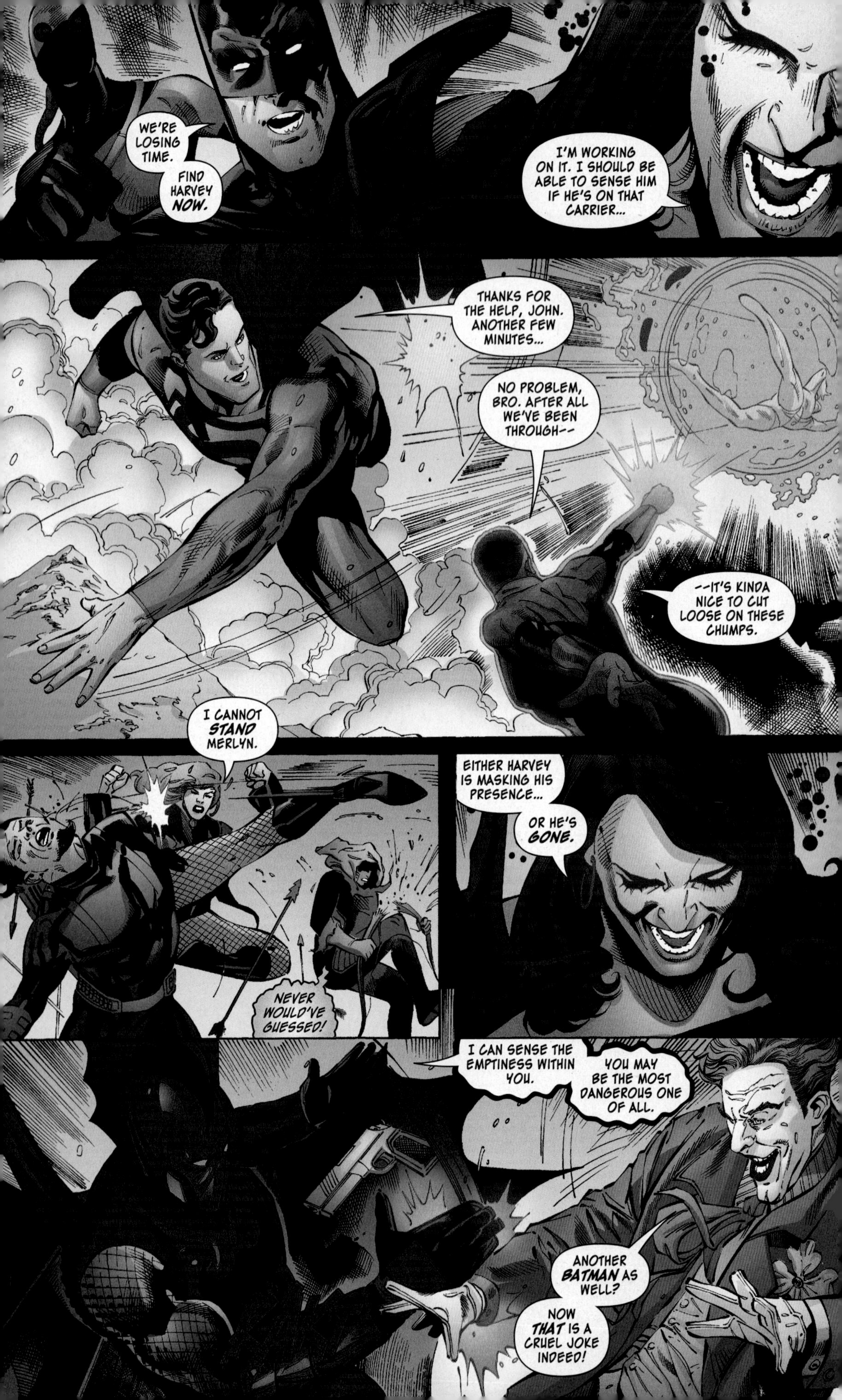
WE'RE LOSING TIME.
FIND HARVEY NOW.
I'M WORKING ON IT. I SHOULD BE ABLE TO SENSE HIM IF HE'S ON THAT CARRIER...
THANKS FOR THE HELP, JOHN. ANOTHER FEW MINUTES...
NO PROBLEM, BRO. AFTER ALL WE'VE BEEN THROUGH--
--IT'S KINDA NICE TO CUT LOOSE ON THESE CHUMPS.
I CANNOT STAND MERLYN.
NEVER WOULD'VE GUESSED!
EITHER HARVEY IS MASKING HIS PRESENCE...
OR HE'S GONE.
I CAN SENSE THE EMPTINESS WITHIN YOU.
YOU MAY BE THE MOST DANGEROUS ONE OF ALL.
ANOTHER BATMAN AS WELL?
NOW THAT IS A CRUEL JOKE INDEED!

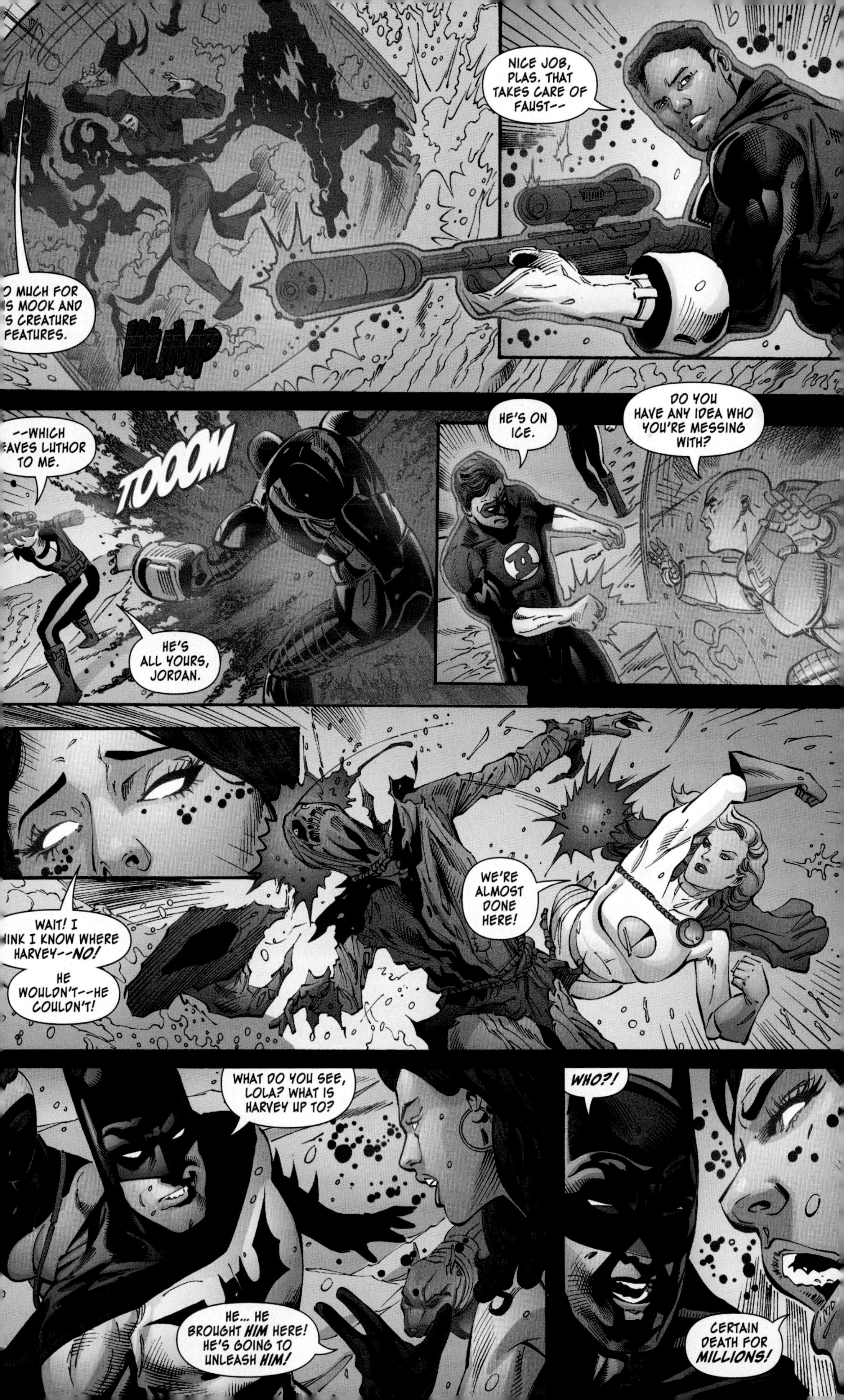
O MUCH FOR S MOOK AND S CREATURE FEATURES.
WUMP
NICE JOB, PLAS. THAT TAKES CARE OF FAUST--
--WHICH EAVES LUTHOR TO ME.
TOOOM
HE'S ALL YOURS, JORDAN.
HE'S ON ICE.
DO YOU HAVE ANY IDEA WHO YOU'RE MESSING WITH?
WAIT! I INK I KNOW WHERE HARVEY--*NO!*
HE WOULDN'T--HE COULDN'T!
WE'RE ALMOST DONE HERE!
WHAT DO YOU SEE, LOLA? WHAT IS HARVEY UP TO?
HE... HE BROUGHT *HIM* HERE! HE'S GOING TO UNLEASH *HIM!*
WHO?!
CERTAIN DEATH FOR *MILLIONS!*

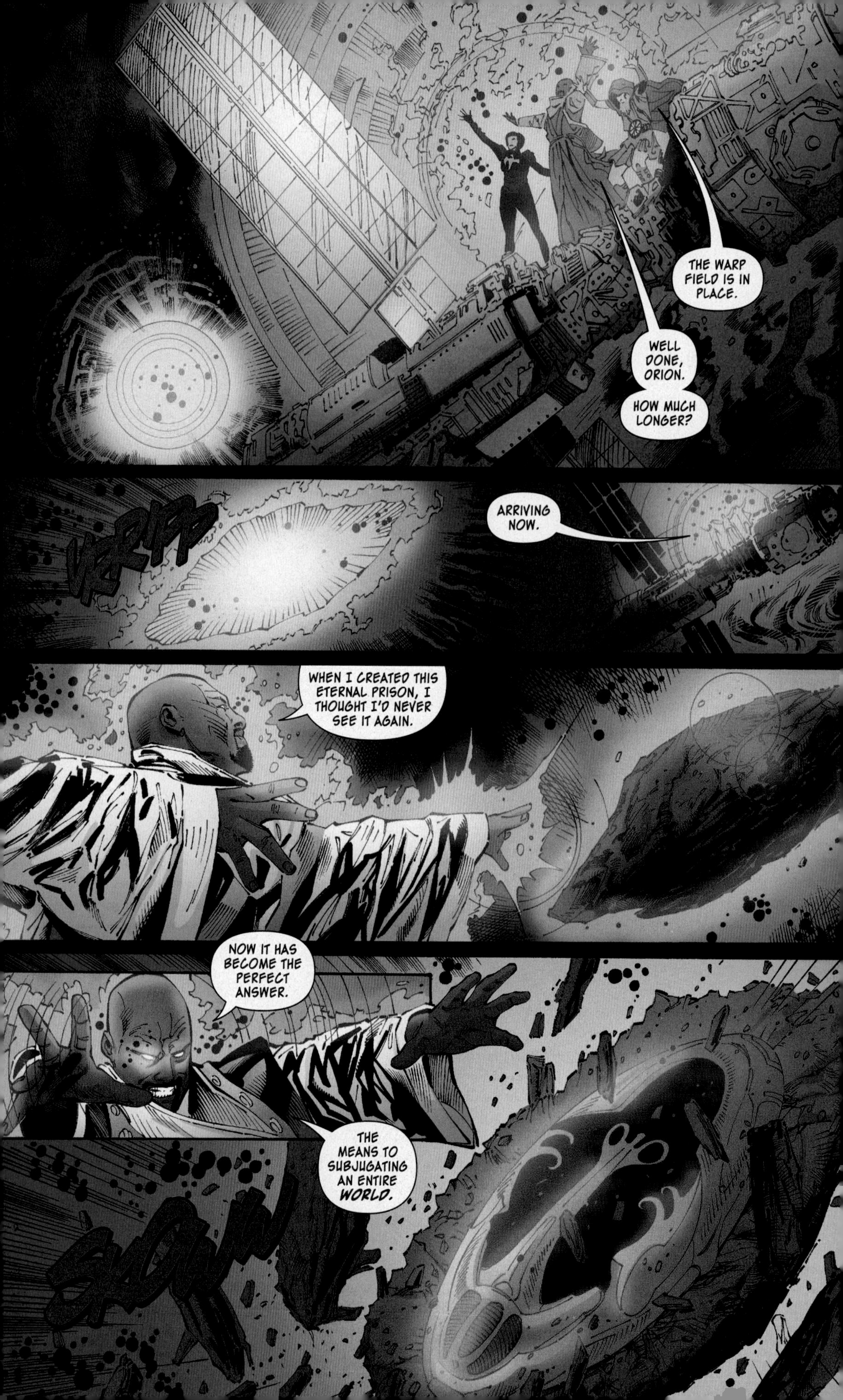

THE WARP FIELD IS IN PLACE.
WELL DONE, ORION.
HOW MUCH LONGER?
VRRIPP
ARRIVING NOW.
WHEN I CREATED THIS ETERNAL PRISON, I THOUGHT I'D NEVER SEE IT AGAIN.
NOW IT HAS BECOME THE PERFECT ANSWER.
THE MEANS TO SUBJUGATING AN ENTIRE WORLD.

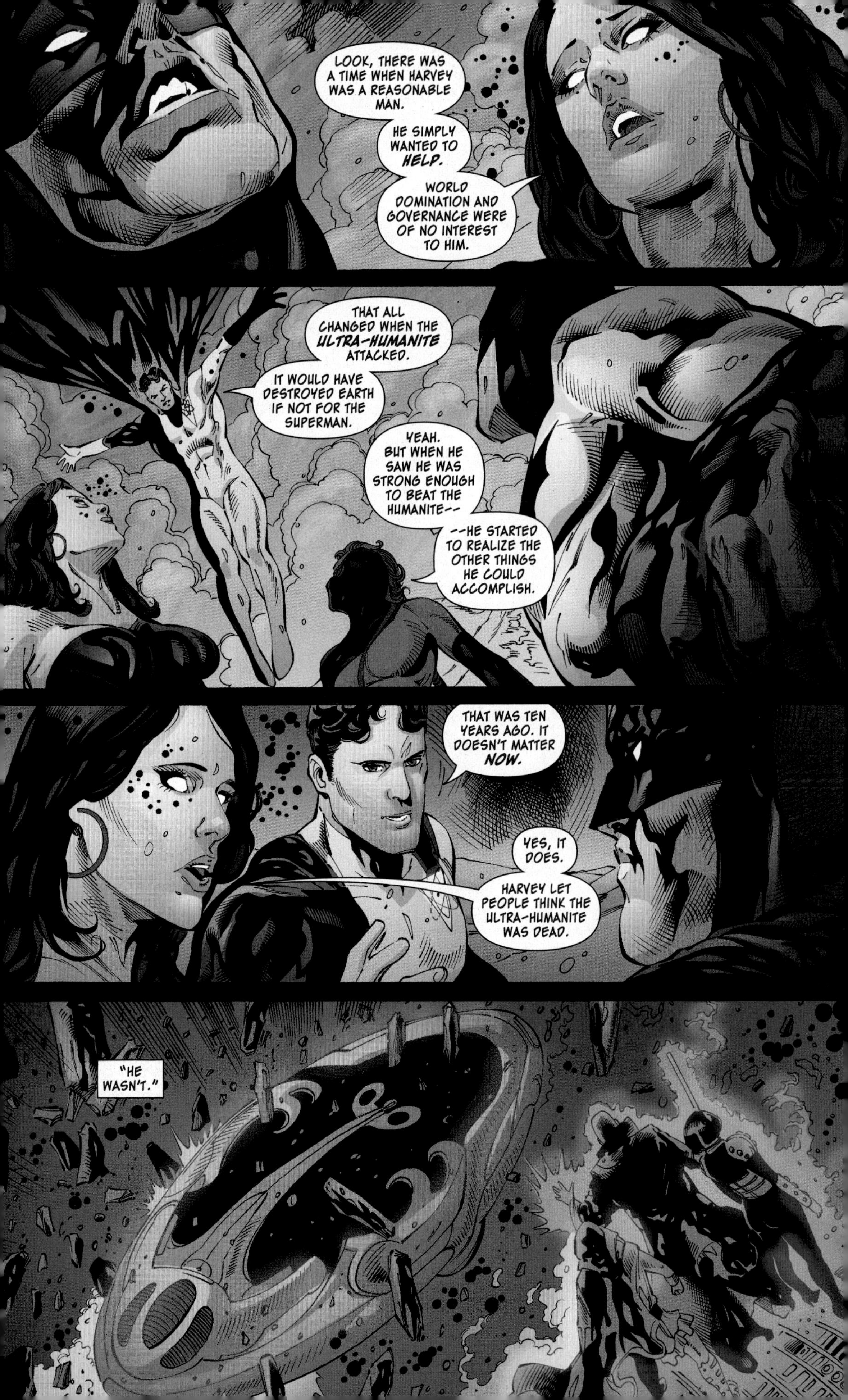

LOOK, THERE WAS A TIME WHEN HARVEY WAS A REASONABLE MAN.
HE SIMPLY WANTED TO HELP.
WORLD DOMINATION AND GOVERNANCE WERE OF NO INTEREST TO HIM.
THAT ALL CHANGED WHEN THE ULTRA-HUMANITE ATTACKED.
IT WOULD HAVE DESTROYED EARTH IF NOT FOR THE SUPERMAN.
YEAH. BUT WHEN HE SAW HE WAS STRONG ENOUGH TO BEAT THE HUMANITE--
--HE STARTED TO REALIZE THE OTHER THINGS HE COULD ACCOMPLISH.
THAT WAS TEN YEARS AGO. IT DOESN'T MATTER NOW.
YES, IT DOES.
HARVEY LET PEOPLE THINK THE ULTRA-HUMANITE WAS DEAD.
"HE WASN'T."

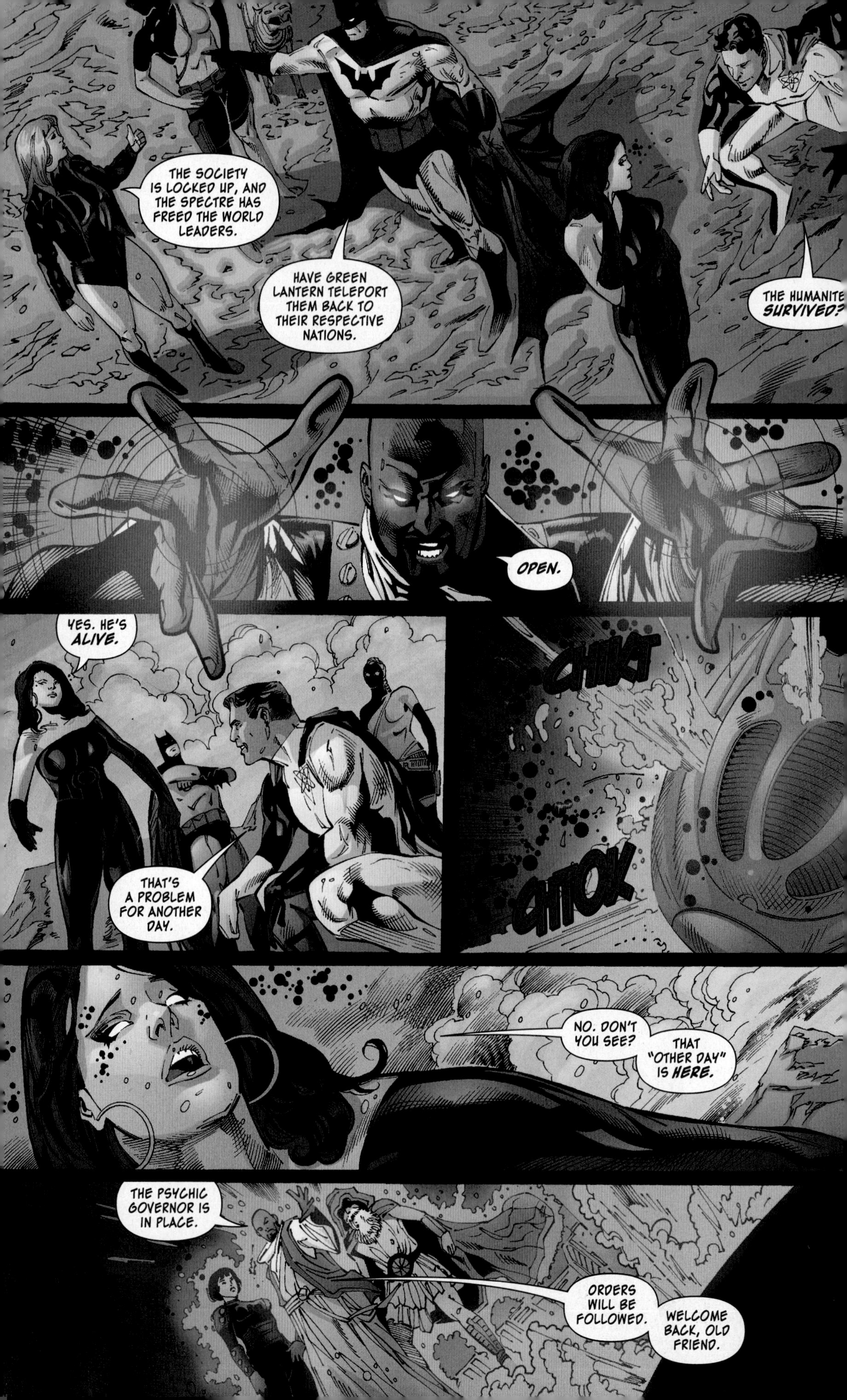

THE SOCIETY IS LOCKED UP, AND THE SPECTRE HAS FREED THE WORLD LEADERS.
HAVE GREEN LANTERN TELEPORT THEM BACK TO THEIR RESPECTIVE NATIONS.
THE HUMANITE SURVIVED?
OPEN.
YES. HE'S ALIVE.
THAT'S A PROBLEM FOR ANOTHER DAY.
CHKT
CHTOK
NO. DON'T YOU SEE?
THAT "OTHER DAY" IS HERE.
THE PSYCHIC GOVERNOR IS IN PLACE.
ORDERS WILL BE FOLLOWED.
WELCOME BACK, OLD FRIEND.

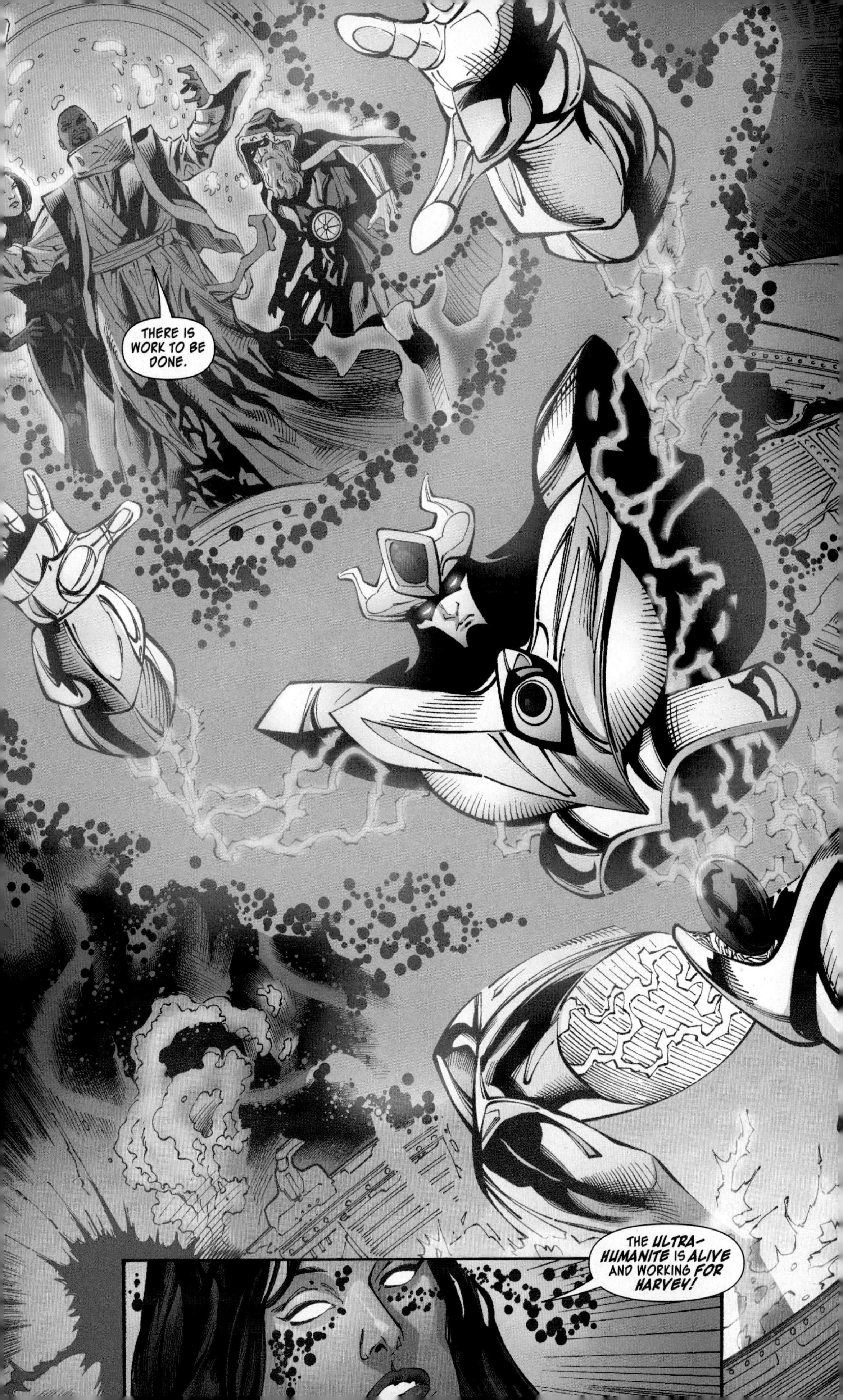
THERE IS WORK TO BE DONE.
THE ULTRA-HUMANITE IS ALIVE AND WORKING FOR HARVEY!

TangentComics™

Cover art by Dan Jurgens and Kevin Conrad.

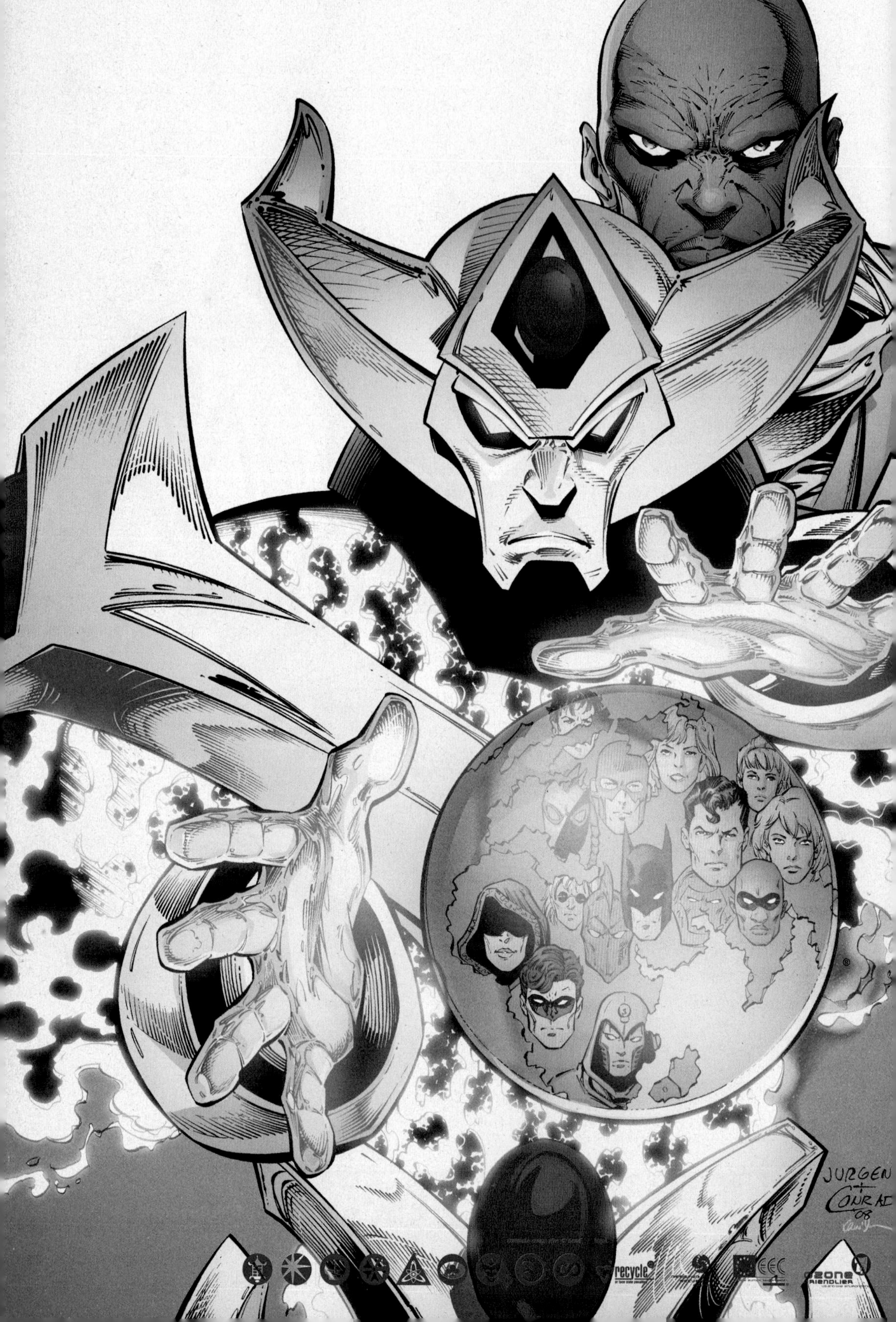

JURGEN + CONRAD '08

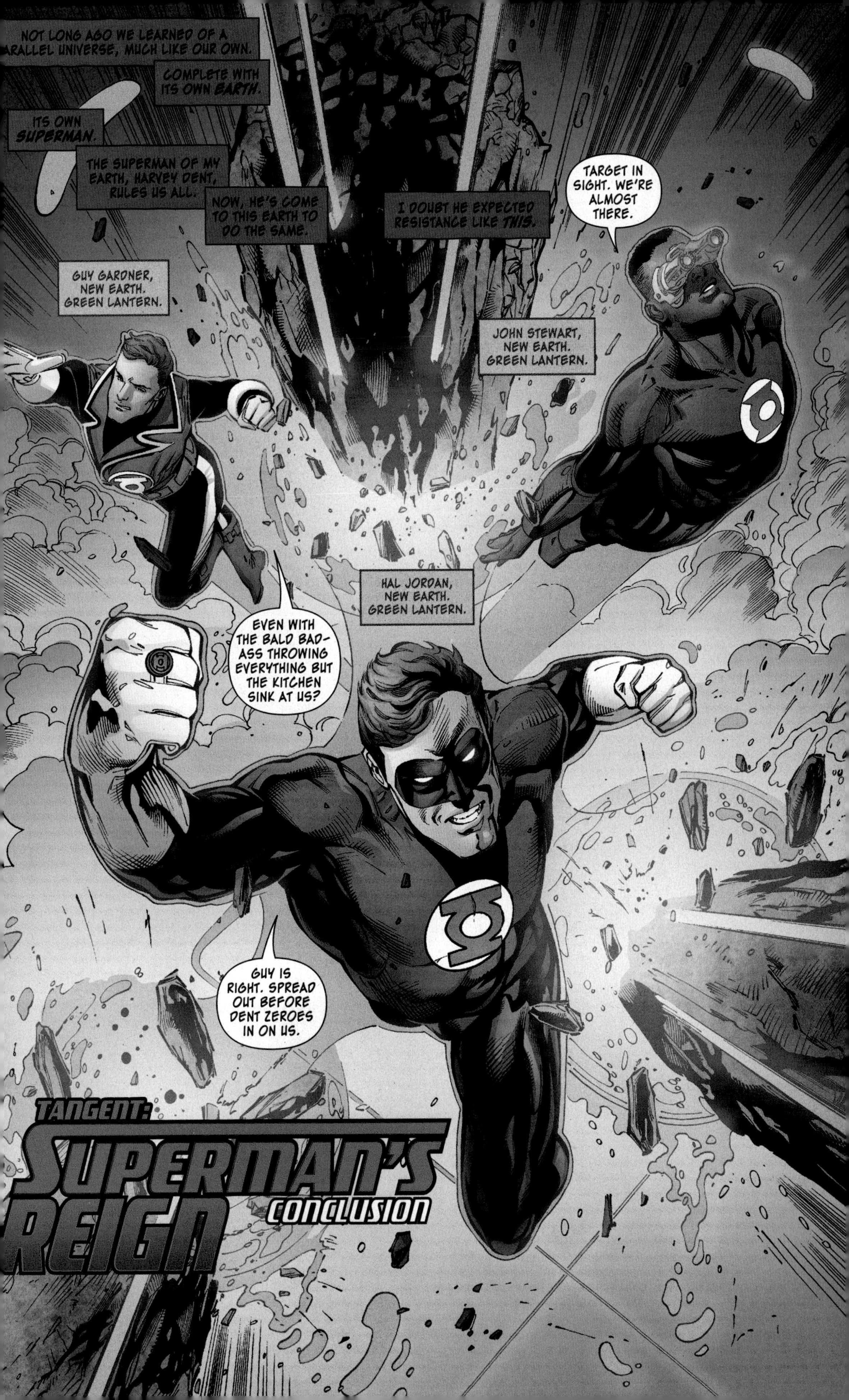

NOT LONG AGO WE LEARNED OF A PARALLEL UNIVERSE, MUCH LIKE OUR OWN.
COMPLETE WITH ITS OWN EARTH.
ITS OWN SUPERMAN.
THE SUPERMAN OF MY EARTH, HARVEY DENT, RULES US ALL.
NOW, HE'S COME TO THIS EARTH TO DO THE SAME.
I DOUBT HE EXPECTED RESISTANCE LIKE THIS.
TARGET IN SIGHT. WE'RE ALMOST THERE.
GUY GARDNER, NEW EARTH. GREEN LANTERN.
JOHN STEWART, NEW EARTH. GREEN LANTERN.
HAL JORDAN, NEW EARTH. GREEN LANTERN.
EVEN WITH THE BALD BAD-ASS THROWING EVERYTHING BUT THE KITCHEN SINK AT US?
GUY IS RIGHT. SPREAD OUT BEFORE DENT ZEROES IN ON US.
TANGENT: SUPERMAN'S REIGN
CONCLUSION

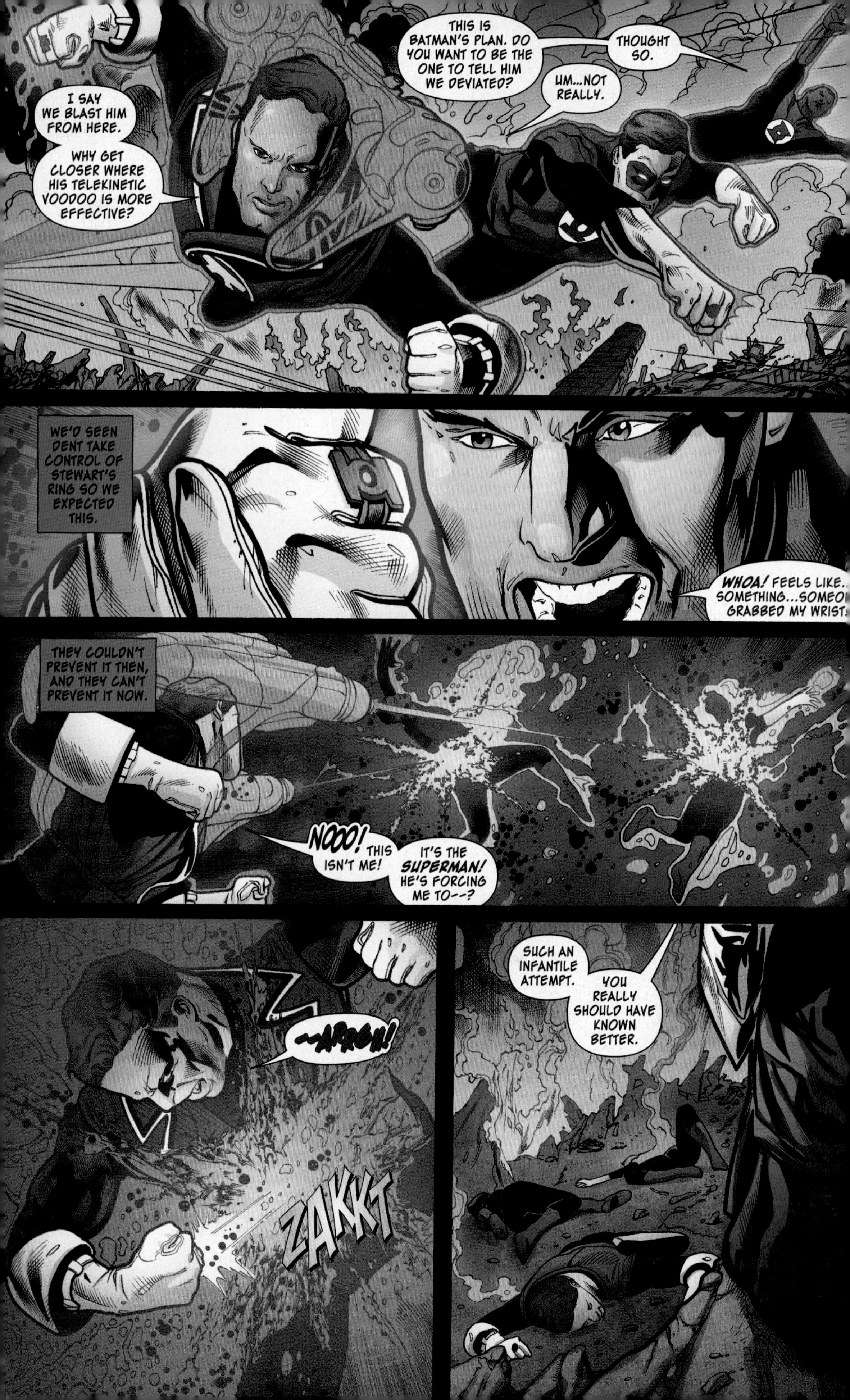
I SAY WE BLAST HIM FROM HERE.
WHY GET CLOSER WHERE HIS TELEKINETIC VOODOO IS MORE EFFECTIVE?
THIS IS BATMAN'S PLAN. DO YOU WANT TO BE THE ONE TO TELL HIM WE DEVIATED?
UM...NOT REALLY.
THOUGHT SO.
WE'D SEEN DENT TAKE CONTROL OF STEWART'S RING SO WE EXPECTED THIS.
WHOA! FEELS LIKE... SOMETHING...SOMEO GRABBED MY WRIST.
THEY COULDN'T PREVENT IT THEN, AND THEY CAN'T PREVENT IT NOW.
NOOO! THIS ISN'T ME!
IT'S THE SUPERMAN! HE'S FORCING ME TO--?
--ARRGH!
ZAKKT
SUCH AN INFANTILE ATTEMPT.
YOU REALLY SHOULD HAVE KNOWN BETTER.

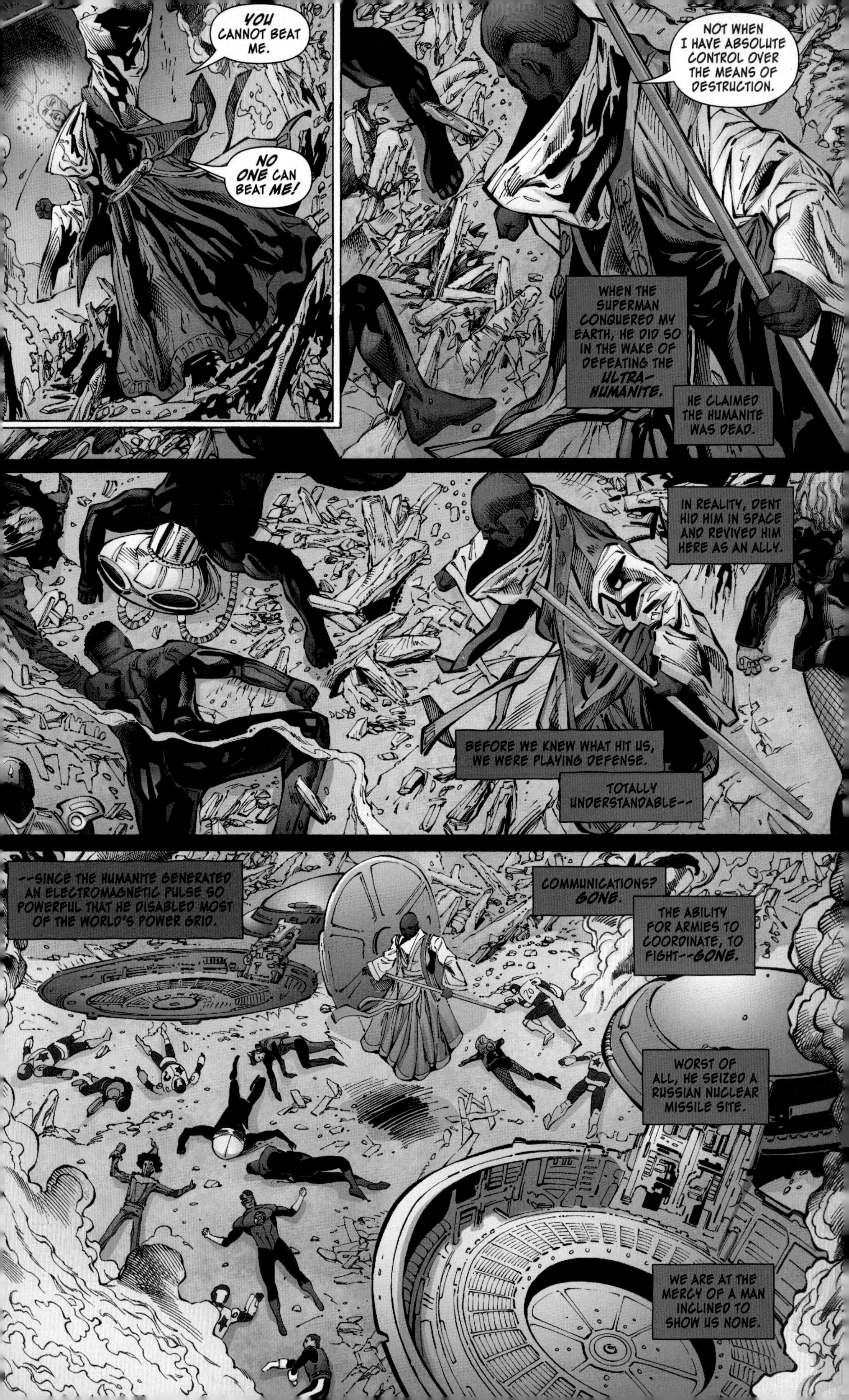
YOU CANNOT BEAT ME.
NO ONE CAN BEAT ME!
NOT WHEN I HAVE ABSOLUTE CONTROL OVER THE MEANS OF DESTRUCTION.
WHEN THE SUPERMAN CONQUERED MY EARTH, HE DID SO IN THE WAKE OF DEFEATING THE ULTRA-HUMANITE.
HE CLAIMED THE HUMANITE WAS DEAD.
IN REALITY, DENT HID HIM IN SPACE AND REVIVED HIM HERE AS AN ALLY.
BEFORE WE KNEW WHAT HIT US, WE WERE PLAYING DEFENSE.
TOTALLY UNDERSTANDABLE--
--SINCE THE HUMANITE GENERATED AN ELECTROMAGNETIC PULSE SO POWERFUL THAT HE DISABLED MOST OF THE WORLD'S POWER GRID.
COMMUNICATIONS? GONE.
THE ABILITY FOR ARMIES TO COORDINATE, TO FIGHT--GONE.
WORST OF ALL, HE SEIZED A RUSSIAN NUCLEAR MISSILE SITE.
WE ARE AT THE MERCY OF A MAN INCLINED TO SHOW US NONE.

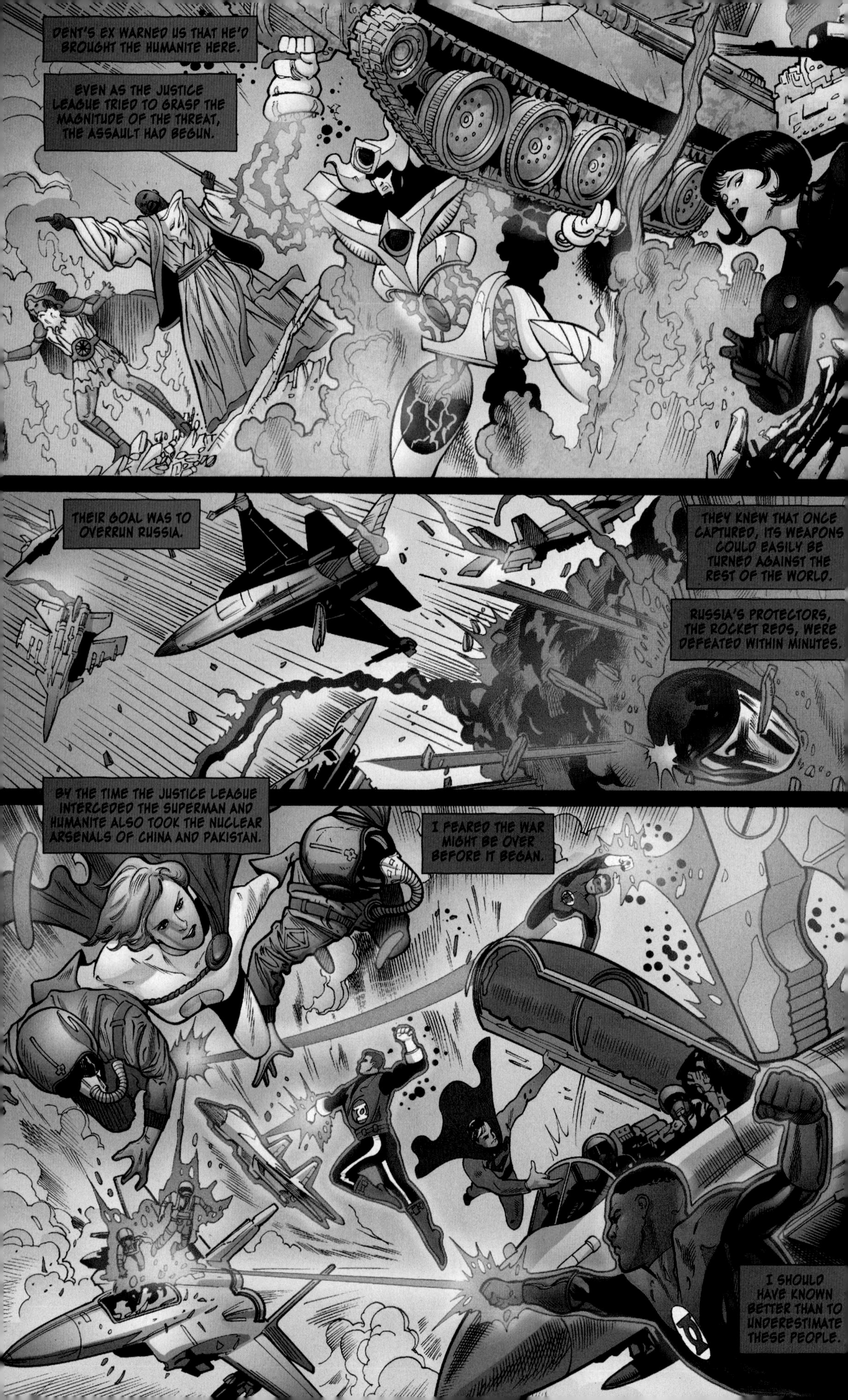
DENT'S EX WARNED US THAT HE'D BROUGHT THE HUMANITE HERE.
EVEN AS THE JUSTICE LEAGUE TRIED TO GRASP THE MAGNITUDE OF THE THREAT, THE ASSAULT HAD BEGUN.
THEIR GOAL WAS TO OVERRUN RUSSIA.
THEY KNEW THAT ONCE CAPTURED, ITS WEAPONS COULD EASILY BE TURNED AGAINST THE REST OF THE WORLD.
RUSSIA'S PROTECTORS, THE ROCKET REDS, WERE DEFEATED WITHIN MINUTES.
BY THE TIME THE JUSTICE LEAGUE INTERCEDED THE SUPERMAN AND HUMANITE ALSO TOOK THE NUCLEAR ARSENALS OF CHINA AND PAKISTAN.
I FEARED THE WAR MIGHT BE OVER BEFORE IT BEGAN.
I SHOULD HAVE KNOWN BETTER THAN TO UNDERESTIMATE THESE PEOPLE.

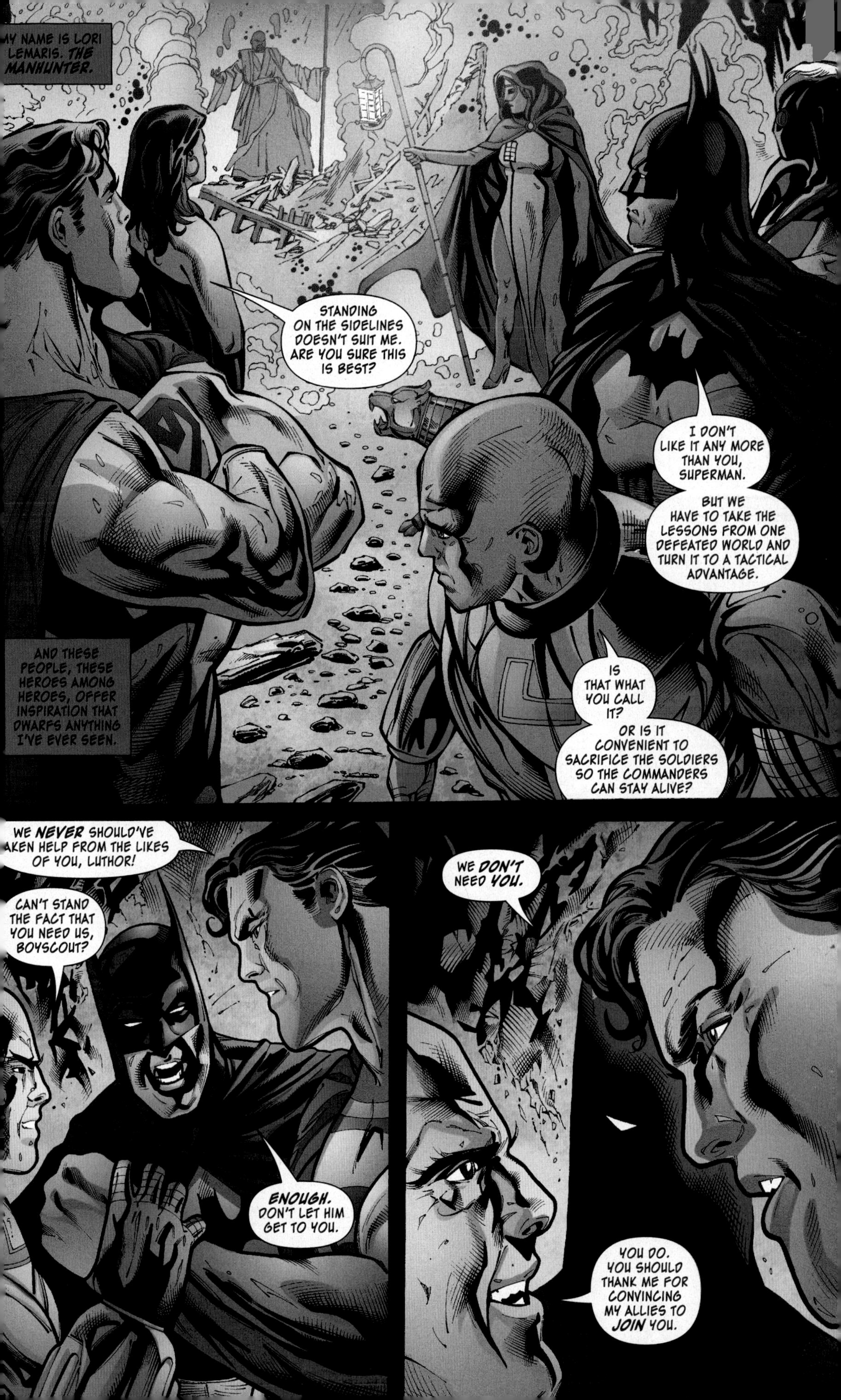

MY NAME IS LORI LEMARIS. THE MANHUNTER.
STANDING ON THE SIDELINES DOESN'T SUIT ME. ARE YOU SURE THIS IS BEST?
I DON'T LIKE IT ANY MORE THAN YOU, SUPERMAN.
BUT WE HAVE TO TAKE THE LESSONS FROM ONE DEFEATED WORLD AND TURN IT TO A TACTICAL ADVANTAGE.
AND THESE PEOPLE, THESE HEROES AMONG HEROES, OFFER INSPIRATION THAT DWARFS ANYTHING I'VE EVER SEEN.
IS THAT WHAT YOU CALL IT?
OR IS IT CONVENIENT TO SACRIFICE THE SOLDIERS SO THE COMMANDERS CAN STAY ALIVE?
WE NEVER SHOULD'VE AKEN HELP FROM THE LIKES OF YOU, LUTHOR!
CAN'T STAND THE FACT THAT YOU NEED US, BOYSCOUT?
ENOUGH. DON'T LET HIM GET TO YOU.
WE DON'T NEED YOU.
YOU DO. YOU SHOULD THANK ME FOR CONVINCING MY ALLIES TO JOIN YOU.

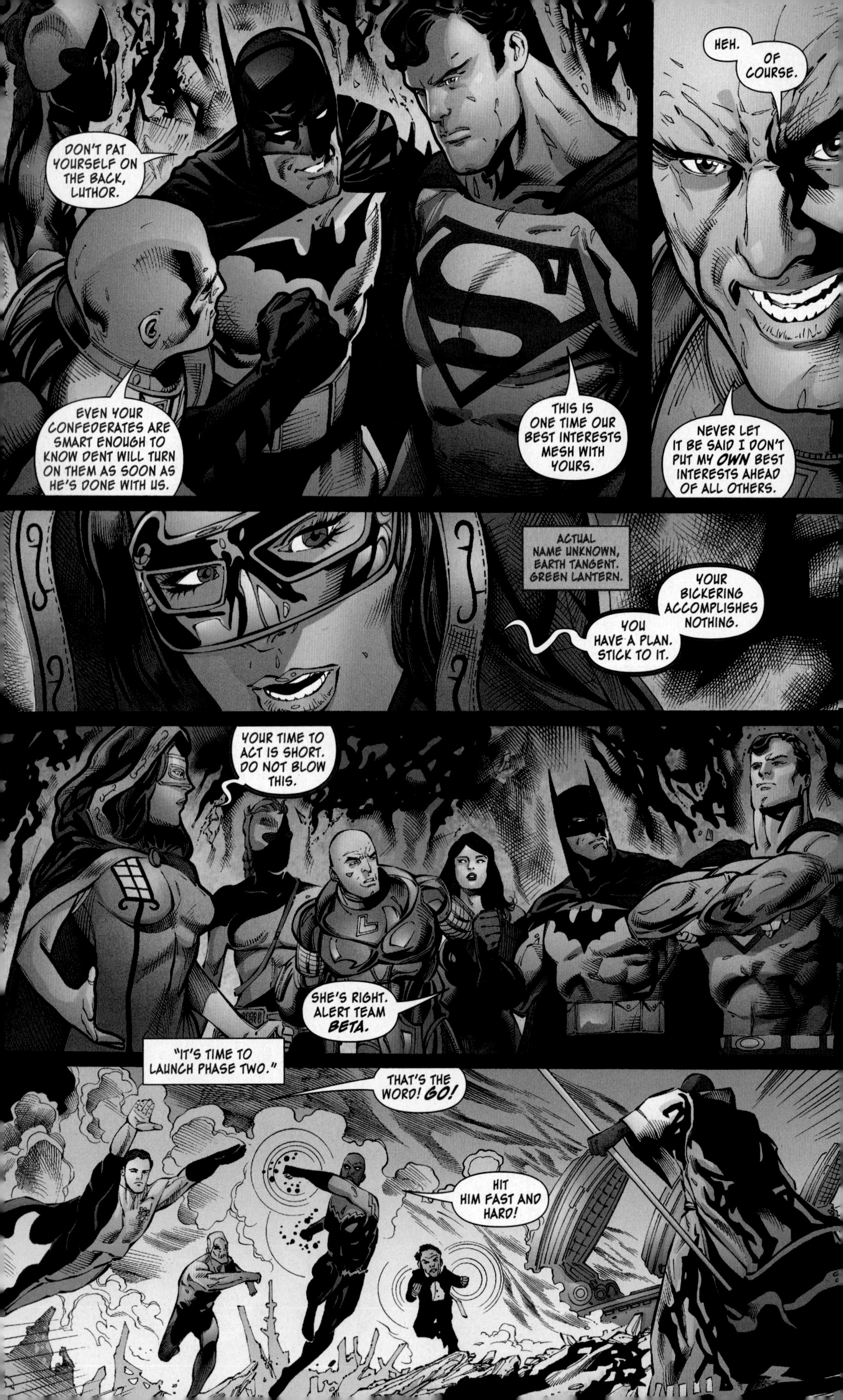
DON'T PAT YOURSELF ON THE BACK, LUTHOR.
EVEN YOUR CONFEDERATES ARE SMART ENOUGH TO KNOW DENT WILL TURN ON THEM AS SOON AS HE'S DONE WITH US.
THIS IS ONE TIME OUR BEST INTERESTS MESH WITH YOURS.
HEH.
OF COURSE.
NEVER LET IT BE SAID I DON'T PUT MY OWN BEST INTERESTS AHEAD OF ALL OTHERS.
ACTUAL NAME UNKNOWN, EARTH TANGENT. GREEN LANTERN.
YOUR BICKERING ACCOMPLISHES NOTHING.
YOU HAVE A PLAN. STICK TO IT.
YOUR TIME TO ACT IS SHORT. DO NOT BLOW THIS.
SHE'S RIGHT. ALERT TEAM BETA.
"IT'S TIME TO LAUNCH PHASE TWO."
THAT'S THE WORD! GO!
HIT HIM FAST AND HARD!

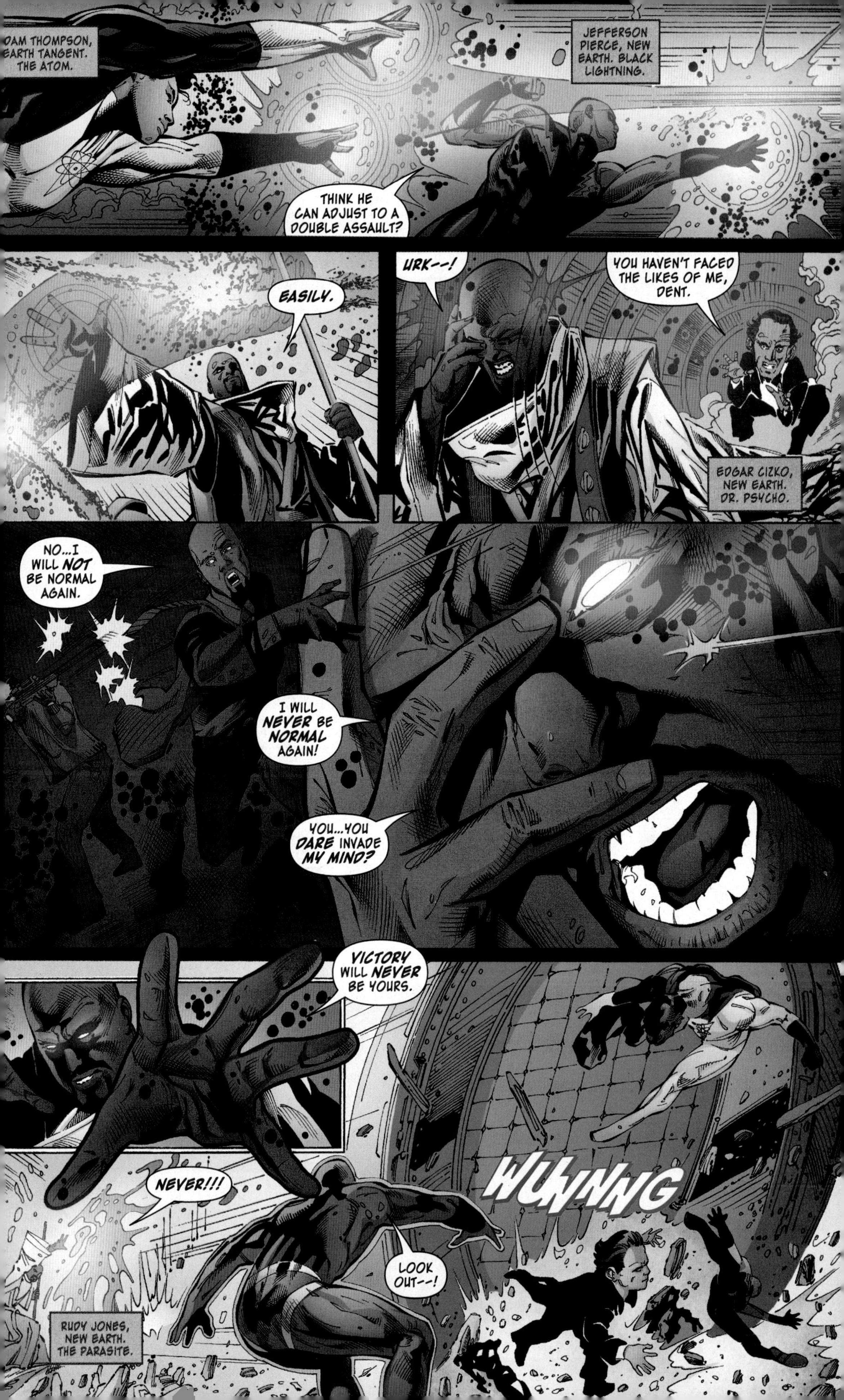

OAM THOMPSON, EARTH TANGENT. THE ATOM.
JEFFERSON PIERCE, NEW EARTH. BLACK LIGHTNING.
THINK HE CAN ADJUST TO A DOUBLE ASSAULT?
EASILY.
URK--!
YOU HAVEN'T FACED THE LIKES OF ME, DENT.
EDGAR CIZKO, NEW EARTH. DR. PSYCHO.
NO...I WILL NOT BE NORMAL AGAIN.
I WILL NEVER BE NORMAL AGAIN!
YOU...YOU DARE INVADE MY MIND?
VICTORY WILL NEVER BE YOURS.
NEVER!!!
WUNNNG
LOOK OUT--!
RUDY JONES, NEW EARTH. THE PARASITE.

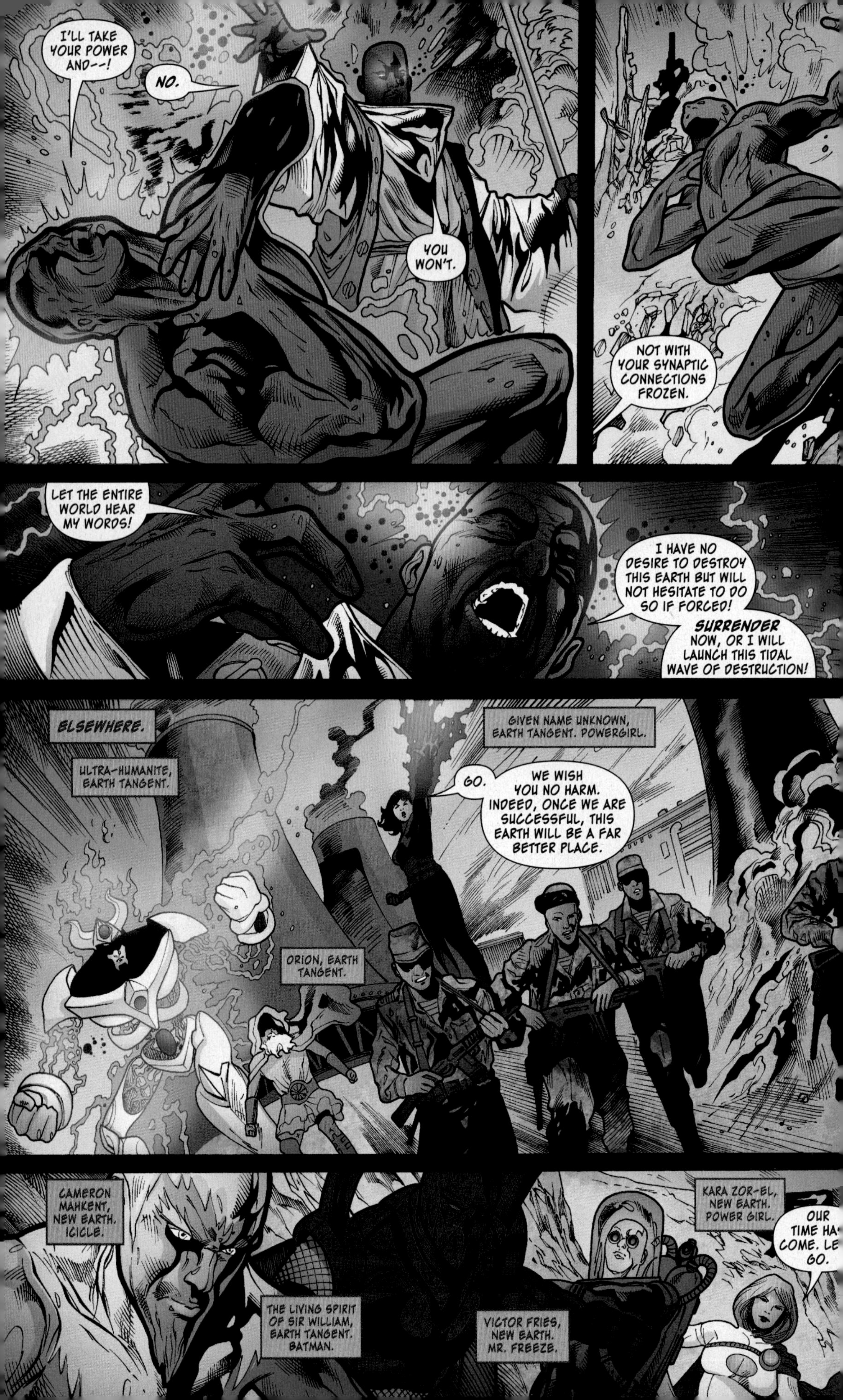

I'LL TAKE YOUR POWER AND--!
NO.
YOU WON'T.
NOT WITH YOUR SYNAPTIC CONNECTIONS FROZEN.
LET THE ENTIRE WORLD HEAR MY WORDS!
I HAVE NO DESIRE TO DESTROY THIS EARTH BUT WILL NOT HESITATE TO DO SO IF FORCED!
SURRENDER NOW, OR I WILL LAUNCH THIS TIDAL WAVE OF DESTRUCTION!
ELSEWHERE.
ULTRA-HUMANITE, EARTH TANGENT.
GIVEN NAME UNKNOWN, EARTH TANGENT. POWERGIRL.
GO.
WE WISH YOU NO HARM. INDEED, ONCE WE ARE SUCCESSFUL, THIS EARTH WILL BE A FAR BETTER PLACE.
ORION, EARTH TANGENT.
CAMERON MAHKENT, NEW EARTH. ICICLE.
THE LIVING SPIRIT OF SIR WILLIAM, EARTH TANGENT. BATMAN.
VICTOR FRIES, NEW EARTH. MR. FREEZE.
KARA ZOR-EL, NEW EARTH. POWER GIRL.
OUR TIME HA COME. LE GO.

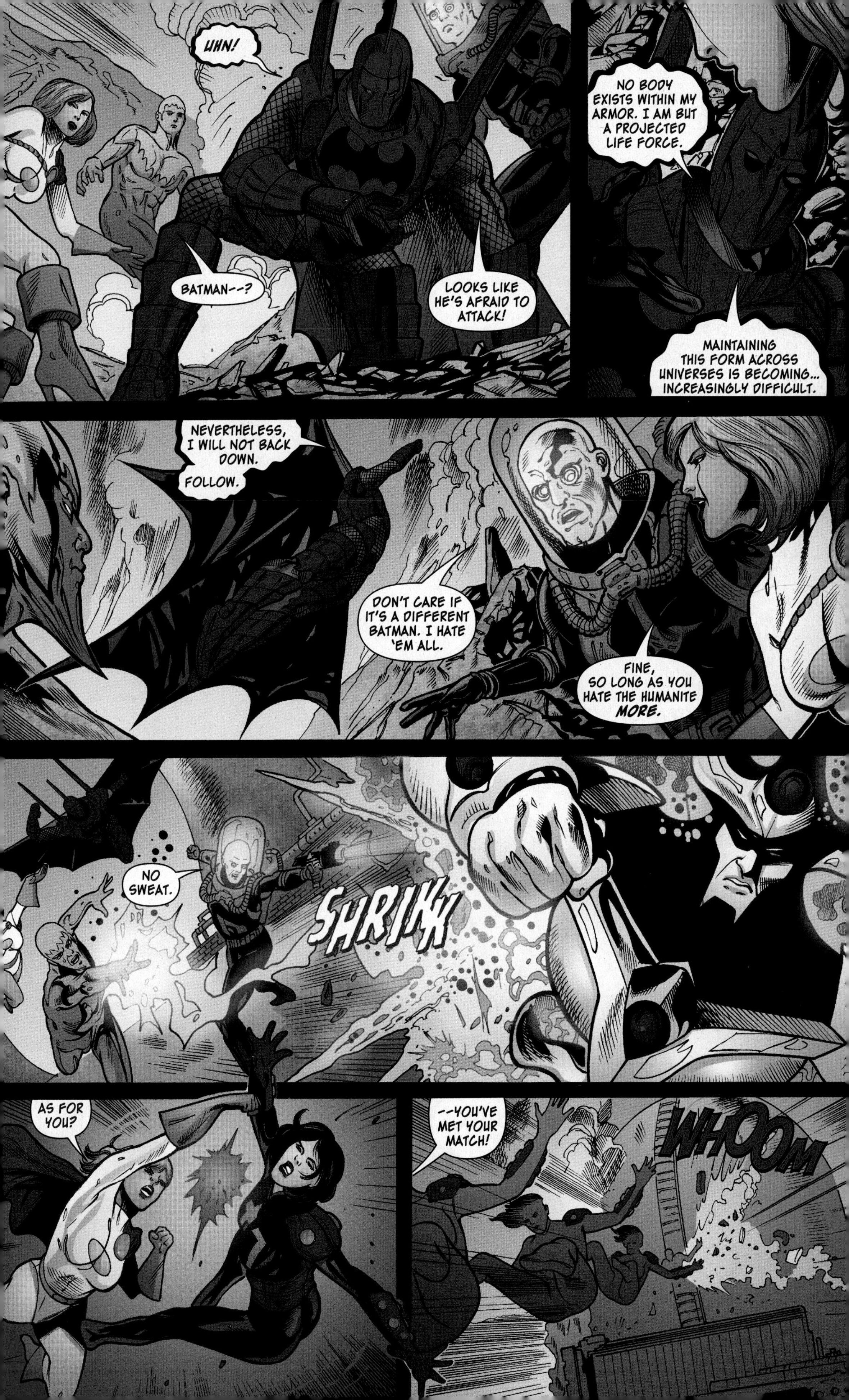
UHN!
BATMAN--?
LOOKS LIKE HE'S AFRAID TO ATTACK!
NO BODY EXISTS WITHIN MY ARMOR. I AM BUT A PROJECTED LIFE FORCE.
MAINTAINING THIS FORM ACROSS UNIVERSES IS BECOMING... INCREASINGLY DIFFICULT.
NEVERTHELESS, I WILL NOT BACK DOWN.
FOLLOW.
DON'T CARE IF IT'S A DIFFERENT BATMAN. I HATE 'EM ALL.
FINE, SO LONG AS YOU HATE THE HUMANITE MORE.
NO SWEAT.
SHRIKK
AS FOR YOU?
--YOU'VE MET YOUR MATCH!
WHOOM

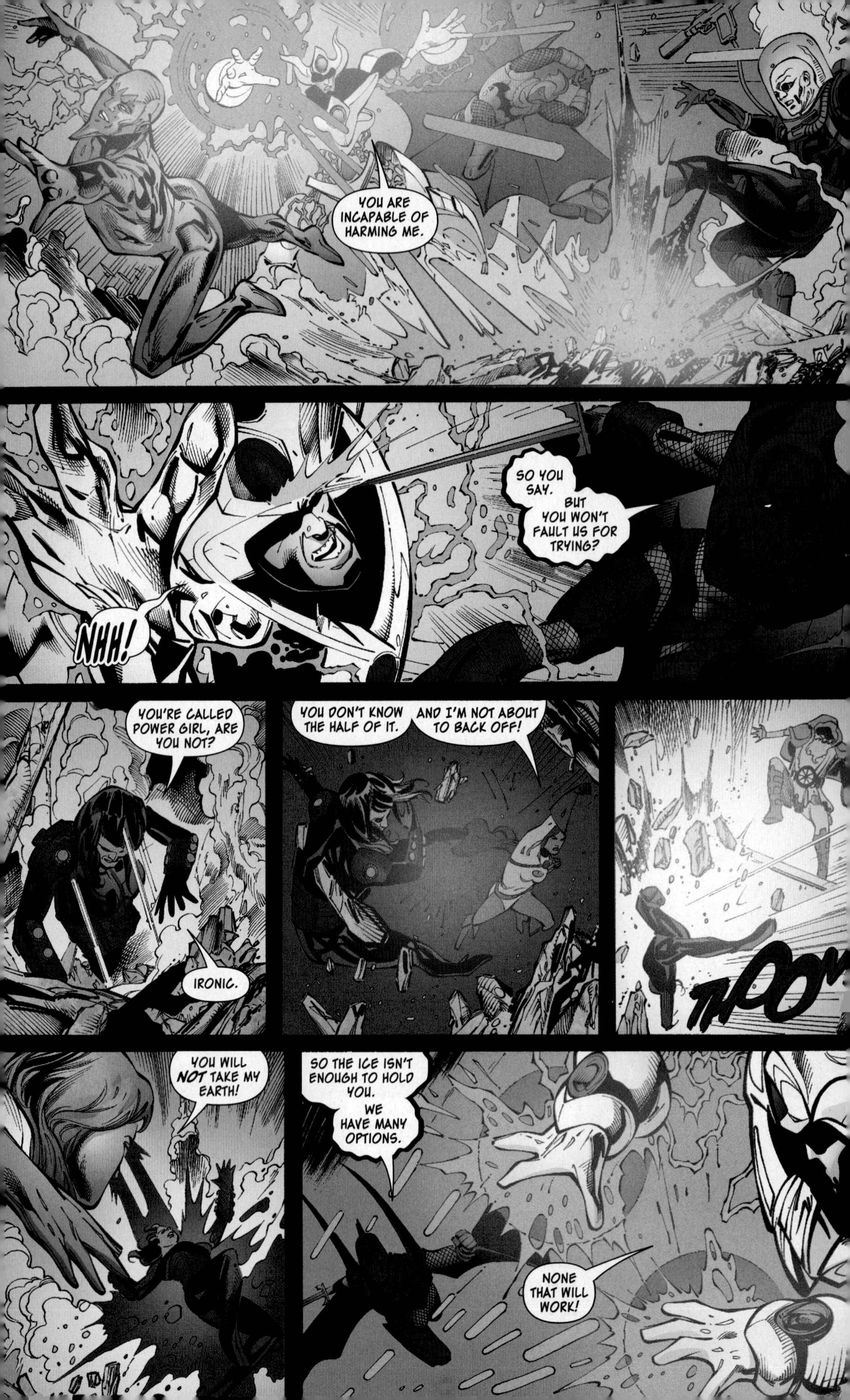
YOU ARE INCAPABLE OF HARMING ME.
SO YOU SAY.
BUT YOU WON'T FAULT US FOR TRYING?
NHH!
YOU'RE CALLED POWER GIRL, ARE YOU NOT?
IRONIC.
YOU DON'T KNOW THE HALF OF IT.
AND I'M NOT ABOUT TO BACK OFF!
YOU WILL NOT TAKE MY EARTH!
SO THE ICE ISN'T ENOUGH TO HOLD YOU.
WE HAVE MANY OPTIONS.
NONE THAT WILL WORK!

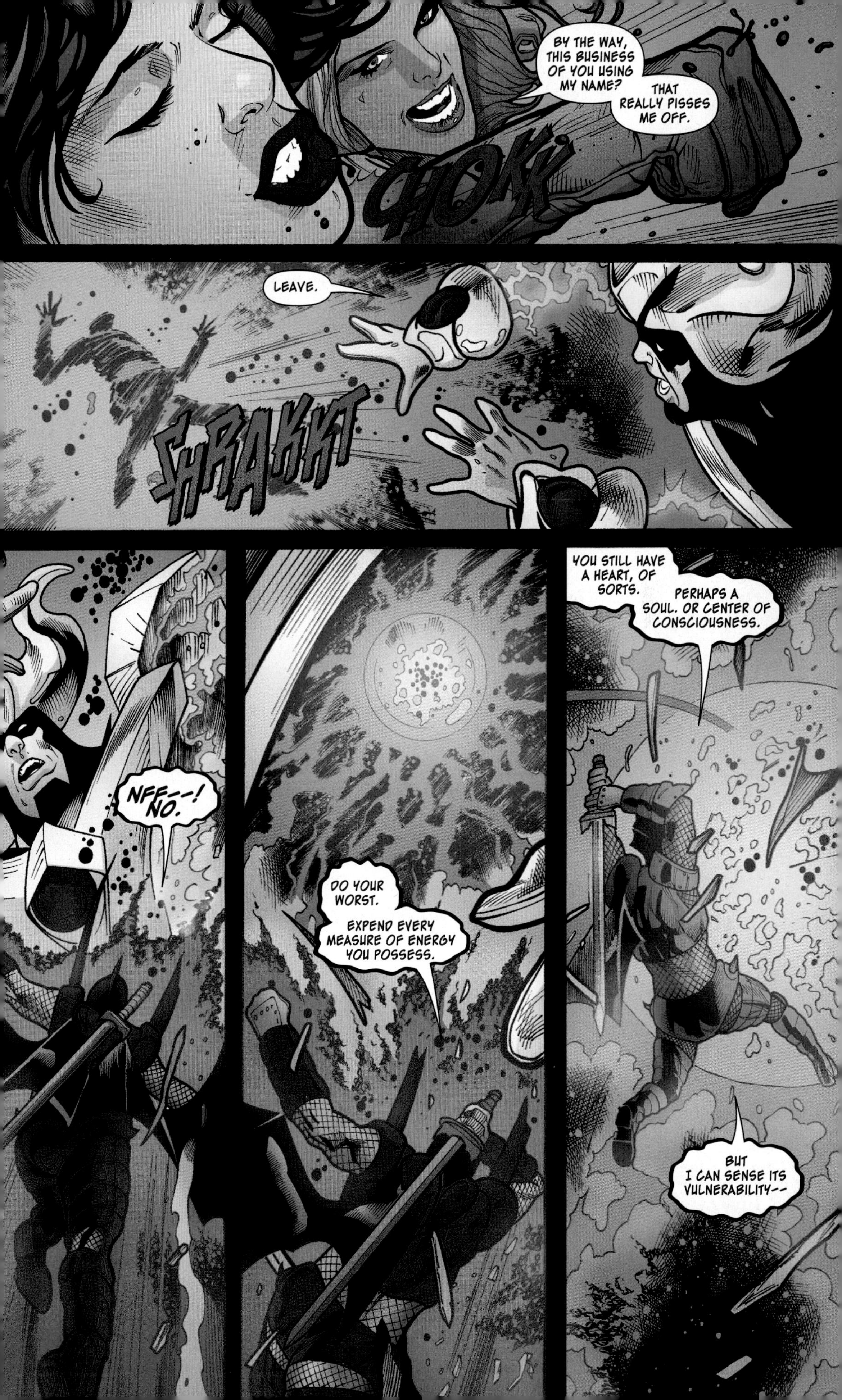
BY THE WAY, THIS BUSINESS OF YOU USING MY NAME?
THAT REALLY PISSES ME OFF.
CHOK!
LEAVE.
SHRAKKT
NFF--! NO.
DO YOUR WORST.
EXPEND EVERY MEASURE OF ENERGY YOU POSSESS.
YOU STILL HAVE A HEART, OF SORTS.
PERHAPS A SOUL. OR CENTER OF CONSCIOUSNESS.
BUT I CAN SENSE ITS VULNERABILITY--

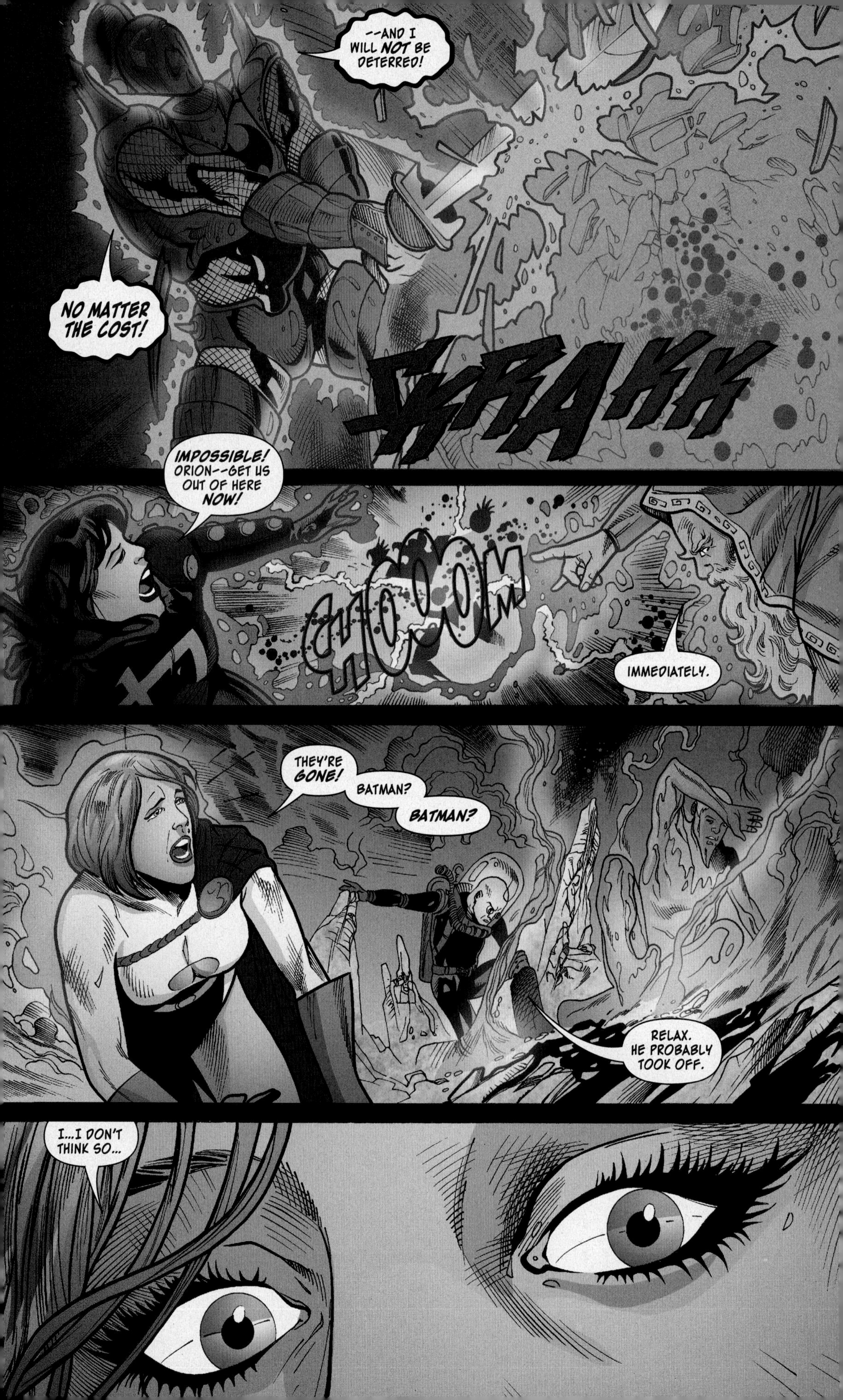

--AND I WILL NOT BE DETERRED!
NO MATTER THE COST!
SKRAKK
IMPOSSIBLE! ORION--GET US OUT OF HERE NOW!
CHOOOM
IMMEDIATELY.
THEY'RE GONE!
BATMAN?
BATMAN?
RELAX. HE PROBABLY TOOK OFF.
I...I DON'T THINK SO...

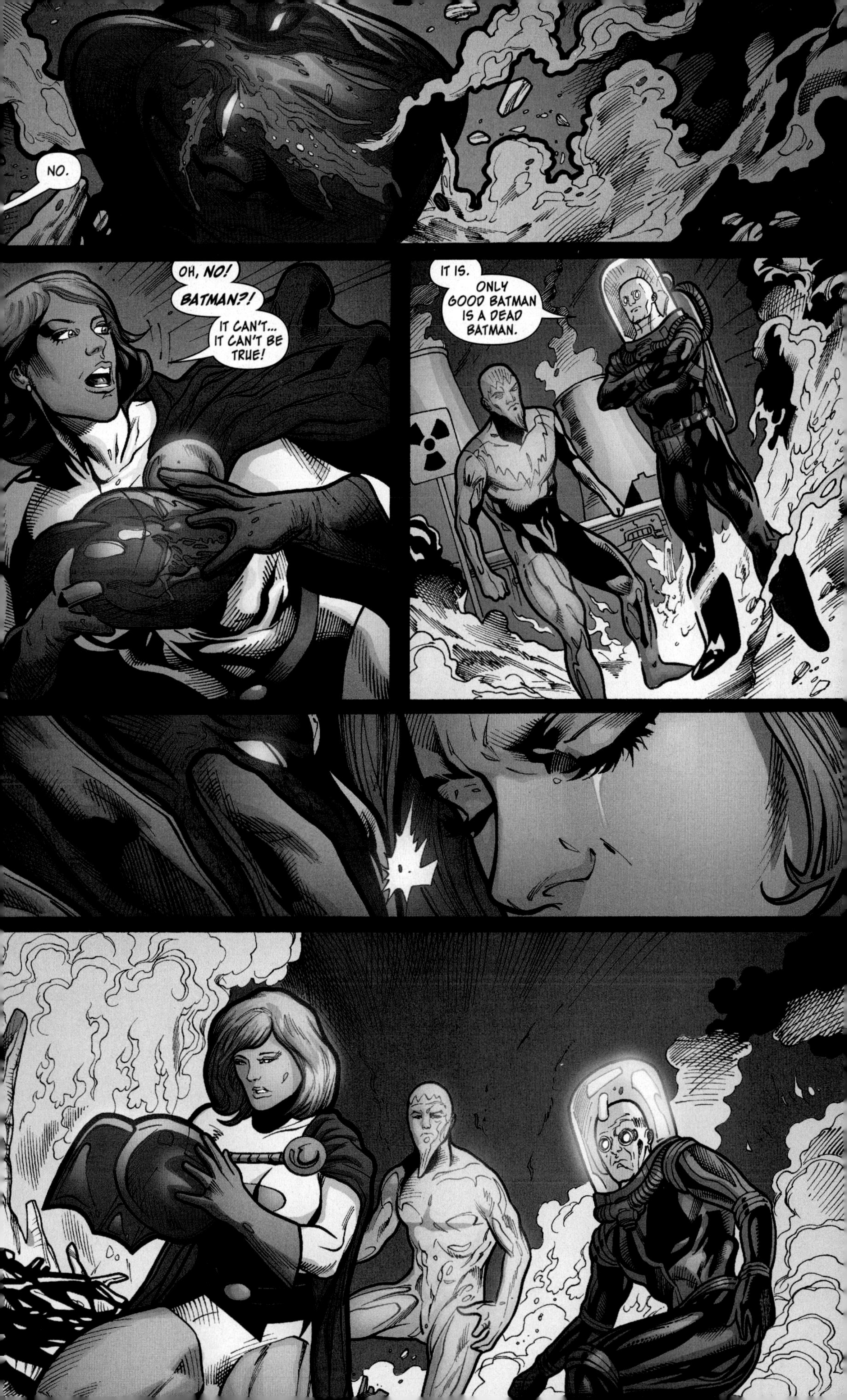
NO.
OH, NO!
BATMAN?!
IT CAN'T... IT CAN'T BE TRUE!
IT IS.
ONLY GOOD BATMAN IS A DEAD BATMAN.

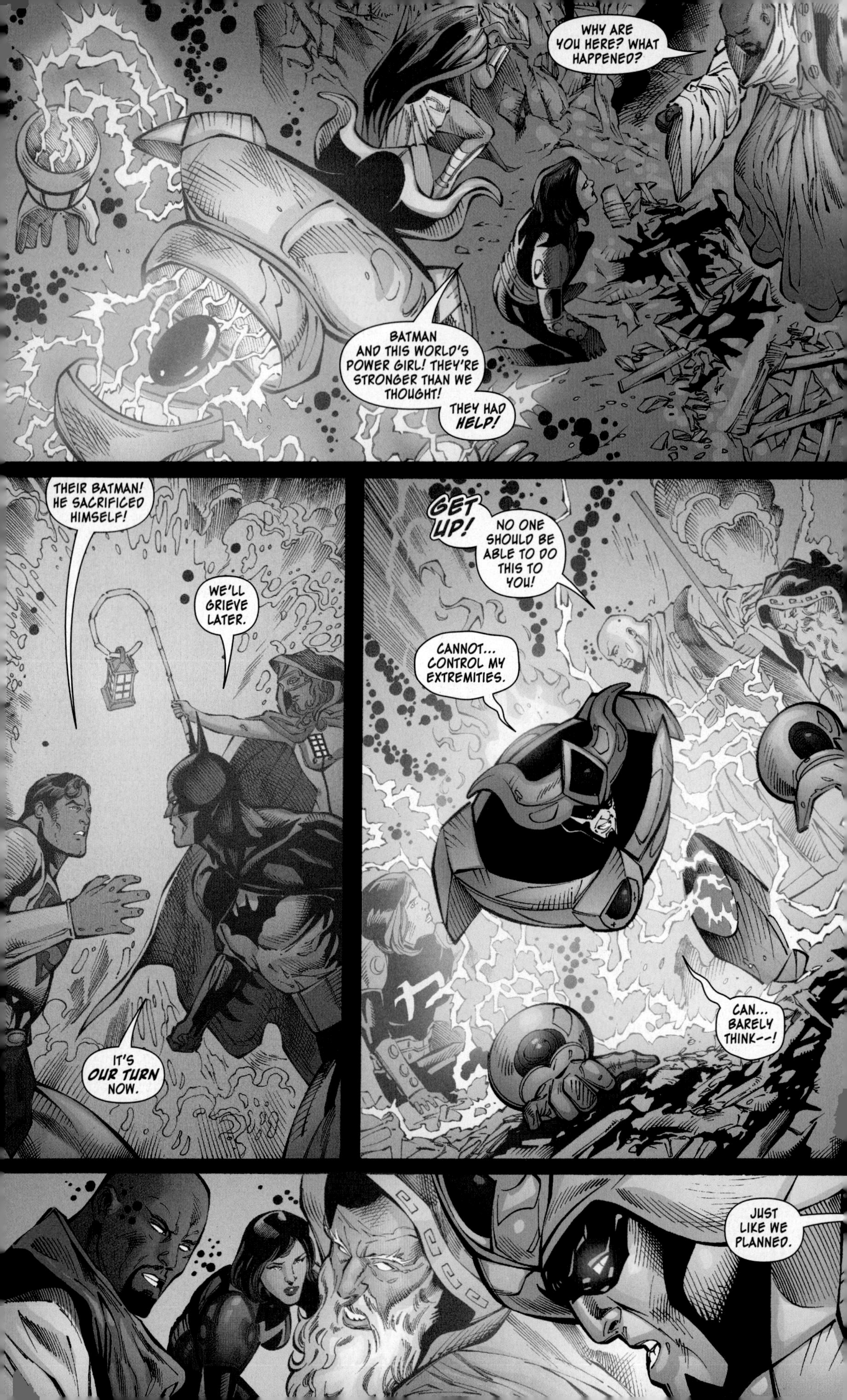
WHY ARE YOU HERE? WHAT HAPPENED?
BATMAN AND THIS WORLD'S POWER GIRL! THEY'RE STRONGER THAN WE THOUGHT!
THEY HAD HELP!
THEIR BATMAN! HE SACRIFICED HIMSELF!
WE'LL GRIEVE LATER.
IT'S OUR TURN NOW.
GET UP!
NO ONE SHOULD BE ABLE TO DO THIS TO YOU!
CANNOT... CONTROL MY EXTREMITIES.
CAN... BARELY THINK--!
JUST LIKE WE PLANNED.

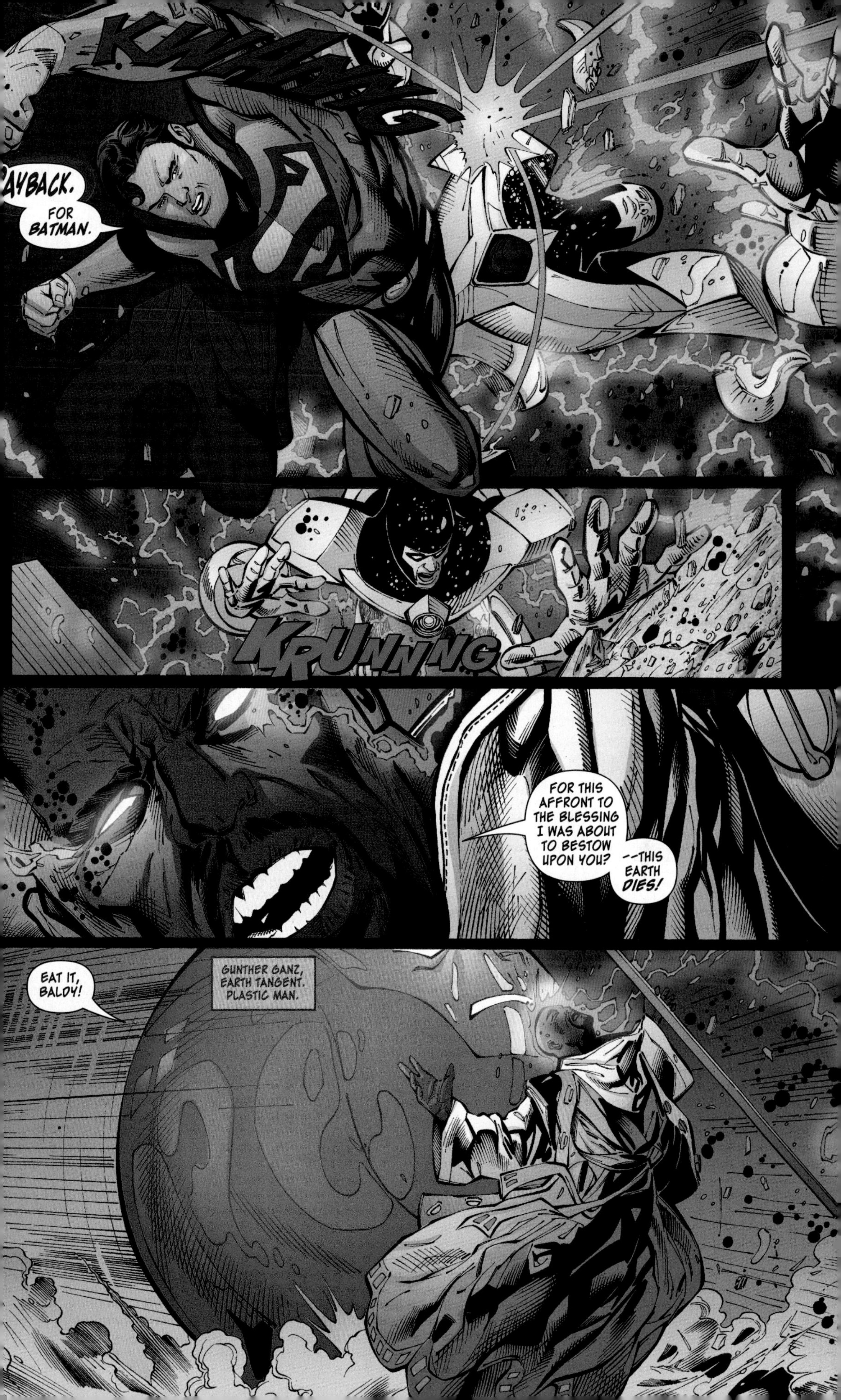
KWHAMG
AYBACK.
FOR BATMAN.
KRUNNNG
FOR THIS AFFRONT TO THE BLESSING I WAS ABOUT TO BESTOW UPON YOU?
--THIS EARTH DIES!
EAT IT, BALDY!
GUNTHER GANZ, EARTH TANGENT. PLASTIC MAN.

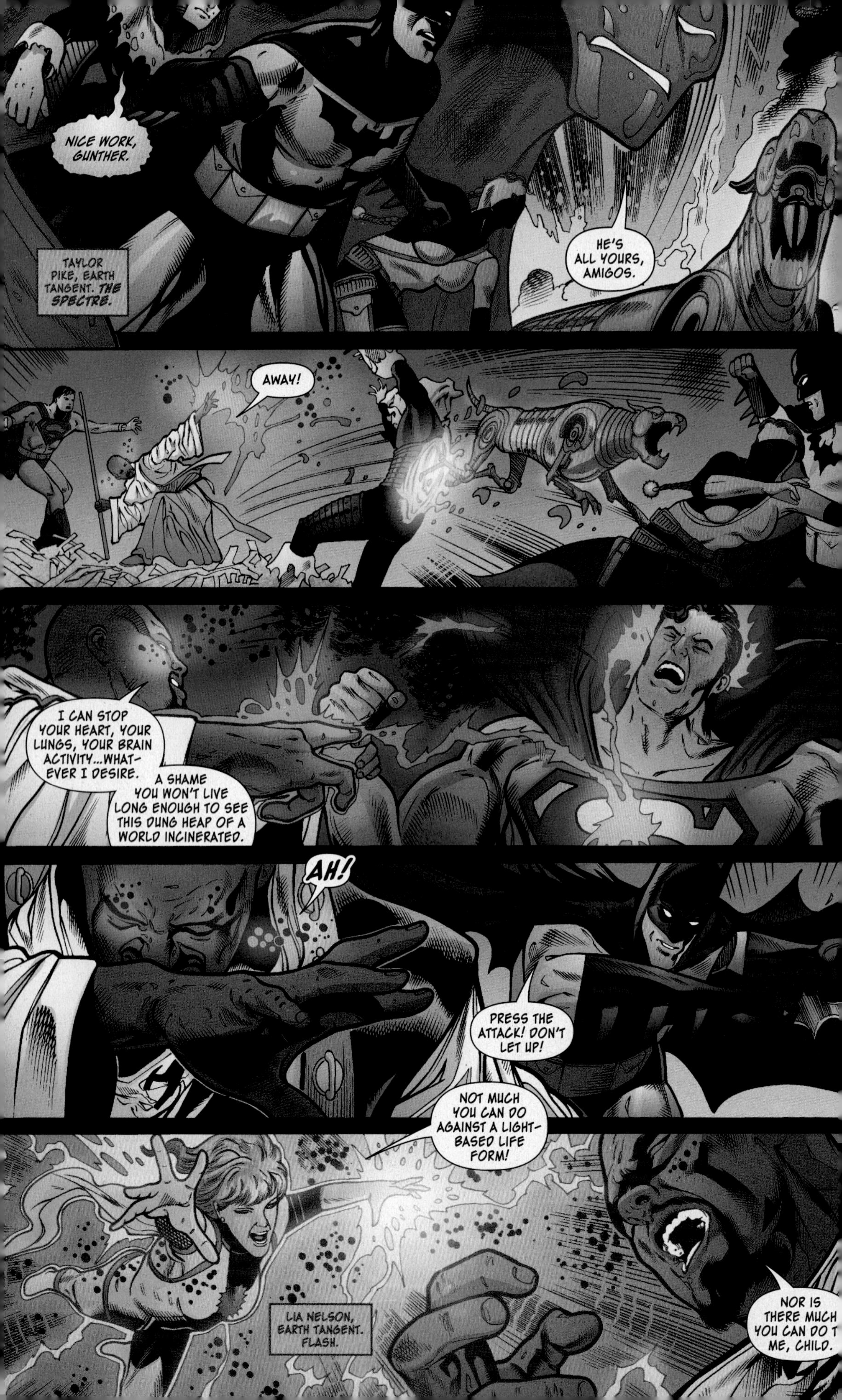

NICE WORK, GUNTHER.
TAYLOR PIKE, EARTH TANGENT. THE SPECTRE.
HE'S ALL YOURS, AMIGOS.
AWAY!
I CAN STOP YOUR HEART, YOUR LUNGS, YOUR BRAIN ACTIVITY...WHATEVER I DESIRE.
A SHAME YOU WON'T LIVE LONG ENOUGH TO SEE THIS DUNG HEAP OF A WORLD INCINERATED.
AH!
PRESS THE ATTACK! DON'T LET UP!
NOT MUCH YOU CAN DO AGAINST A LIGHT-BASED LIFE FORM!
LIA NELSON, EARTH TANGENT. FLASH.
NOR IS THERE MUCH YOU CAN DO T ME, CHILD.

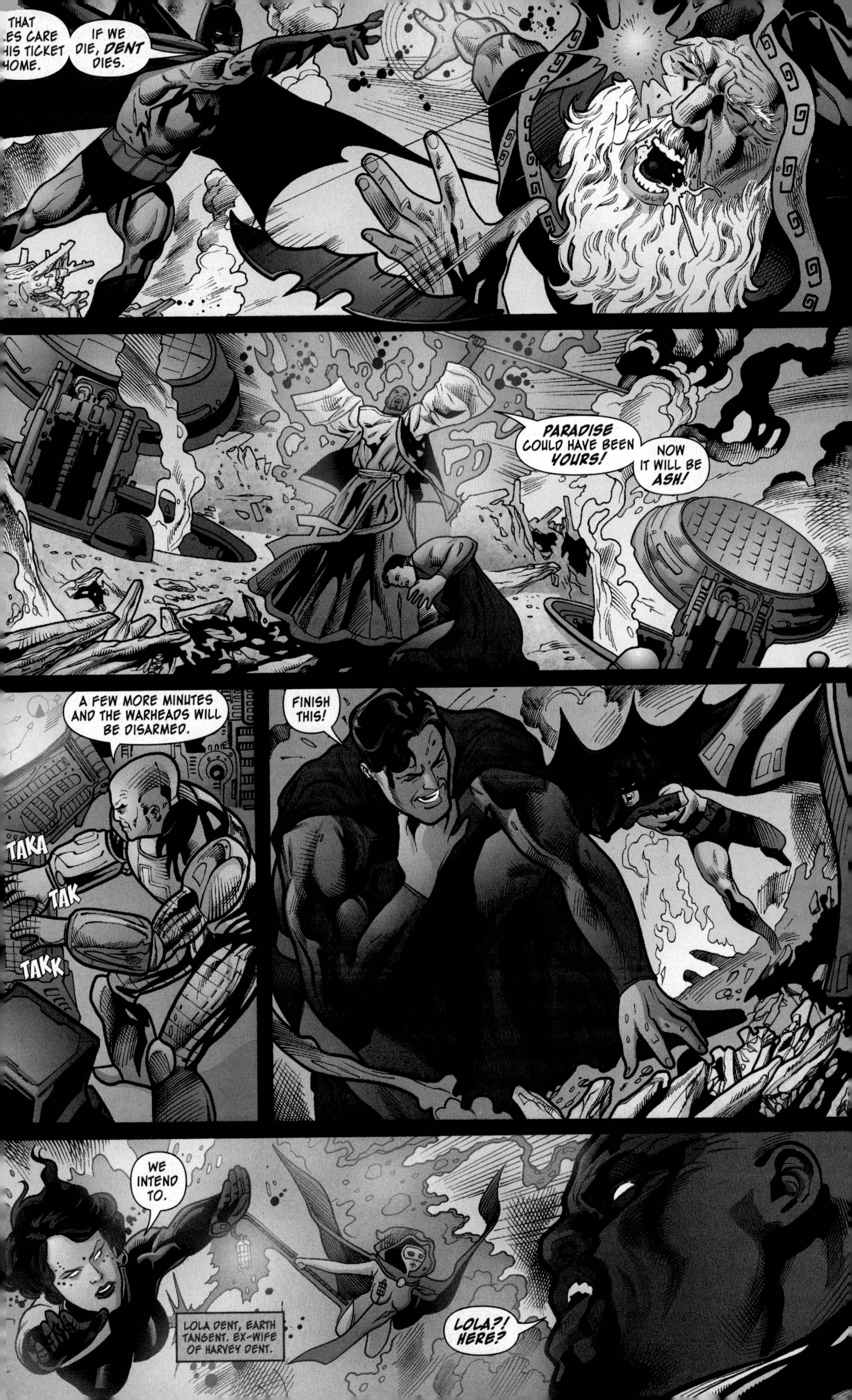

THAT ES CARE HIS TICKET HOME.
IF WE DIE, DENT DIES.
PARADISE COULD HAVE BEEN YOURS!
NOW IT WILL BE ASH!
A FEW MORE MINUTES AND THE WARHEADS WILL BE DISARMED.
TAKA
TAK
TAKK
FINISH THIS!
WE INTEND TO.
LOLA DENT, EARTH TANGENT. EX-WIFE OF HARVEY DENT.
LOLA?! HERE?

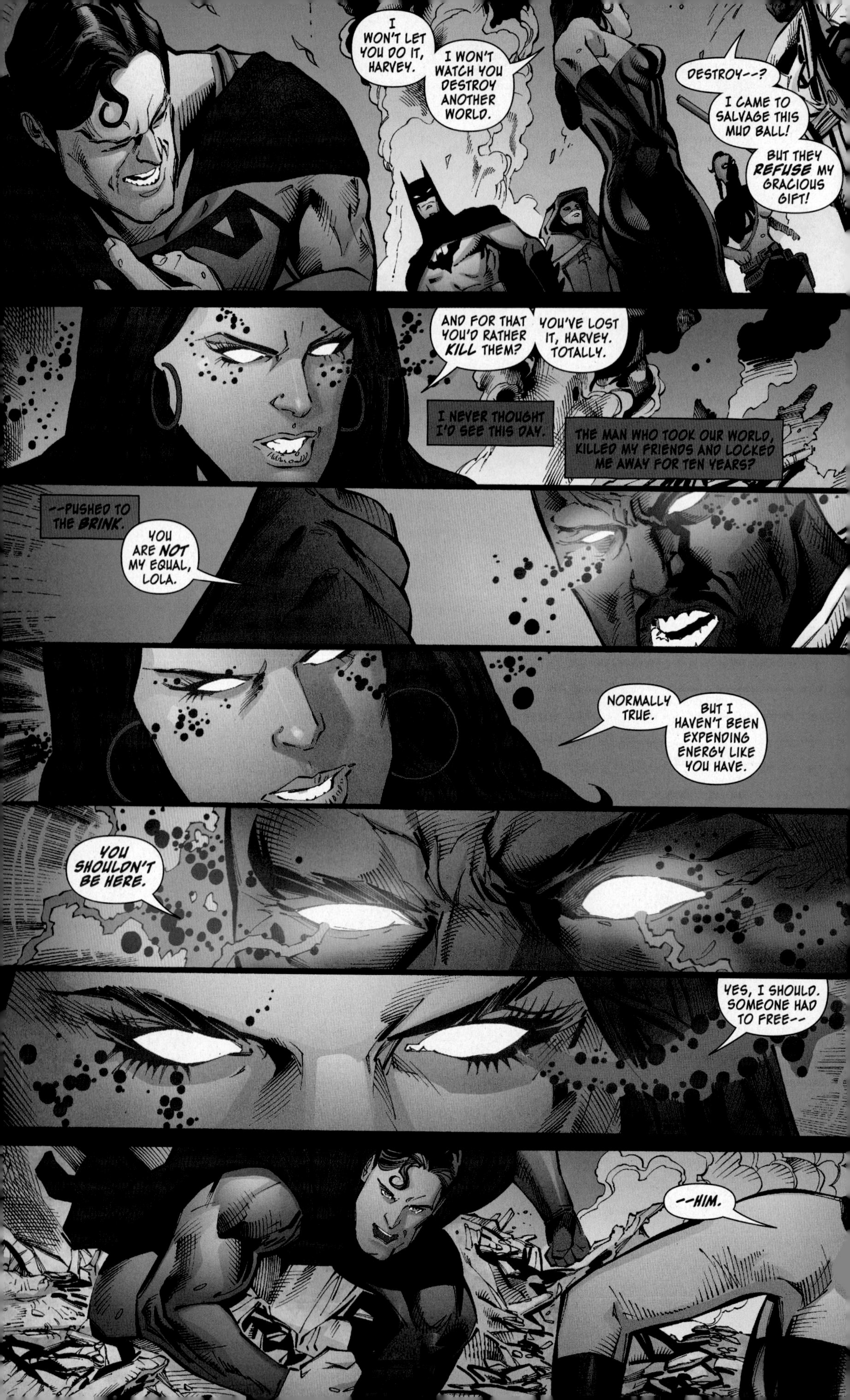
I WON'T LET YOU DO IT, HARVEY.
I WON'T WATCH YOU DESTROY ANOTHER WORLD.
DESTROY--?
I CAME TO SALVAGE THIS MUD BALL!
BUT THEY REFUSE MY GRACIOUS GIFT!
AND FOR THAT YOU'D RATHER KILL THEM?
YOU'VE LOST IT, HARVEY. TOTALLY.
I NEVER THOUGHT I'D SEE THIS DAY.
THE MAN WHO TOOK OUR WORLD, KILLED MY FRIENDS AND LOCKED ME AWAY FOR TEN YEARS?
--PUSHED TO THE BRINK.
YOU ARE NOT MY EQUAL, LOLA.
NORMALLY TRUE.
BUT I HAVEN'T BEEN EXPENDING ENERGY LIKE YOU HAVE.
YOU SHOULDN'T BE HERE.
YES, I SHOULD. SOMEONE HAD TO FREE--
--HIM.

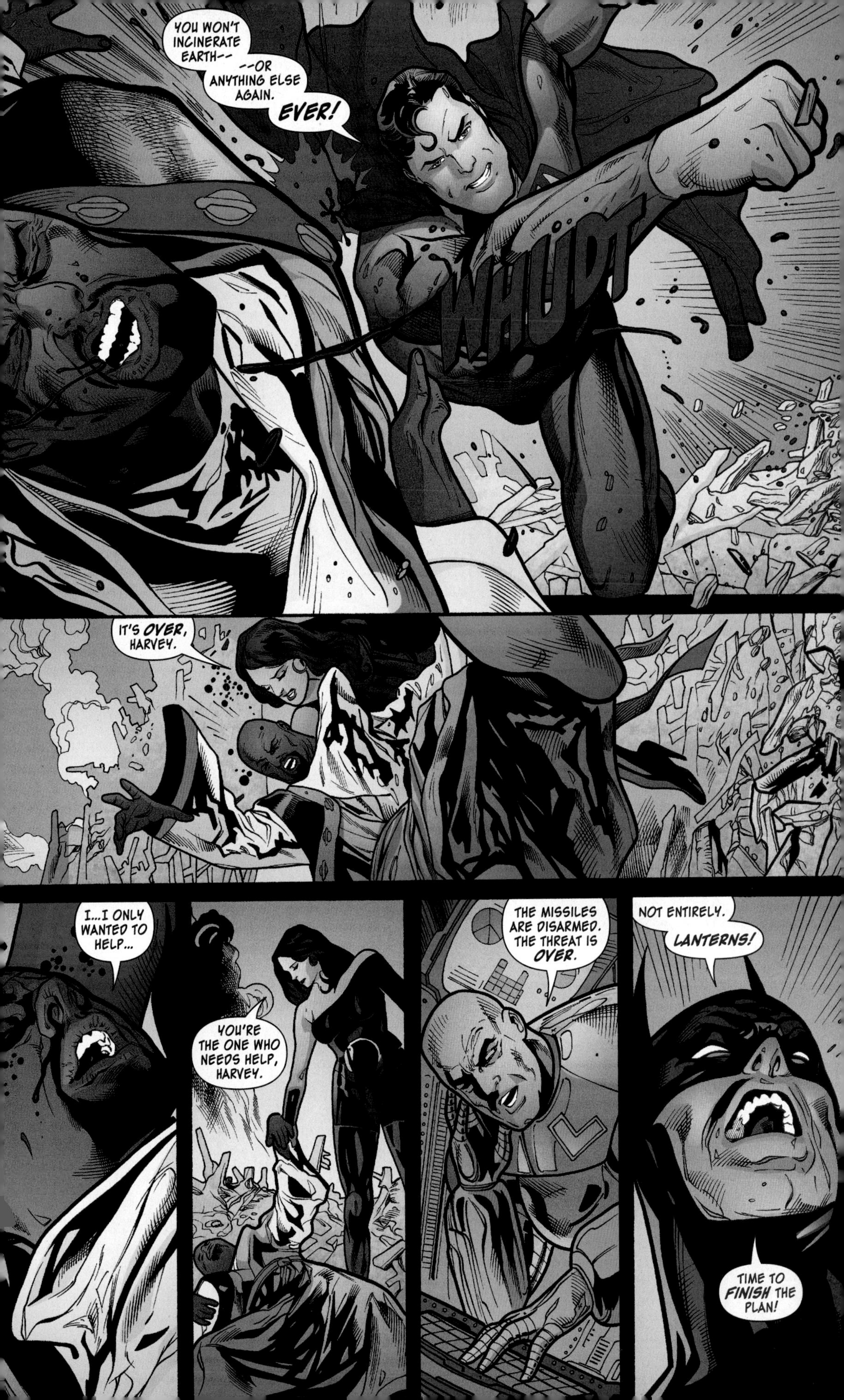
YOU WON'T INCINERATE EARTH--
--OR ANYTHING ELSE AGAIN. EVER!
WHUDT
IT'S OVER, HARVEY.
I...I ONLY WANTED TO HELP...
YOU'RE THE ONE WHO NEEDS HELP, HARVEY.
THE MISSILES ARE DISARMED. THE THREAT IS OVER.
NOT ENTIRELY.
LANTERNS!
TIME TO FINISH THE PLAN!

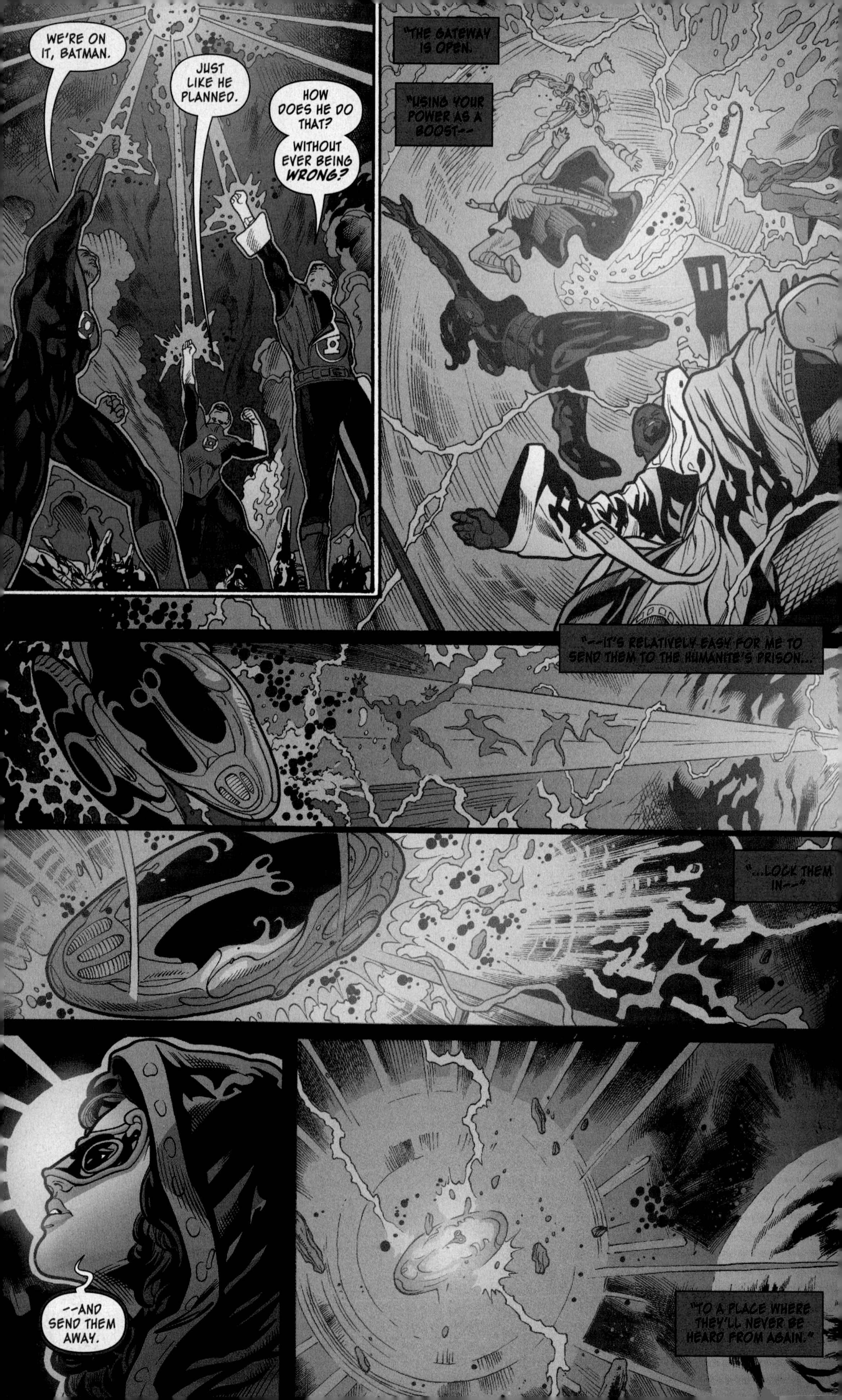

WE'RE ON IT, BATMAN.
JUST LIKE HE PLANNED.
HOW DOES HE DO THAT?
WITHOUT EVER BEING *WRONG?*
"THE GATEWAY IS OPEN.
"USING YOUR POWER AS A BOOST--
"--IT'S RELATIVELY EASY FOR ME TO SEND THEM TO THE HUMANITE'S PRISON...
"...LOCK THEM IN--"
--AND SEND THEM AWAY.
"TO A PLACE WHERE THEY'LL NEVER BE HEARD FROM AGAIN."

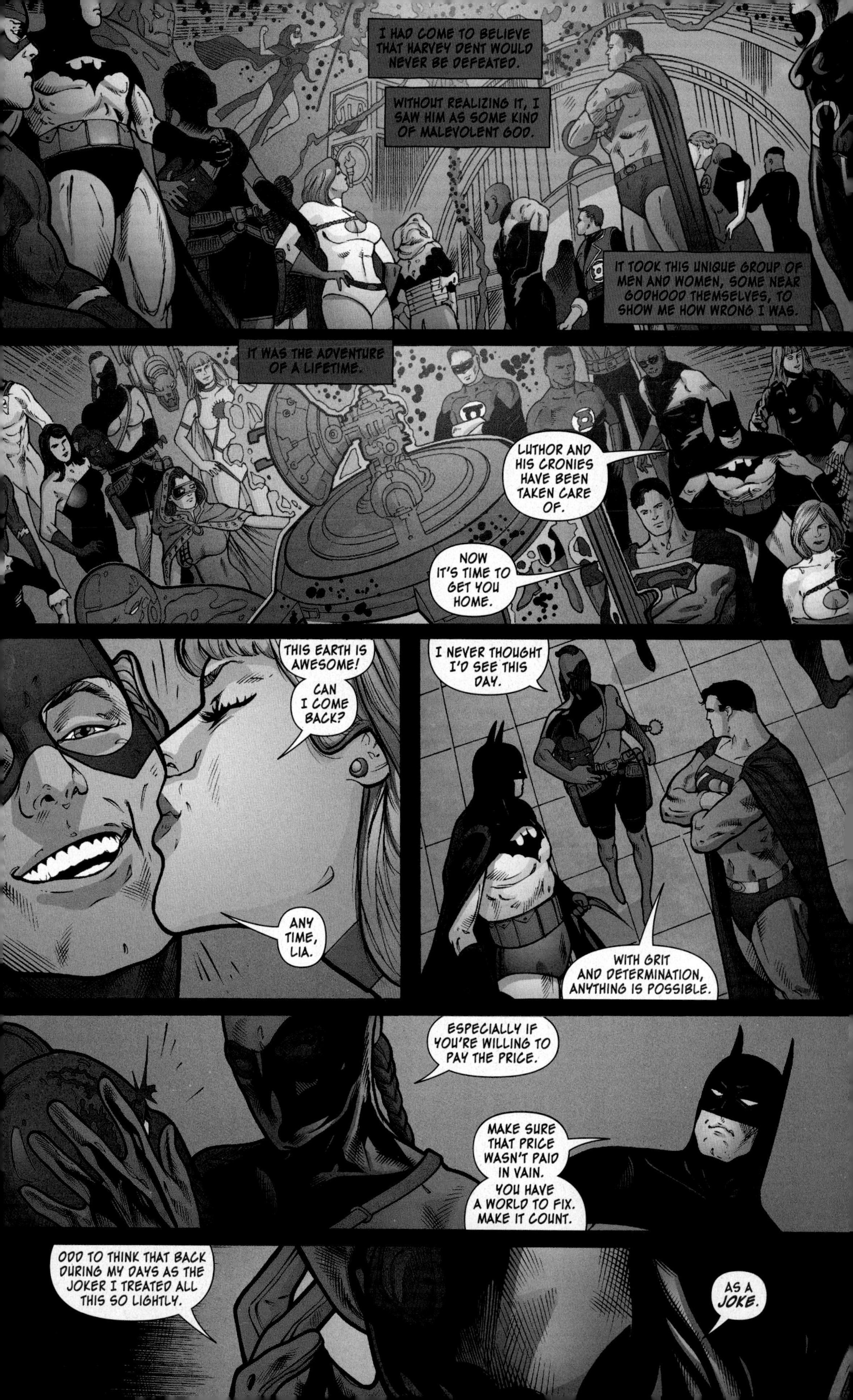
I HAD COME TO BELIEVE THAT HARVEY DENT WOULD NEVER BE DEFEATED.
WITHOUT REALIZING IT, I SAW HIM AS SOME KIND OF MALEVOLENT GOD.
IT TOOK THIS UNIQUE GROUP OF MEN AND WOMEN, SOME NEAR GODHOOD THEMSELVES, TO SHOW ME HOW WRONG I WAS.
IT WAS THE ADVENTURE OF A LIFETIME.
LUTHOR AND HIS CRONIES HAVE BEEN TAKEN CARE OF.
NOW IT'S TIME TO GET YOU HOME.
THIS EARTH IS AWESOME!
CAN I COME BACK?
ANY TIME, LIA.
I NEVER THOUGHT I'D SEE THIS DAY.
WITH GRIT AND DETERMINATION, ANYTHING IS POSSIBLE.
ESPECIALLY IF YOU'RE WILLING TO PAY THE PRICE.
MAKE SURE THAT PRICE WASN'T PAID IN VAIN.
YOU HAVE A WORLD TO FIX. MAKE IT COUNT.
ODD TO THINK THAT BACK DURING MY DAYS AS THE JOKER I TREATED ALL THIS SO LIGHTLY.
AS A *JOKE*.

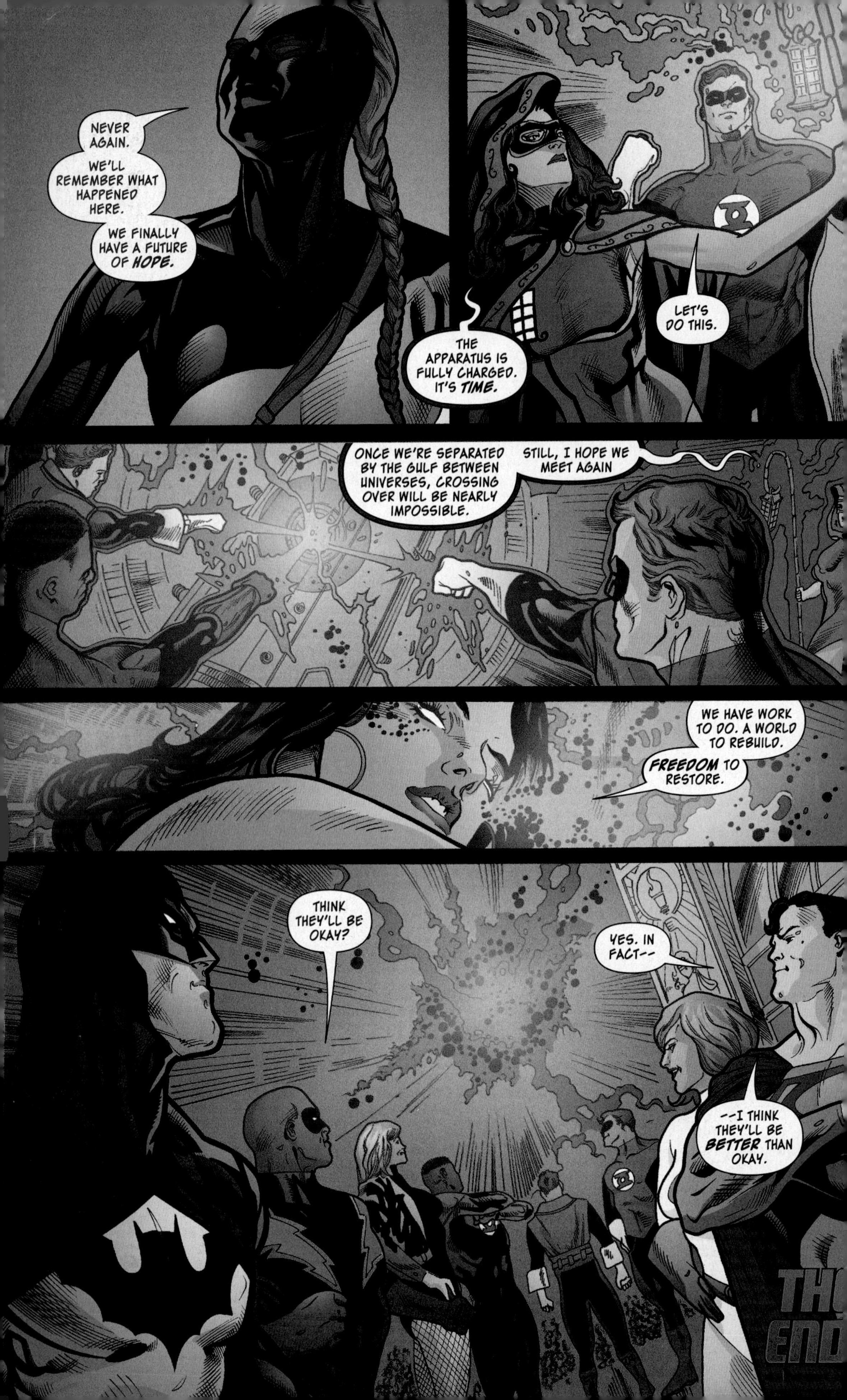
NEVER AGAIN.
WE'LL REMEMBER WHAT HAPPENED HERE.
WE FINALLY HAVE A FUTURE OF HOPE.
THE APPARATUS IS FULLY CHARGED. IT'S TIME.
LET'S DO THIS.
ONCE WE'RE SEPARATED BY THE GULF BETWEEN UNIVERSES, CROSSING OVER WILL BE NEARLY IMPOSSIBLE.
STILL, I HOPE WE MEET AGAIN
WE HAVE WORK TO DO. A WORLD TO REBUILD.
FREEDOM TO RESTORE.
THINK THEY'LL BE OKAY?
YES. IN FACT--
--I THINK THEY'LL BE BETTER THAN OKAY.

MORE CLASSIC TALES OF THE MAN OF STEEL

SUPERMAN:
THE MAN OF STEEL
VOLS. 1 - 6

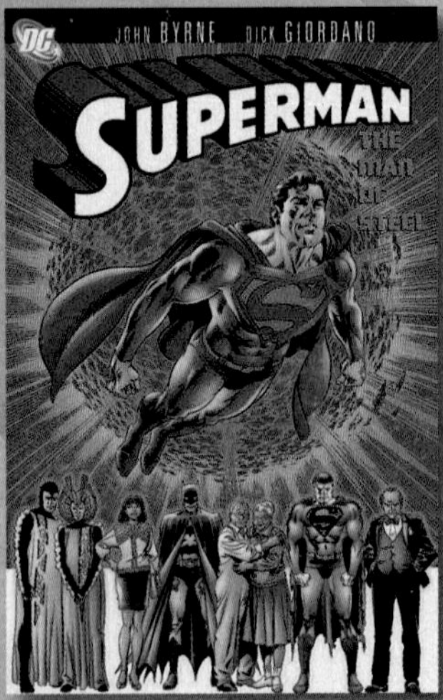
JOHN BYRNE
DICK GIORDANO
SUPERMAN
THE MAN OF STEEL

JOHN BYRNE

SUPERMAN:
BIRTHRIGHT

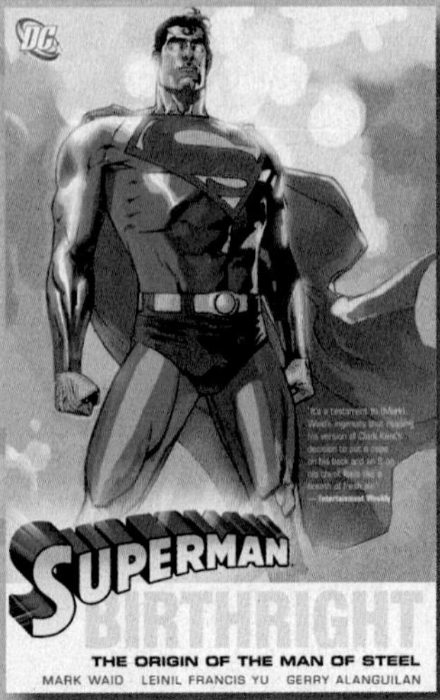
SUPERMAN
BIRTHRIGHT
THE ORIGIN OF THE MAN OF STEEL
MARK WAID · LEINIL FRANCIS YU · GERRY ALANGUILAN

MARK WAID
LEINIL YU

SUPERMAN:
CAMELOT FALLS
VOLS. 1 - 2

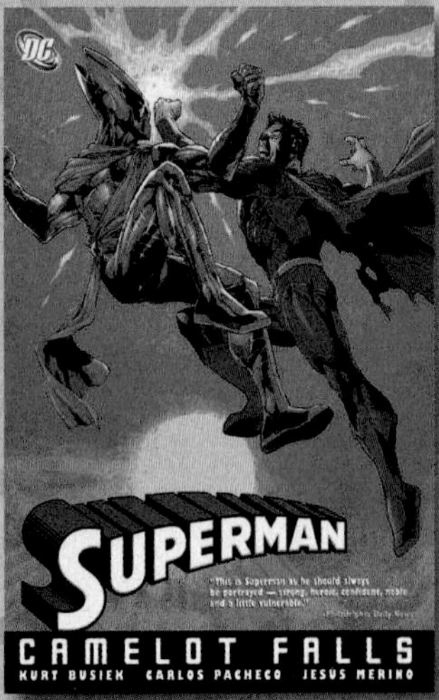
SUPERMAN
CAMELOT FALLS
KURT BUSIEK CARLOS PACHECO JESUS MERINO

KURT BUSIEK
CARLOS PACHECO

SUPERMAN:
OUR WORLDS AT WAR

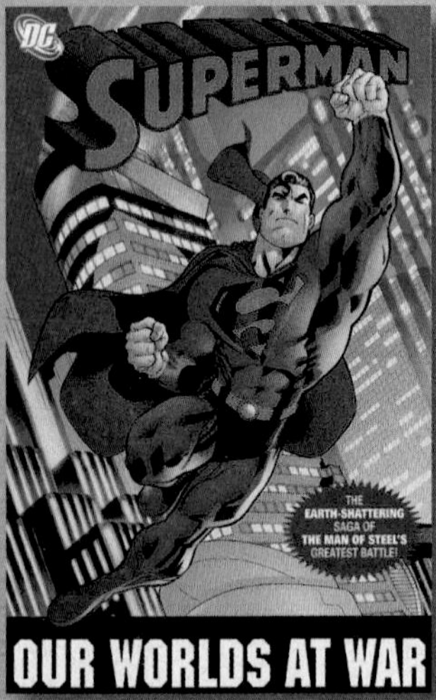
SUPERMAN
THE EARTH-SHATTERING SAGA OF THE MAN OF STEEL'S GREATEST BATTLE!
OUR WORLDS AT WAR

VARIOUS
WRITERS & ARTISTS

SUPERMAN:
RED SON

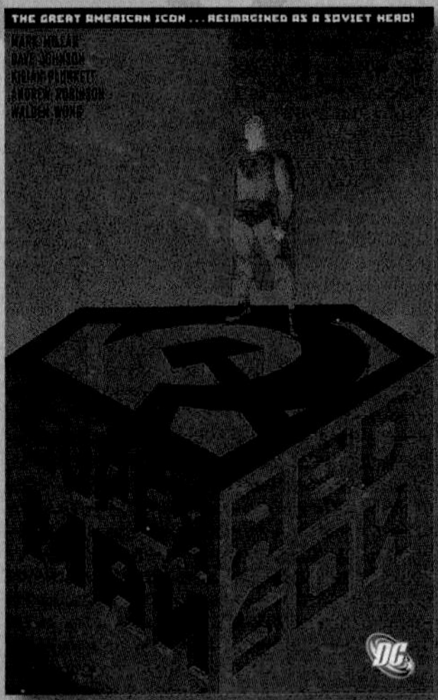
THE GREAT AMERICAN ICON... REIMAGINED AS A SOVIET HERO!

MARK MILLAR
DAVE JOHNSON
KILLIAN PLUNKETT

SUPERMAN:
SECRET IDENTITY

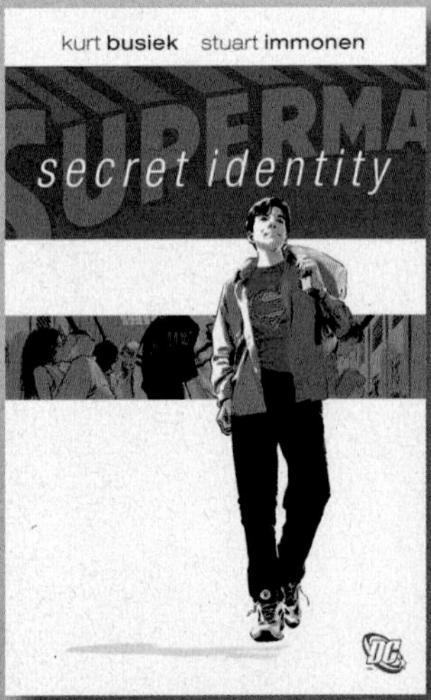
kurt busiek stuart immonen
secret identity

KURT BUSIEK
STUART IMMONEN

SEARCH THE GRAPHIC NOVELS SECTION OF
DCCOMICS.COM
FOR ART AND INFORMATION ON ALL OF OUR BOOKS!